The
BUSINESS
of CRAFTS

The
BUSINESS
of CRAFTS

∾

The COMPLETE
DIRECTORY
of RESOURCES
for ARTISANS

∾

The Crafts Center
with Kathy Borrus, Lloyd Herman, and John Wilson

∾

WATSON-GUPTILL PUBLICATIONS/NEW YORK

Senior Editor: Candace Raney
Edited by Alisa Palazzo
Designed by Areta Buk
Graphic production by Hector Campbell

First published in 1996 in the United States
by Watson-Guptill Publications,
a division of BPI Communications, Inc.,
1515 Broadway, New York, N.Y. 10036.

Library of Congress Cataloging-in-Publication Data

    The business of crafts : the complete directory of resources for artisans /
Crafts Center.
      p. cm.
    Includes bibliographical references and index.
    ISBN 0-8230-0542-9
    1. Handicraft—Marketing.   I. Crafts Center (Washington, D.C.)
    HD2341.B875   1996
    745.5'068'8—dc20   96-33293
                                            CIP

Printed in the United States of America

First printing, 1996

1 2 3 4 5 6 7 8 / 03 02 01 00 99 98 97 96

CONTENTS

FOREWORD

The Business of Crafts is a valuable source of information and guidance that will help folk artists organize, create, and market their work successfully. There are so many talented artisans lacking the necessary funds and information to expedite the entrepreneurial process. This book suggests effective methods for marketing creatively through a mix of traditional and non-traditional venues. It is designed to help folk artists, who rely on crafts as a primary source of income, strengthen the network of artisans and resources. The volume suggests a broad range of markets and provides pertinent information on developing ongoing merchandising arrangements for the working artist. At a time when funds are few for both art and social programs, this book is a valuable tool for folk artists in their efforts to achieve both artistic excellence and financial security.

As someone who loves folk art and perceives it as a unique expression of this country's heritage and diversity, I appreciate this book and recommend it to others.

Jane Alexander

INTRODUCTION

As the founder and president of The Crafts Center, a nonprofit organization that helps low-income artisans worldwide, I am pleased to write the introduction to *The Business of Crafts.* Although The Crafts Center is primarily an advocate of economically marginal artisans around the world, it is nevertheless concerned with assisting the many craftspeople and groups in the United States, as well. In general, The Crafts Center seeks to ensure that producers receive a fair share of the profits for their crafts and that human rights, such as safe and healthy working conditions, and environmental considerations are respected.

Managing a crafts enterprise and manufacturing and marketing products comprise a complicated process. In my experience, it is the management and marketing that require the most attention. Craft businesses often fail less for lack of quality design than for lack of administration, which can include insufficient accounting, failure to answer or fill orders in a timely fashion, unsuitable packing of merchandise, and a lack of market analysis and targeting. Since it is often hard to strike a fair compromise between production costs and what the market is willing to pay, The Crafts Center tends to recommend "high end" or "high niche" markets, such as interior design firms and boutiques, which require only small quantities and pay higher prices. Nevertheless, this book attempts to describe every identifiable craft market.

We are lucky to have a foreword by Jane Alexander, the distinguished actress and arts advocate. The book's first section, a history of American crafts, has been contributed by Lloyd Herman, a noted curator and the director of our first national crafts collection, the Renwick Gallery, a treasured part of Washington's Smithsonian Institution. Over the years Mr. Herman's creative talents, enthusiasm, and aesthetic sensibilities have provided a great boost to crafts in the United States and in Canada, whose national gallery he helped to establish.

The second and third sections are by Kathy Borrus, a talented freelance writer and retail marketing consultant, who was for many years the merchandise manager of the Smithsonian Institution shops, and has worked with many specialty retailers and artisans throughout the United States and overseas. In the second part, she concentrates on merchandising and product development, and also writes about mission definition, careful project development, sound and reliable management, high-quality and efficient production, and various marketing strategies and methods. She was ably assisted in her work by John Wilson, an British anthropologist and crafts importer who has worked in the Middle East, Morocco, West Africa, Indonesia, Guatemala, and Jamaica, and has run crafts businesses in both London and Washington, D.C.

In the third section, she describes the many different market types and recounts interesting and helpful interviews with buyers and producers. Complementing each market description are address listings of many corresponding American businesses, which craftspeople may want to contact. The lists were compiled by The Crafts Center staff—Nina Smith, Executive Director; Christine Brawdy, Assistant Director; Hedy Buzan, Research Coordinator and Librarian; Evelyn Mendoza, Membership Director; and myself—and we hope they prove helpful.

Also included is a glossary of business terms commonly used in the crafts market. Understanding the language of the crafts business world is essential to the success of your endeavors, and this section should serve as a practical guide through the maze of commercial terms.

I hope that *The Business of Crafts* will serve you well in your pursuits. The work of the artisan truly bonds the people of the world and also serves to remind us of our national heritage and the many links between us.

Caroline Ramsay Merriam
President and Founder
The Crafts Center

AMERICAN CRAFTS: TOWARD A NEW CENTURY

North American crafts are not what they used to be. Handmade things are not necessary in our homes or to clothe our bodies. Now, machines make our necessities. In the past century, North American crafts have matured and become sophisticated, moving from the popular perception of rustic chairs, ceramic pots, and colorful quilts to expressive objects of great technical virtuosity and expressive power—as stylish as decorative arts, from any place or period, in museum collections.

"Decorative art" is an interesting term. Scorned by modern artisans as denoting frivolous, unnecessary decoration on functional objects, its use has been revived. The term, never abandoned by museums and historians, is resurfacing to describe utilitarian objects for the home that go beyond the merely functional. The best of these home furnishings add verve and originality to usefulness. They are a vital element of American visual history in this century. They are art—art that is practical, as well as decorative.

Many people are puzzled, if not downright alienated, by much of the art that contemporary fine artists produce. The aesthetic challenges and messages of painting, sculpture, drawing, and printmaking are beyond many of us who simply want to be surrounded by things of beauty. Using craft materials and techniques, artists may make objects that provoke and question, eschewing utilitarian tradition to be purely expressive, but American craftspeople have not abandoned beauty. Far from it. Contemporary decorative arts are colorful, richly textured, and elegant in surface and form. They wed down-to-earth practicality with high-style sheen; they are the new heirlooms—to be used or admired and preserved for future generations.

THE 1880s: THE DEVELOPMENT OF THE ARTS AND CRAFTS MOVEMENT

In the last 100 years, American crafts have changed yet, in many ways, have remained the same. In the second half of the 19th century, English and American artisans were losing ground to industrialization; factories were churning out furniture, silver plate, ceramic statues, and other extravagantly embellished goods for the home. It was a time of showmanship for the machine—printed fabrics and wallpapers, carved and embossed wood furniture, molded and painted ceramic figurines and tableware was all heavily ornamented. Unfortunately, many were grossly overdecorated in inappropriate ways. It was a period of excess.

However, along with the excesses of the 1880s and '90s came the work of significant designers, and many of them looked back at other times for their inspiration. The Philadelphia Centennial Exhibition of 1876 revived patriotic fervor and extolled America's colonial past. Soon, Victorian-flavored adaptations of earlier styles surfaced, and the spinning-wheel—an anachronism in the 1880s—became a decorative reminder of the past in many family parlors. Other styles that were revived, often with the exaggeration we associate with Victorian pomposity, included the rococo, Gothic, Renaissance, exotic Asian, Egyptian, and Neo-Greco. Such exuberant fantasies weren't limited to high-style, expensive furniture but could be found in mass-produced goods, affordable to the growing middle-class.

In England, social reformer John Ruskin (1819–1900) and his disciple, poet and artist William Morris (1834–1896), led the reaction to the garish excesses and shoddy workmanship of the new manufactured housewares. In founding the Arts and Crafts movement, they strove to return dignity to handcraftsmanship, improving both the quality of life for the artisan and the caliber of the work created. According to craft historian Edward Lucie-Smith, in his book *Craft Today: Poetry of the Physical* (Weidenfeld & Nicolson, 1986), as this wave of positive activity crested in England, the American Arts and Crafts movement was often negative, rejecting the dominance of industry rather than stressing the revival of hand skills.

This American movement was also not characterized by a single modern style, for it incorporated strains of art nouveau, a late-19th-century French design trend with Japanese influences characterized by sinuous lines and organic forms and linked to the Aesthetic movement in England. Direct Japanese influence appears in the designs of American architects and brothers Henry Mather Greene and Charles Sumner Greene (active just after 1900), and in the rectilinear style of Scottish architect and designer Charles Rennie Mackintosh (1868–1928). Gustav Stickley (1858–1942), one of the foremost American furniture-makers of the movement, gave it voice through publication of *The Craftsman.*

Arts and crafts societies sprang up in numerous American cities, and exhibitions gave visibility to the new artistic products. Designs emphasized simplicity of form and naturalized decoration, usually flowers and plants represented realistically or only gently stylized. Ceramics often had subtle matte surfaces, and greens and soft, natural colors predominated over strong reds, purples, and the gilded adornments of popular manufactured wares. Those who subscribed to the crafts philosophy prized honesty of workmanship not only in household furnishings, but in architecture as well. Henry Mather Greene and Charles Sumner Greene exemplified and even made a fetish of this; they connected beams with wood pegs and commonly made deliberate use of joinery for decorative effect.

Objects were made by individuals and small factories, which provided dignified work opportunities for young women with artistic talent. The art potteries of the late 19th and early 20th centuries employed men to throw the pots and young women to decorate them. One of the ceramicists who rose to prominence, Adelaide Alsop Robineau, not only carved intricate designs into her porcelain vases, but helped to unite ceramics with the Arts and Crafts movement by founding the publication *Keramic Studio* in 1899.

While Robineau, Maria Longworth Nichols (founder of the Rookwood Pottery), and other art potters were establishing the American Arts and Crafts movement style, an Englishman, Charles Fergus Binns, was hired to originate the curriculum at the New York State School of Clayworking and Ceramics at Alfred University in Alfred, New York, in 1900. As models for his students, he chose the classic forms of Chinese, Greek, and Persian ceramics, rather than examples from English pottery. It is reported that he taught his students to use jiggers to ensure that the curves and proportions of their work matched those of the prototypes—perhaps leading the way to the future profession of industrial design.

Though some art potteries were in New York, most were in Ohio. The Arts and Crafts movement was not solely an East Coast phenomenon, however. In California, the Greene brothers invented the California bungalow-style house and also designed the interior furnishings for wealthy clients. Arthur and Lucia Mathews, working in the San Francisco Bay area, designed furniture, picture frames, and decorative objects that often incorporated historical references but were usually decorated with flowers indigenous to California.

Ironically, the well-designed, well-made, handcrafted household goods, produced as an alternative to garish manufactured stuff, never reached the market. Then, as now, most people want what they think rich people own. Those who respected the handmade, and understood the philosophical ideals of the Arts and Crafts movement, embraced this artistry, but without broad support, the movement waned. *The Craftsman* ceased publication in 1916. World War I reduced the availability of some materials, such as precious metals, and made the purchase of luxuries unfashionable. The period finally petered out before the 1920s.

Not all American artisans and crafts were associated with the Arts and Crafts movement. Far from it. Folk crafts had survived from the colonial era, and the artistry diversified with each successive wave of European immigration. Though manufactured goods replaced many handmade products, people who revered the craft heritage found ways to help preserve it. For example, in the early 1900s a few weavers took steps to preserve the tradition of coverlet weaving, which was being supplanted by machine-woven items. They introduced coarser yarns and tried other methods to reduce handweaving time and labor. Others recorded patterns for future generations. To preserve colonial furniture styles, Reverend Wallace Nutting produced high-quality replicas of what he dubbed "pilgrim" furniture, due to its simple treatment of materials and design that harked back to the ideals of the nation's founding fathers. Philadelphian Samuel Yellin, who won commissions in various cities to create handsome iron grilles, screens, and gates for buildings, adapted many medieval decorative designs for his work.

Louis Comfort Tiffany (1848–1933), fueled by the success of his art glass, introduced his ceramics at the St. Louis World Fair in 1903, the same year that Englishman Frederick Carder founded Steuben Glass Works in Corning, New York. Their rivalry over similar iridescent glass surfaces led to a lawsuit and, eventually, friendship, and the promotion of the art of glasswork.

THE REDISCOVERY OF CRAFTS
IN THE EARLY 20TH CENTURY

Little has been recorded about American crafts between the two world wars, with the exception of ceramics, but even in this discipline, no evidence has been cited that a major stylistic influence united American crafts artists. The 1920s brought recognition, by artists and collectors, to Native American crafts and folk art. Later in that decade, America's most famous native potter, María Martínez of San Ildefonso Pueblo, New Mexico, rediscovered the previously lost secret of the black-on-black pottery that brought fame to their pueblo.

Wharton Esherick, who by 1950 was considered the dean of American furniture artisans, displayed a distinctive Art Deco influence in some of the pieces he made in his Paoli, Pennsylvania, studio (now the Wharton Esherick Museum). The Art Deco style, named for the International Exposition of Decorative Arts in Paris in 1925, wasn't strongly felt in the United States until the 1930s, when, as with the mission-style furniture of the Arts and Crafts movement, manufacturers began copying it. Art Deco wasn't the only stylistic influence on ceramics in the 1930s; also evident were strong links to the Wiener Werkstatte in Vienna, which exemplified a modern style similar to the Bauhaus movement in Germany. This influence was most strongly felt in Cleveland, where artists who had studied in Vienna infused their ceramic sculpture with European style and wit.

Among the Cleveland ceramicists active in the 1930s, Edris Eckhardt and Viktor Schreckengost were still active more than 50 years later. Eckhardt was strongly associated with another phenomenon of the '30s, the Work Projects Administration (WPA). The WPA, a federal government program to provide employment for artists during the Depression, generated projects involving crafts and craftspeople across the nation. In Oregon, for example, skilled artisans designed and made furnishings and decorations for Timberline Lodge on Mount Hood. They wove draperies, bedspreads, and rugs for the guestrooms; constructed furniture; forged decorative gates and fireplace fittings; and created wood mosaics and other ornamental surfaces for public rooms.

In another WPA project in New York State, Seneca Indians were employed by the WPA to re-create objects of the Iroquois culture for posterity. In Connecticut, the WPA sponsored a toy-making project. And in Cleveland, Eckhardt directed a WPA office that offered employment to artists who would handcraft pieces of furniture, fabrics, and playground sculptures. Eckhardt also personally created a series of figurines depicting familiar storybook characters, which were replicated and distributed to public libraries to encourage reading. Another major effort of the WPA was the *Index of American Design,* which employed artists to make meticulous watercolor renditions of American crafts and folk arts from the colonial era through the end of the 19th century. These 16,000 images, housed in the National Gallery of Art in Washington, D.C., provide both a reminder of America's craft history and a design inspiration to artisans today.

It is easy to think of the Depression as a time only of deprivation, when few had the luxury of making or buying handmade goods, but it was a vital time for American crafts in two ways—there was a reverence for a national craft heritage, and also a new perspective on craftmaking and craft education brought by the new immigrants. The necessities made by rural craftspeople probably helped to sustain them during the Depression, even though money for nonessentials was short.

In 1939, writer and researcher Allan Eaton's rural crafts research was published in the book *Crafts of the Southern Highlands.* It validated the crafts of that region and helped to renew interest in them. He followed this up in 1946 with his book *Crafts of New England.* Both remain valuable references to the craftmaking of this era. Along with the *Index of American Design,* these books served to revive artisans' pride in their work and bring national attention to an important part of the country's heritage. Exhibitions of regional crafts and other events soon followed. Both the Southern Highlands Handicraft Guild and the New Hampshire League of Craftsmen were founded in the 1930s and remain vital in promoting the crafts in their regions.

At the other end of the spectrum of American crafts were sophisticated art objects made by immigrants from Europe. The threat of Nazism drove many Jewish artisans to the United States to make new lives. Austrian ceramicists Gertrud and Otto Natzler settled in Los Angeles and won their first award in 1938 at the Syracuse Ceramic National exhibitions—a series of shows that remained important for decades in recording the best of American ceramics. Also around 1938, Trude Guermonprez, another Austrian, immigrated with her weaving studio to northern California. Frans and Marguerite Wildenhain, Dutch and German respectively, also moved their pottery to northern California. Marguerite, educated at the Bauhaus and a respected ceramic designer in Germany, was revered by many as a "potter's potter" up until her death in the 1980s. When the Bauhaus closed, German painter Josef Albers (1888–1976) came from Germany to add substance to the experimental Black Mountain College in North Carolina.

Not all European immigrants came to escape Nazism, however. George Boothe, a newspaper publisher from Detroit, founded the Cranbrook Academy of Art and attracted renowned Finnish architect Eliel Saarinen (1873–1950) as its first director in 1930. Other European artists composed the first faculty: Marianne Strengel, who directed the textiles program, and Maija Grotell, head of ceramics, were both Finnish artists and teachers who influenced generations of American craftspeople; Arthur Nevill Kirk, an English goldsmith, brought to America the "Liberty's look," a somewhat Scandinavianized Art Deco style popularized by the Liberty department store in London. In fact, the entire Cranbrook campus, designed by Eliel Saarinen, continues to exemplify a distinctive '30s style, just as the academy remains one of the most important educational institutions for modern American craftsmakers.

WPA programs gave crafts and architecture visibility. The establishment of membership organizations for craftspeople began to help them publicize and market their work. And, the new immigrants provided fresh viewpoints on artistic style and craft education that would exert a lasting influence.

THE ALLIANCE OF CRAFTS AND ART AFTER WORLD WAR II

Crafts artisan became a less popular occupational choice during the 1940s while the nation was at war, but after World War II, a new era dawned for American crafts. Handy and Harmon, a smelter and supplier of precious metals, sponsored a series of workshops that taught metal holloware techniques. The ripple effect generated by this, and by jeweler/metalsmith Margaret Craver's use of metalsmithing in rehabilitation programs for veterans, was significant. But perhaps of greatest importance was the increased educational opportunity available through the GI Bill. Veterans could return to college to earn university degrees subsidized by the United States government. To serve their needs, universities expanded their curriculums and many added art and crafts courses.

In the 1950s, craftspeople, who had previously worked in relative isolation, began to find a common voice through the American Craftsmen's Cooperative Council, now the American Craft Council (ACC). The ACC sponsored the first national craft conference, a nationally circulated publication, and the Museum of Contemporary Crafts (opened in 1956 in New York and now known as the American Craft Museum). The membership services of these groups provided the first national link through which people could learn what fellow artisans were making. They opened the doors to a national exchange of technical information and stylistic influences.

While artisans were caught up in the general spirit of optimism and economic growth of the '50s, their objects remained tied to functional usage. Only in such traditionally narrative and decorative works as tapestries and stained-glass windows was a purely expressive art apparent. Modernism, however, was very much in vogue. New forms abounded in virtually every medium, though the materials and techniques used were far more limited than they are today. The principal mediums for more modern creations were clay and fiber, and the resulting crafts were notable and influential. Mariska Karacz, whose abstract forms in stitchery had wide visibility in nationally circulated magazines such as *House Beautiful* and *Woman's Day*, and Peter Voulkos, who taught ceramics at the Otis Art Institute and later the University of California at Berkeley, gave the Abstract Expressionist painting movement a position in the craft world. Lenore Tawney hung her loom-woven hangings away from the wall, creating see-through fiber sculpture. Margaret DePatta veered away from traditional jewelry making, choosing eccentrically cut gems and smooth river pebbles for her sculptural brooches. John Paul Miller revived the ancient art of granulation, but the jewelry forms to which he applied the tiny gold spheres were definitely modern.

In the 1960s, artists in the United States began to look forward, as well as back to the past. In this period of great social unrest, people were polarized by grave issues, such as the war in Vietnam, the civil rights movement in the South, and assassinations of political leaders. Alienated by big business and unsympathetic government, many young people chose a simpler life in the country, where they believed they could survive on homegrown vegetables and local sales of their handmade crafts. Macramé plant hangers and tie-dyed T-shirts characterized do-it-yourself crafts. Many amateur artists were skilled at promotion, and the large quantities of these mediocre objects flooding the market undermined the acceptance of university-educated craftpeople as true artists. These artisans struggled to prove that artistic expression wasn't limited to paint and canvas.

The '60s built upon the acceptance of modern craft styles from the '50s and also nurtured the freedom to experiment. Many artisans and academics were lured by foreign cultures, and not only adapted their techniques and materials to their own uses, but also found a source of sustenance for their souls (especially from Asian cultures and religions). The peace corps, Fulbright fellowships, and other international programs provided opportunities for living abroad. And, at home, a plethora of influences—international, social, and political—provided inspiration for contemporary crafts. An emphasis on content and an independence from primarily functional craft traditions separated the new craft artists from those who made utilitarian objects.

This decade can also be characterized in several other ways. An offhand, sometimes outrageous, humor characterized the "funk" movement in ceramics, which emanated from the San Francisco Bay area and from Robert Arneson's work. There was an exploration of familiar textile techniques, such as knitting and crochet. And, more exotic methods—such as Scandinavian card-weaving, knotless netting from New Guinea, weaving from ancient Peru, pile carpet-making from Finland, and the introduction of such untraditional weaving materials as plastic and newspapers—all found credibility in the 1960s.

The first international tapestry biennial was held in Lausanne, Switzerland, in 1963 and provided an international focus on large-scale sculptural fiber art. As much prominence as the new "art fabric" received in the '60s, it isn't easy to characterize the textile art of this period. Crafters embraced the quilt and renewed its vigor. "Soft sculpture" joined the textile lexicon, appearing in both new off-loom woven sculptures and padded-fabric constructions. The aforementioned macramé and tie-dyed fabrics were so ubiquitous that they came to characterize the counterculture of the decade.

In 1962, Harvey Littleton, a ceramicist from Wisconsin, and Dominick Labino, a glass engineer in Ohio, conducted a workshop at the Toledo Museum of Art. There they introduced artists to the possibilities offered by a small glass furnace.

Labino used glass marbles made from a formula that would melt easily. That workshop led to the formation of glassblowing programs in more than 100 art schools and universities within that decade alone. Glass moved out of the factory and into the art studio.

The freedom to explore methods and materials continued into the 1970s. Jewelers, led by teacher Stanley Lechtzin at the Tyler School of Art in Philadelphia, experimented with electroforming. With this technique, commonly used to bronze baby shoes, artists could build up thin films of metal on virtually any surface, creating the appearance of massive, organic jewelry that was very lightweight. A landmark 1970 workshop at Southern Illinois University in Carbondale introduced traditional blacksmithing to jewelers and other metalworkers; organized by Professor L. Brent Kington, it led to a renewed interest in the application of forging iron to architectural ornamentation, as well as to the creation of tables, plantstands, torchères, and other such objects.

Just as ironwork began to find its way into the art world, basketry was explored for the expressive potential of various rigid structural forms. Artisans also investigated the artistic possibilities of felting and hand-papermaking, which were popularized through workshops and craft schools. Handsewn clothing moved away from the shapeless poncho of the 1960s toward haute couture, as the "wearable art" movement developed momentum and craftspeople specializing in textiles expressed themselves through theatrical, humorous, or style-conscious garments. Related to this, the surface design movement compelled fiber artists to examine the uses of pattern and color on fabrics. Painting and printing took their places in the catalog of acceptable textile techniques, along with color xerography, heat transfer of photographic images, and a wealth of dyeing methods, including batik, ikat, and tie-dye, to name just a few. Appliquéd and pieced quilts, beading, stitchery, and other surface embellishments were all accepted as part of this developing craft movement.

Organizations and publications were part of the new network of information now available to the crafts community. *Surface Design Journal, Fiberarts, Fine Woodworking, Metalsmith,* and *The Bead Journal* (now *Ornament*) all began publishing in the 1970s. Artists formed new organizations and began to hold conferences to share their mutual need for information and supplement the American Craft Council, which was the only national voice for America's craftspeople. The Society of North American Goldsmiths (SNAG), the Glass Art Society (GAS), the National Council on Education in the Ceramic Arts (NCECA), and the Artist Blacksmith Association of North America (ABANA) still continue today, and other more specialized organizations represent enamelists, quiltmakers, and wood turners. All have been instrumental in the development of diverse techniques, permitting practitioners to expand their technical vocabularies in the service of ideas.

Ideas, content, and meaning were all important to craftspeople in the 1970s. The art world had been given high visibility when the landmark exhibition "Objects: USA" premiered in 1969. This national exhibition traveled across the United States and internationally through the early 1970s and presented an eye-filling array of handcrafted objects that illustrated the artistic potential of common clay, glass, fiber, metal, and wood. Museums and galleries began to take notice, and new galleries opened and began to cultivate the collector market.

Galleries were only one avenue through which craftspeople began to sell their work. The country craft fair grew into a major wholesale/retail marketing opportunity, especially as the ACC's northeast regional fair grew into the national Craft Fair in Rhinebeck, New York. This fair attracted buyers from quality gift shops, department stores, and a burgeoning number of craft shops across the country; their need for quantities of a single design made artisans rethink their production methods. Deadlines for deliveries had to be met, and shortcuts for production had to be implemented to speed manufacturing. The Rhinebeck fair spurred wholesale and retail markets in several cities, all initiated by the ACC and copied widely.

Other selling opportunities presented themselves as percent-for-art programs in which state, county, and city governments recommended or required that a percentage of their construction budgets for public works projects be allocated for the purchase of art. This gave artisans the chance to create ceramic murals, stained-glass windows, ornamental iron grilles, and dramatic fiber hangings to humanize public buildings. Some crafters found that interior designers, often accustomed to designing a room or space for an important antique, began to see contemporary handmade objects as distinctive accents. Whether purely expressive or functional, American crafts became new symbols of quality and originality.

AMERICAN CRAFTS AT THE DAWN OF THE NEW CENTURY

The new opportunities to sell crafts in the 1980s made it necessary for craftspeople to learn business practices and marketing skills. Many became entrepreneurs, enlarging their studios to include several employees, who made or finished the stylish new products they originated. Competition for booth space in a growing number of craft fairs—including ACC's wholesale/retail shows and new nationally juried retail fairs sponsored by museums as fund-raisers—necessitated professional-quality photographic presentations, since fair organizers selected artists from slides of their work. To compete in this widening market, artisans had to find their own market niche, improve product design to attract the jaded eyes of wholesale buyers, and be aware of fashion and consumer trends.

Handcrafted items, even those made using production shortcuts and a division of labor, can rarely compete in price with comparative manufactured goods. But many American artisans found that by refining their designs and creating luxurious effects by selecting fine materials or finishing techniques, they could justify their prices to consumers.

Just who are these consumers? Many were craft-fair shoppers in the '60s, whose tastes have now grown as handmade merchandise improved. Others are drawn to craft galleries that, along with museums, have performed an important educational function in bringing contemporary crafts to the mainstream public. Many collectors are self-made businesspeople—a notable number are real estate developers—who acquired an interest in collecting after they became prosperous enough to afford such an indulgence.

Collecting is not necessarily expensive today, but prices are definitely up. Investment potential attracts the kind of collector who has seen prices escalate for decorative objects from the Arts and Crafts movement and later periods, and hopes that over time contemporary crafts will also increase in value. And, unlike collectors of paintings or prints, craft collectors find social satisfaction and prestige in such educational and collectors' groups as the American Craft Museum's Collectors Circle and the James Renwick Alliance. They also often belong to, and attend conferences of, the major medium organizations, such as NCECA and GAS.

Their refinement of tastes also causes many collectors to seek works by established craftpeople. Galleries and auction houses often sell earlier works by living artisans, providing a secondary market for crafts. An element of competition among collectors adds stamina to the market and some, to show off their prizes, even remodel or construct their homes specifically to present museum-style installations. Acquiring the best of American crafts brings status (and possible investment appreciation) to collectors. They may also pass heirloom-quality objects on to their families or ensure their own recognition as collectors by donating pieces to museums.

Museum collections today verify the importance of American crafts to our nation's visual heritage. Some museums collect contemporary crafts because their curators recognize the validity of ceramics or glass and the relationship of these mediums to contemporary sculptural expression. Others link these new functional objects to historical decorative arts, or collect them because of the materials with which they are made. Art museums that have in the past only exhibited or collected Asian ceramics and crafts, medieval carved furniture and stained glass, or other historic crafts, finally see that American artisans are creating objects worthy of their interest. Except in conservative art museums unwilling to consider the artistic worth of anything but paintings, drawings, prints, and sculpture, crafts are finding a place in exhibition programs and permanent collections. All are part of the constant, ongoing recategorization of art, which, in this century, has embraced printmaking and photography more quickly than the craft mediums. Museums, like the private collectors who serve on their boards of trustees, are wooed by galleries wishing to sell them craft items.

With the introduction in the 1980s of the International New Art Forms Exposition and its successor, Sculpture Objects and Functional Arts (SOFA), a major Chicago retail art fair at which major craft galleries from across the nation promote their artists, both public and private collectors have found a single marketplace for these new items. A second SOFA exposition in Miami made its debut in 1995 and suggests future growth of the craft-gallery exposition concept.

So, who are the craftmakers of today, and how do they differ from their kin of the past? They are older than the artisans of the 1960s, because fewer young people are making the lifestyle decisions of earlier decades, instead preferring occupations with greater, more dependable earnings. Consequently, enrollment in craft programs has dropped, and several universities and art schools have reduced or curtailed their craft curriculums. Those that do retain craft programs are adding business and marketing courses to accompany the purely artistic disciplines and give their graduates an edge in today's marketplace.

Some craftspeople are taking advantage of opportunities to design, but not necessarily make, their goods. Others increase their options by participating in industry programs, such as the Kohler Company's Arts/Industry program in which ceramic artists worked with skilled technicians in the company's toilet and sink factory to create new, large-scale art objects cast in industrial porcelain. This program evolved, in the 1980s, into Artist Editions—toilets and sinks decorated by artists. Others artisans design and make limited edition objects.

More so than at any previous time, artisans are enjoying the success of sales of their work for increasingly large figures. A network of collectors who prize these products, museums that exhibit and acquire the work, magazines that publicize it, and architects and designers who secure commissions are all measures of this success.

As further evidence of this growth in the craft world, women are no longer only in the ceramics and fibers fields; they are carving and turning wood, making furniture, and forging iron. Crafters are gaining recognition as designers and artists, and are crossing the boundaries that ghettoized crafts in the past. Some are becoming superstars, whose craft prices escalate toward those for contemporary paintings.

Yet, the oft-heard refrain that crafts are now accepted as art is overstated. Not all collectors or curators pigeonhole expressive objects according to their mediums, but there still exists a definite curatorial bias against artworks made with craft materials and techniques. Established painters or artists may make odd creations in clay and have them seen as equal to their major works, but craftspeople encounter more difficulty in gaining acceptance for their craft pieces. Perhaps as a result, craftmakers are now edging across medium lines. In the 1980s for example, the two luminaries in the glass-art field, Harvey K. Littleton and Dale Chihuly, each produced drawings and prints to complement their glass sculptures. Ceramicists also sometimes make prints or drawings. Established ceramicists Peter Voulkos, Robert Arneson, and Michael Lucero also cast their work in bronze, possibly to associate themselves with a more "serious" art medium.

Many artisans scorn the very term "craft," believing that it hinders their full acceptance by others as artists. Realizing the controversy the word inspires, the British Crafts Centre in London changed its name to Contemporary Applied Arts in 1987. The major art fair representing America's premier craft galleries calls itself the "Sculpture Objects Functional Arts Exhibition". Even the American Craft Council's for-profit division, which produces five major wholesale/retail fairs, sells the slogan "Handmade in America" and soft-pedals the word "craft." British ceramicist Allison Britton, speaking at the World Crafts Council in Australia in 1988, advocated dropping the word "craft" in favor of "art" to denote purely expressive objects and using "design" for those that are utilitarian.

TRENDS IN THE CRAFTS WORLD: PAST AND PRESENT

In many ways, the close of this century can be compared to the end of the previous one, with both similarities and differences. Both were periods of relative prosperity and peace. Artistic products were often made by small factories—not only by individual craftspeople. Affluent consumers could afford to ally themselves with culture and taste by acquiring objects for their homes that would identify their social aspirations. Often, their choices were ornate, with refined forms and patterned surfaces—truly "decorative" arts.

However, while objects from the Arts and Crafts movement of the late 19th century were in decided contrast to the prevalent, highly ornamented manufactured goods of that time, the modern craft revival since World War II has increasingly joined with the mass market. In fact, much of the merchandise offered at ACC fairs is as slick and devoid of personality as its factory-made counterparts.

But in contrast to this (and unlike the 1880s, when crafts provided a streamlined antidote to garish ornament of manufactured goods) today the simple, often sterile, unadorned forms are also often those produced in factories, and the luxurious, ornate, exotic items are the work of artisans. Nowadays, craftsmakers may face competition from copycat manufacturers because their designs for functional objects aren't protected by copyright. It is not uncommon for a foreign entrepreneur to buy a handmade American item, have it copied in Taiwan or Hong Kong, and then sell it (back to Americans or in their own countries) for far less than its American originator can offer it. In the decades following the 1880s, Gustav Stickley's early modernist designs were also copied and offered nationwide by catalog retailers. Some contemporary craftsmakers make furniture so special or complex that their markets are too small or their designs too costly and difficult to replicate profitably.

An interesting question that we must raise today (as borderlines become less distinct) is, What is handcraft and when does it become manufacturing? Art glass was actually factory-made until 1962, when the development of the small glass furnace and a glass formula with a lower melting temperature made it possible for artists to blow glass in their own studios. Today, many artists only direct the blowing and forming of molten glass shapes, which are made by a skilled team of technicians. It is a curious circle.

The word "handmade" no longer means "made only by hand." No one questions furniture-makers for using machine-driven saws, sanders, and other power equipment, or modern glues, for that matter. The artisan is still in control, and the machine functions only as a tool. Potters don't build every piece by hand, or throw them on a wheel—slipcast forms are quite acceptable and their consistently identical shapes satisfy retailers. Wall hangings can be woven on computer-controlled looms from computer-generated patterns. Clothing is sewn together on electric sewing machines and made of machine-knit fabric. Perhaps only purist quiltmakers will insist on hand-quilting their patterned tops, which are often pieced on sewing machines!

While the machine takes on what was previously the role of the hand, new materials offer color and surface alternatives not possible before the present era.

Gold and silver continue to impress us with their rich, gleaming surfaces, but anodized aluminum provides metallic color, too. Titanium, a refractory metal borrowed by modern craftmakers from the space program, is one of the newest substance to add interest to handmade objects. It is dull gray until electric current is applied to its surface, resulting in a variety of different colors. Patination of metal surfaces also provides colorful effects. Other vivid modern materials include resins, used as inlays in wood furniture and decorative accessories; tinted plastic laminates, usually associated with kitchen counters; and dichroic glass for a rainbow of color.

Inspiration traditionally came to craftsmakers from their materials, and it still does. Today, however, it usually comes from more diverse sources. Unlike most other countries, the United States has no single craft tradition. Consequently, its artisans aren't limited to a single style or prescribed way of working. Instead, they consider the world and its visual history fair game for their own interpretation.

In the 1920s and '30s craftspeople rediscovered Native American and vernacular or folk art. And each new generation continues to reinterpret, and draw inspiration from, previous artistic styles. Just as the quilt remains the quintessential craft tradition while being constantly updated, other forms of "naive" American art are continually being rediscovered by furniture-makers, weavers, potters—and consumers.

The ideals of American craftsmakers are certainly diverse, but diversity is a characteristic of our people and the forms of their expression. What lies ahead in the next century? Perhaps a renewed interest in the ruggedness of frontier crafts and traditional rural chairs, jugs, and rugs. Certainly, manufacturers respond to each current design inspiration, whether it is country French, high-tech, or American Southwest. American artisans, competing for the consumer dollar, will follow such trends, but they also will lead; they must be aware that the temptation to create only for the tastes of others can leave their work barren of personal meaning and energy. But, since American crafts have survived war and depression, I believe that they can survive fashion, too.

THE ART AND CRAFT OF BUSINESS

One appealing aspect of having your own crafts business is the freedom to create a working environment that complements your lifestyle. While the opportunity to define what you want from your business and from your life is quite attractive, you need to be realistic about the market for your crafts and your ability to produce for, and sell to, that market. You must design a workable plan that allows you to make a living through your own company. This guide will help you identify the most promising outlets for your merchandise and plan a strategy to maximize your chances of success.

The first step is a careful analysis of what you want to do now and in the future, how you want to work, and what you're capable of producing. Decide what you want, then work toward that goal.

DEFINING YOUR OBJECTIVES

As when planning a trip, if you want to start a crafts business, you need to have an idea of where you're going and how to get there. State a destination, and plan a route to control your progress. This allows you to concentrate on the business aspects that will move you along your course. To define your strengths and objectives and decide where you want to go, consider where you are now.

- What is your skill level compared to that of other craftspeople in your market?
- What are your strengths and weaknesses?
- Are you more of a creative designer or a skilled technician? Do you want to fashion your work yourself or contract the labor out?

- Do you like to experiment with new processes and techniques or are you content to create the same product repeatedly?
- Do you mind pressure?
- How well do you work with other people? Would you rather manage a large studio and workshop or work alone?
- Do you want to fit your family life or outside interests into your working life?

These questions will help you define your overall objectives. You should also write a *mission statement.* This will give you direction. Start by thinking about what you would like to achieve several years from now. Work backward to the present. Share your mission with your friends, family, and colleagues, and encourage them to contribute their ideas. Consider the following factors:

- *Business size.* Do you see yourself in a big workshop with 10 workers and large orders from department stores? Or, do you see yourself working alone quietly on a new piece for a local gallery or on a special commission for a valued client?
- *Location.* Do you want a loft in a big city or a workshop in a rural setting close to a town? Do you want to work alone from your house or with a group of craftspeople in a shared space?
- *Travel.* How much traveling will you do for your business? Do you yourself want to participate in fairs and trade shows or would you prefer to hire a sales representative?
- *People.* How many people do you want to work with? Do you want to employ them full-time or hire them on a freelance basis?
- *Skill level.* How do your skills compare with those of other craftspeople? Where in the market should you try to compete?

Everybody's situation is different, so you may find other variables to consider, but basically this is the process. Look carefully at what you want, and give your imagination free rein for a while. Then distill your aims into a simple mission statement, as short as two sentences. A statement such as, "Working from my home in the country making specialized metal sculptures, I want to express my creativity and have enough time for my garden and family," is enough to start. If this is your fantasy, translate it into a plan, and design a strategy based on the information in this guide; for example, you should examine the types of market, described in later sections, which require low production levels. However, if your statement is, "I will work hard for five years creating a craft production facility with a 10-person workshop," then your approach will be completely different. You should read the information on the larger-scale production and marketing opportunities. Either way, your ultimate choice of your craft, production facilities, markets, organizational structure, and location will be determined by your objectives, so give these issues concentrated thought.

IDENTIFYING YOUR SKILLS

As an entrepreneur, you want to build a business on your creative talent, aesthetic sense of design, and managerial ability. The skill level of you and your employees helps determine the way you shape your business. Your production choices and product designs are integrally related to this skill level and should be part of a total strategy.

If you are the creative designer, for example, you may want a staff of technical craftspeople to concentrate on production. If you intend to have employees, you should evaluate your managerial skills and cultivate them for growth. Identifying a market opportunity is as much of a skill as making the actual product. By carefully analyzing your product potential and manufacturing capacity, you will be able to ascertain which market most closely matches your expertise.

To achieve what you articulate in your mission statement, you must focus on all these factors. But to accomplish anything, you need more than your statement— you need a game plan. Organizing your business is essential to success. Once you have articulated your vision, the next step is to develop a marketing strategy and structure your operation around it.

PLANNING A MARKETING STRATEGY

Business literature is rife with military similes that talk of setting a course and planning an attack on the market, as if it was an impenetrable fortress to be scaled. The assumption is that consumers are defending themselves against your assaults, and you must outflank or outsmart them to win. Think of your selling efforts more as guides for your customers, much like road signs to a destination. By analyzing your product, place in the market, and pricing potential, and then designing your promotional materials, you will give visual signposts to your customers, leading them to their, as well as your, "destination"—the purchase of your goods and the start of a profitable business relationship.

With so many competing retail craft fairs (an estimated 30,000 each year) and dozens of wholesale trade shows, you must be selective and plan your approach to the market carefully. What will you sell and at what venue? Who are your customers and how will you reach them? How much can you charge for your product? The most crucial part of any venture is being able to stay on course, set your own limits, and focus on a particular market segment, achieving small successes rather than attempting everything at once.

DEFINING YOUR MARKET

The two basic elements of a crafts business are the product and buyer, and they need to be successfully matched. Look at your endeavors as a whole process, not a series of isolated actions. To help determine the best markets for your goods, think about your product. Based on your interests, experience, and skill level, you have created a desirable craft item that has several appealing characteristics: quality construction, aesthetic appeal, utility, uniqueness, and fair pricing. Then consider the customers who will part with their money to own your work and develop an emotional attachment to it. What kind of people are they? Where do they live? What will appeal most to them about your product?

Identifying your customers is an essential step. Imagine the people you would like to identify with your product. Write down all their characteristics, including their occupations and levels of education, how often they travel, what kind of magazines they read, and the entertainment they choose. Think about their aesthetic preferences, which will in turn determine their shopping habits. Since consumer purchasing trends change seasonally, you will need to make continual product development and marketing adjustments to meet market demands.

An example of a successful craft business that has geared its product development and selling efforts to a particular market is Guy Wolfe Pottery, located in New Preston, Connecticut. Guy Wolfe creates unglazed earthenware flower pots based on old English garden designs. They are all hand thrown and range in size from small seed pots to large planting pots. He has also resurrected some old Victorian flower pot designs. His packaging is a masterpiece of simplicity that targets one particular, receptive segment of the market—upscale garden customers. But the real stroke of genius is the way he builds on the nostalgic appeal of his pots; he stamps each one with a seal displaying his name, the date, and the weight of the original clay ball used for the pot. With this presentation, he elevates the perceived quality and value of his handcrafted work, and this allows him to charge very high prices.

This is an example of product analysis and market definition leading to product redefinition. Guy Wolfe did not start out being successful. He started with a skill and an idea and then narrowed his market to focus on customers with an interest in gardening and nostalgia and adapted his craft accordingly. He sells through the *Smith & Hawken* catalog (targeted to gardeners and socially responsible customers), retail outlets, and his studio.

ANALYZING THE COMPETITION

In some ways, you are better off ignoring what anyone else is doing, because outside influences can distract you from what *you* want to do. Of course, your own skills and vision shape your work, but on the other hand, understanding the competition gives you invaluable insight into the market and a reference point from which to operate.

For instance, almost every potter makes coffee mugs. The generally accepted price ceiling for this item is $10 retail, because competition drives the price down. Yet Gil Wilson, at the Chatham Pottery in Cape Cod, gets between $18 and $22 for his mugs. What is the difference?

Regular coffee mug	Chatham Pottery coffee mug	Chatham's value added
plain earth tone glaze	fish or morning glory design	unique design
sale at craft show	sale in retail store	continual name recognition
individual pieces	part of a consistent look and set	integrated product with related component parts
retail location with mass-market customers	retail location with upscale customers	environment adds to perceived value

In the chart above, you can see the aspects that enable Chatham Pottery to charge more for their products. A look at the competition indicates that the market for $10 mugs is already saturated. There is, however, room for an upscale version. Consider how you can add value to your product to distinguish it from others on the market and increase the price. For instance, if you think that people are looking for original coffee mugs—a fair assumption—you could experiment with glazes and designs. This might be especially appropriate at retail craft fairs where customers buy gift items or impulse purchases; these consumers are unlikely to shop for complete sets of earthenware to transport home. On the other hand, if you are selling through a retail outlet, you might be better off designing your mugs as part of a whole set of dinnerware, and this may be a way of selling a larger quantity at one time. Certainly, making the same cups as everyone else will not distinguish your line or increase sales.

CREATING A SALABLE PRODUCT

Finding out what will sell is at the heart of what you are doing. Before reviewing the details of design and product development, analyze the circumstances of making a sale and the conditions under which people will buy certain crafts. Time, convenience, context, and price are among the variables that a customer thinks about.

- *Time.* Are the buyers in a hurry or looking for a spur-of-the-moment purchase? Or, are they casually browsing?
- *Convenience.* Will it be easy or cumbersome for them to carry or transport your products?
- *Context.* How appropriate are your items for the location in which you are selling them? Does your work match the atmosphere or theme of the shop, fair, or event?
- *Price.* Does your price fit your target audience? What are the prices of any competing crafts?

As an example, consider context. Crafts that sell successfully in certain contexts don't necessarily sell well in others. Customers at tourist locations might select small items, such as handcrafted jewelry, but are unlikely to purchase large or expensive pieces of ironwork, while consumers in high-priced craft galleries might choose large pieces of pottery or custom-made furniture because the shop provides good customer service.

Utilitarian products might have mass appeal in either location. In general, useful crafts sell better than purely decorative items. If you are a weaver, you are more likely to sell bags, rugs, and clothing than wall hangings. Keeping this in mind, you could adapt an ordinary, mass-produced item to your own style. For instance, Katohna (New York) craftsperson John McLeod has taken the wooden kitchen utensil to a fine art; his unique designs and smooth wooden serving spoons, forks, and the like are in great demand. Many people prefer to own attractive household items that have character and integrity, and they are also willing to pay more money for a quality product that they know they need.

Adapting historical designs to fit modern needs is another way to make your work more unique and salable. The Mica Lamp Company, in California, fabricates Mission-style lighting fixtures using slices of mica for the shades. They successfully integrate a contemporary style with an established aesthetic.

Design your work with these factors in mind: The complex web of human desires and perceptions motivates purchases. The more accurately you anticipate your market, the more likely you are to succeed with the right item in the right place at the right time.

There are certain principles you can follow to focus on your goals and business opportunities. As a starting point, review your mission, skills, and experience. Consider the market and think about which products best suit it. Structure your design, prices, and presentation accordingly. Also, identify your target customers and their buying desires, and consider the circumstances and environment in which you are going to be selling. Understand the limits and opportunities; this provides clues on size, price, and presentation.

PRICING FOR THE MARKET

The ultimate test of whether you have a salable product is whether it sells, and pricing plays a key role in a successful marketing program. Once you have defined your craft line and considered the market potential, you must determine price. Understandably, you would like to get a certain price to justify your time and creative effort, not to mention the years of training involved in mastering your skills. If you price too high, you will put yourself out of the market and not make any sales. If your pricing is unrealistically low, you won't earn enough money to make ends meet.

Pricing is one of the trickiest parts of the whole business process. You have two competing forces influencing the final price of your item. There is the price you would like to get for your work versus the effects of competition and price resistance, which are driving the price down. The final retail cost, which will appeal to the customer, lies somewhere in the middle. You can assess your retail-price options by comparative shopping. To determine if there will be demand for your work, even if you plan to wholesale only, you must understand the perceived retail value of similar goods and where your work fits into the spectrum.

Note that, there is a difference between pricing and costing your work. *Costing* incorporates labor, time, materials, and overhead; this is discussed on pages 45–47 under Production for Profit. Retail *pricing* reveals the value of your product based on the market demand, availability, and perceived value. The following pricing suggestions are for determining the retail-market value.

- Research the prices of similar products in your target market. Look at catalogs and brochures and visit craft shops and shows to get a range of prices. Also check prices at import stores; if something similar is being made overseas for a fraction of your costs, you might want to consider revising your product design.
- Maximize the appeal of your goods. The only way craftspeople can justify the higher prices they need to charge is by providing better design, quality, presentation, and service.
- Offer a range of prices, sizes, designs, and colors. Once you narrow down your market, create a line that gives buyers maximum choice and captures differing tastes. Big pieces round out a collection, but smaller, less expensive pieces are more salable.
- Give yourself a realistic profit margin based on an analysis of your costs. It is more important to price your items realistically and devise an appropriate marketing strategy than to price too cheaply and lose money.

IMAGE AND PROMOTION

Presentation is a part of market identification. It is an exciting part of the business and gives you the opportunity to control your image in a positive, or negative, way. How you present yourself and your work to the public distinguishes your operation from others. A polished, professional image is as important as the quality of your product line.

Promoting yourself is an art. It is a critical factor in your success, and it is worth your time and effort. Your visual signals are road signs to your customers; your work and presentation communicate at a glance if you are selling something that fits into their life. Without promotion no one will know where to discover your work. You need to develop a whole package that articulates your vision, enhances your image, and presents consumers with a road map to your crafts.

If your strength does not lie in promotion, you might want to consider hiring a professional who believes in your work. As you will discover by reading the third chapter of this book (see page 52), various markets require different approaches.

You need to custom design a strategy and select advertising methods that effectively communicate your image and product line to buyers. In this section, we'll consider various approaches.

POSTCARDS

A postcard may be one of the most effective ways to present your work. It should be one of your first promotional investments. Since there is space for messages and buyer notes, postcards are often more useful to buyers than business cards. You can design your own or hire a public relations expert to create an image that will promote your crafts. A targeted mailing list is necessary for maximizing your return; before each trade show or exhibition, send out postcards with your booth number as a reminder to buyers. Often customers visit with postcard in hand, so you might offer a special incentive on the postcard to visit the booth—for example, a five percent discount on all retail purchases over $100. A well-conceived postcard should have the following features:

- A color image (either a photo or drawing) that is the best representation of your product, or a photograph of you at work on your craft.
- The standard postcard format on the reverse side.
- A brief description of your craft.
- Your name, address, and telephone number.
- A printed line that says, "Visit us at the (trade show, fair, etc.), Booth #." Alternatively, you could print a label that lists all the shows in which you participate, and adhere it to the postcard.

BROCHURES

A well-designed brochure, which describes your company and product line, is essential for several reasons. To start, it establishes your presence as a serious enterprise. This may seem to be only a subtle advantage, but you can project how professional and focused you are by how skillfully you articulate your vision and present your crafts. A brochure gives customers a permanent record of your merchandise that they can refer to when ordering or reordering. It can create sales opportunities through the mail or second-hand contact, especially if you cannot personally meet the customer to make a sale.

A successful brochure doesn't need to be expensive or fancy, but it does have to represent your line well. It should contain the following elements:

- A statement about the aims of the organization.
- A brief description of the company history.
- A clear statement of the product line describing the materials used. Include illustrations here, either line drawings or photographs. At least one color photograph is useful for an immediate impression.

- A separate price list with reference numbers that correspond to numbered illustrations. (The advantage to this approach is that you can reprint the price sheet separately from the brochure at a considerable savings. You can also print two different price sheets—one for wholesale and one for retail—to accommodate various markets.
- Information on any quantity discounts.
- Information on production capacity and/or time of delivery after order is placed.
- Optional: A detachable return postcard to request a sample (this can be complimentary or for a fee, depending on your craft).

BIO SHEETS

A common buyer complaint is the lack of simple data on the craftspeople and their processes. A bio sheet is particularly useful if you have not yet developed a brochure but feel you are ready to test-market your goods. It costs considerably less to produce than a brochure and provides buyers with a reminder of who you are. Moreover, it is a useful selling tool for consumers who want to learn more about the artist in whose work they are investing. A bio sheet should include:

- Your personal background information as an artisan, including your education.
- A list of the shows in which you have exhibited.
- A list of select customers.
- Information on the process you use to create your pieces.
- An attached line drawing or photograph of your product line or you at work.

Bio sheets can be as long (or short) as you need and should be handed out at trade shows or should accompany items sold to retail outlets.

HANG TAGS

Hang tags, or cards that provide product information such as materials or descriptions of the artistic process, are useful selling tools for a retail outlet. They add value to your crafts and help educate your customers by explaining background sources or cultural and historical significance. They are a good way to inform people that your product is handcrafted. Hang tags should contain identification of the product; an explanation of the creative process; your company name, logo, and background information; and, when appropriate, a geographical or historical legend to enhance the product value.

PRESS RELEASES

A good press release provides the artist with a vehicle for media attention. You create the news to attract a reporter's attention. Don't underestimate the value of this writing; it is much easier and faster to use material readily available than to research a story. Reporters are always looking for stories and often need to fill spots. If your press release (instead of someone else's) is in their files, busy writers will quickly adapt it to their needs—they have an instant piece, and you have instant publicity. A press release should be double-spaced and include the date; the words: "For Immediate Release"; a contact with telephone number, fax, and address; a headline that summarizes the news release and captures the reporter's attention; and concise and informative paragraphs that tell who, what, where, when, and how in an interesting manner.

The lead, or first, paragraph of a press release should grab the reader's attention and quickly explain the importance of the news. For example, you might be announcing a new product line, participation in an exhibition, or a move to a new gallery location. Place nonessential information and notes to the editor at the end of the release preceded by three number signs (###) to indicate the end of the actual release information. Include slides, transparencies, or photographs labeled with your name and address, and a self-addressed return envelope if you want them back. Be prepared to have these returned to you.

You should also make a list of the possible resources to send the press releases to. This might include local newspapers, local radio and television stations, trade magazines, local tourist or city-entertainment guide publications, convention and tourist-information centers, and art league centers.

NEWSLETTERS

An informative and entertaining newsletter can be a valuable and effective promotional tool. It can capture the interest of customers, retail craft buyers, galleries, and the press. It can alert them to new products and keep them posted on where you are exhibiting next. It is also another way to build a following of loyal customers, and you can prepare a newsletter on a computer without a major expenditure.

When developing your newsletter, consider incorporating some of the following elements: information written in a personal manner about yourself and your recent work, a look behind the scenes at how you make your crafts, unusual distinctions about your crafts, and updates on new materials or creative techniques. Designing a newsletter as a self-mailer (a piece of mail that doesn't require an envelope) saves both printing and paper costs. Other considerations include quantities needed, up-to-date mailing lists, postage costs, and freelance fees for any special layout or design.

ADVERTISING AND PROMOTION

The best advertising is, of course, free advertising. If you can rely on "word-of-mouth" to bring in sufficient sales and, better yet, some free articles, you have it made. Many trade publications have a "New Products" section in which an editor might show your craft at no charge. Similarly, local newspapers or magazines often have "best buys" pages, which might cover special themes or seasonal interests. Both these venues offer opportunities to feature your work at no cost to you.

How do you take advantage of this free publicity? Especially in your local area, get to know the editor. Find out the schedule and planned themes for the product section. Send in an updated press release with photos periodically or when you introduce something new. If they have this material on file, editors may use it at any time when looking for filler or a story.

You may also want to sell a specific product through an ad (in local or national newspapers or magazines) that provides ordering and detailed product information. Or, you could promote your business in general and offer instructions on how to send away for your brochure. Either way, you should collect the names of those people who respond and add them to your mailing list.

Assuming that you need to attract attention on a more regular basis, you must decide how much money to spend and where to advertise for the greatest return. If you are just starting out, you should develop a budget for promotion. And, you need to decide what audience you must reach. Estimate what percent of your total revenues you want to devote to advertising; figure your past costs and adjust the amount based on your experience and other factors, such as new places to advertise. As a guide, ask other craftspeople in your field what they spend on advertising, or check with an industry source, such as *Advertising Age* magazine, for an average budget. Then investigate the costs of advertising in various media. Ask yourself what kind of advertising you want to do and which are the less expensive media options.

Consider the following venues:

- Classified ad in a trade journal.
- Bounce-back ad (a promotional insert in a package shipped to a customer).
- Magalog ad (a magazine that promotes craft products).
- Ad in a hotel or tourist magazine such as *Where.*
- Direct-mail brochure to previous customers.
- Internet (see page 232 for more information).

Compared to the television, radio, and expensive print media, these options are more affordable and offer a good reach. Keep records on your costs, evaluate your returns from each ad. You may want to start small and increase your exposure gradually. After you develop your promotional material, you can begin the next step of test marketing.

TEST MARKETING

Test marketing will help you to identify what sells well and which outlets buy the most. You can test crafts on an experimental basis first. For example, place your crafts in local fairs, flea markets, and exhibits to see if a demand exists for them. Or, set up a small showroom in your home or studio and invite friends to view and purchase your products. You could also send a mailing to the local community to invite them to a special showing of your crafts. Another option is to offer small quantities of products on consignment to local store owners; the response, measured by sales, will indicate whether or not the particular product is salable. If it is, you can ask the buyers to place orders. After initial, positive test marketing, you will be ready for production.

HOW TO REALLY RUN A BUSINESS

With a salable product and marketing strategy in hand, you are on the way to launching your business. You have a vision, but now you need to structure your work, time, production, and staff. To achieve your goals, set and articulate realistic objectives and establish a reasonable time frame within which to accomplish them.

In any endeavor, planning is the basis for sound management. In this section, we will review the importance of establishing a legal business entity, creating a business strategy, and managing your customers and distribution. Then, in the subsequent section, we'll look at production and inventory management. All of these are essential tools for building a successful business.

ORGANIZATIONAL STRUCTURE

For legal and tax purposes, the first step in developing an organizational structure is to separate business and personal affairs. If you are working from your home and have a fledgling craft business that is an extension of your personal interests, you need to keep distinct records. A separate checking account for business and personal use is an easy beginning.

Learn about the legal and tax implications, then choose a legal identity that best suits your business needs. These range from sole proprietorship to a full corporation. The organizational structure you follow depends on your objectives, desired growth, and the number, if any, of future partners or employees. Another structure that you might consider, particularly if you live in a rural area, is a craft cooperative.

Sole Proprietorship

This is the simplest way to organize a business and often involves no more than going to your local government office to get an operating license, which entitles you to run a business in your area. Local zoning requirements may restrict what a company can do in residential areas, but once you have your occupancy permit, you can start operating your business. Depending on your aims, you may also need to acquire a resale tax number (in states that have sales tax) and federal business identification.

Since you record sales as personal income and deduct legitimate operating expenses from that, the danger with a sole proprietorship is the close proximity of business and personal finances. To avoid financial complications, keep completely separate bookkeeping records for craft sales and expenses, and establish a professional checking account.

Countering the advantages of simplicity and flexibility in this situation, however, is personal liability for business losses. You can insure yourself against damage to capital equipment and personal injury suits, but any debt the company takes on will pass directly to you. Since most banks want the principals of the organization to personally guarantee loans, you would probably be liable even if you had formed a corporation. In a sole proprietorship you would be liable for debts to suppliers, and banks could attach your personal assets to settle a claim.

Overall, though, this form of organization is good if you don't plan to expand much beyond a one- or two-person enterprise, or if, in the early stages of the business, you carry losses over to personal tax status. When the business grows beyond a certain size and generates profits or if you need to raise some more capital, you should look at other options.

Partnerships

The saying "Partnerships are the saddest ships that ever sailed" is an appropriately cautionary note on this form of business. While there are many advantages to pooling resources, experience, contacts, and expertise in a partnership, there are also many hazards. It is extremely important that you articulate fully the aims and the goals of the partnership, and that you restate them regularly. There should be no misconceptions about the direction of the company. Like any marriage, the whole is only as strong as the parts; the more clearly partners understand their roles from the outset, the less confusion there will be later.

There are two types of partnerships: basic and limited liability. The *basic partnership* is simple and requires no formalities for creation. You can outline the basic terms of your alliance with a partner in a simple letter of agreement, which one or both of you draft and then sign in front of a witness. Legal work is not necessary and best avoided, as it could become expensive. In the early stage, it is the strength of the intention of the parties, not fine legal language, that will see the enterprise to success.

In any legal definition, there are certain assumed characteristics of a simple partnership:

- New partners cannot be accepted without the unanimous agreement of all existing partners.
- All partners have equal rights and equal votes.
- All partners share equally in the profits and losses of the venture.
- A majority vote is required for ordinary business decisions, whereas only a unanimous vote can change the basic nature of the partnership.
- A partnership can be terminated at any time by any partner, or you can specify a time period in the agreement.

The *limited liability partnership* is so named because it limits the amount of personal liability of the partners to the amount they have invested in the business. Risking only their initial financial input, investors can share in anticipated profits from the enterprise without being involved in the day-to-day management of the business.

There are two different types of partners in this situation: the general partner, who is active in running the business, and the limited partner, who is a passive investor. Because the finer legal points of a limited partnership are far more complicated than those of a simple partnership, you should seek expert legal advice to establish the framework. The main conditions of a limited liability partnership are as follows:

- Define the business—its scope of operations and its potential for growth—in your original agreement.
- Set a time limit for the duration of the partnership, after which profits and assets will be divided.
- Determine the distribution of profits at the outset with a percentage retained for future investment.
- Partners are prohibited from pursuing other business opportunities related to the business of the partnership that are for the profit of only one partner.
- The partnership ceases to exist on the death or withdrawal of a partner, even though you can make provisions for the continuation of business. This means that partners are not stuck in their investments, and unlike a corporation, they are not obliged to find a buyer for their shares.

Partnerships have the advantages of pooling resources for production and sales and obtaining credit from a lender. In addition, they are more flexible and easier to form and disband than corporations. The disadvantages include mutual liability between partners (especially in a simple partnership) and fewer tax advantages because any disbursements are taxed as ordinary income. A partnership works for people who complement each other's skills. Recognizing and respecting your partner's areas of expertise are essential to the success of the enterprise.

Corporations

Corporations represent the greatest separation of business from personal identity, both legally and financially. The defining characteristics of this structure include the following:

- An entity that can be divided and sold.
- Financial existence completely separate from personal finances.
- Shares that are issued to the investors or founders of the company based on how the ownership is divided. For example, shares can be voting and nonvoting. In apportioning shares, you can allot nonvoting shares to passive investors and voting shares to officers running the corporation. You can also apply other restrictions to issued shares.

The main advantages to a corporation involve financial tax benefits and limited personal liability. For example, health insurance and retirement plans can be paid from pre-tax income, and wages, from the remaining income. Profits can be left in the corporation and taxed at a corporate rate, which is less than personal income tax. In the early years of the corporation, Subchapter S status makes sense because losses from the business may be carried over into personal taxes. Any liability and debt taken on by the corporation remains with the corporate entity and does not pass on to the business owner. This advantage is partly illusory, however, in that most banks require a personal guarantee on any loans, and the business owner is personally liable for unpaid withholding taxes.

The disadvantages of a corporation lie in the complexity of the financial and legal paperwork needed to keep it in good standing. You must file regular state and federal papers, conduct annual meetings with minutes, and keep records. The payroll taxes are due on a regular basis with substantial penalties for late payments.

Cooperatives

A crafts cooperative is a useful structure for craftspeople who want to form a business that pools responsibilities and shares economies of scale for goods or services. Owned and financed by members, cooperatives exist for the mutual benefit of the participants and operate by majority rule. Members have only one vote, regardless of whether they control two or 15 percent of the stock. All partakers have an obligation to assist in the management and decision-making processes, and they benefit in proportion to their use of the cooperative, not their financial investment. Like a corporation, a cooperative has a different legal status than a partnership or a sole proprietorship and is incorporated under state law.

Structures for cooperatives vary according to need. They may be local, regional, or state organizations. A local cooperative usually consists of individuals who know each other and band together to solve common problems and possibly share resources, including marketing and production information. This type of alliance is often useful in more rural areas where access is limited. A combination of individuals and/or local cooperatives compose regional and state cooperatives. Again, the advantages are in combining forces to operate on a more efficient scale than would otherwise be possible at the individual level. For example, cooperative purchases of goods and services are less expensive.

Disadvantages exist whenever groups get together. Politics, bureaucratic inflexibility, and the need for constant communication might adversely affect the cooperative arrangement. Generally, however, the groups that work well together can expect many beneficial activities, including:

- Marketing assistance—links to markets and customers, updates on trends, a shared retail store, and help with wholesale opportunities.
- Technical assistance—training in business and production skills, help in securing loans, information on government regulations and craft industry news and activities.
- Production assistance—purchase of supplies in bulk, joint use of equipment, and production and management training.

PLAN OF ACTION

Before you can start to plan your business, you need to review your personal goals. Ask yourself these questions: What do you envision for your future? What makes you happy? What do you enjoy? How will you integrate your personal life with your business life? How much money do you want to make, and how long are you willing to wait to realize these returns? The answers to these queries will help you develop your business objectives.

Business Plan

A well-thought-out plan is vital to developing a successful business. Writing down your ideas, aims, strategies, and resources forces you to think clearly and realistically about building, organizing, and managing a business. You may discover that your notions are not as appealing as they were before you committed them to paper. Or, you may develop additional ideas that you hadn't previously thought about. Writing the plan gives you a direction. It also gives investors or bankers an overview of your business as a credit or investment risk.

Where do you start? If you go to your local book or computer store, you will find numerous books and software on how to write business plans. Any of these will help, because there is no one correct way to organize yourself. Most business proposals, however, share the following components presented in this order:

- Cover page—a title page with your company name, address, telephone number, and your name as chief executive.
- Table of contents—a list of sections with corresponding page numbers.
- Executive summary—a one-page summary of your business plan.
- Company information—the company description, history, evolution, strategy, and goal. This is a logical place to include your vision and mission statement.
- Market—a description of your target audience, including information on craft trends and interests. You should note both negative and positive elements of your market.
- Product—an explanation of your craft, prices, quality, distinctions, and competition.
- Sales and marketing strategy—a statement of the methods you will use to sell and promote your craft. Include craft fairs and other markets you intend to target.
- Financing—a report of your sales history and anticipated revenues, plus an explanation of how you intend to acquire capital. You will probably want to include a profit-and-loss statement, as well as cash-flow projections (estimates of cash coming in and to be spent at a future time).

Write in your own words as clearly and concisely as possible. Keep your plan focused. If necessary, get assistance for certain sections, but don't delegate the process entirely; the exercise may take a week or longer, but it will help you become more focused and professional.

Implementation

With a simple business proposal that outlines overall goals and company strategy, you are ready to put your plan into action. You want to have a basic organizational structure in place to maximize resources and control your activities so that you don't lose focus.

Let's look at how Pot Luck Studios of Modena, New York, implemented their strategy. Started by Karen Skelton in the late 1980s, Pot Luck Studios makes beautifully designed, glazed flower pots and wholesales them at the major gift shows. The product has a very focused market—garden accessories. A graphic designer by training, Skelton concentrated on the presentation and design of the company, leaving the actual production to potters working for her. Her business plan in the early stages could have read something like this:

Product and Market
Product—flower pots of all sizes
Niche—designer stores, high-end gift shops, urban garden centers

Advantages
High level of design
Unique product
Focused product line with a whole range of flower pots

Strategy
Concentrate on the wholesale market
Invest in printing and promotional materials to create a quality image
Establish an identity in the urban garden market
Invest time and money on a well-designed booth for trade shows
Sell 2,000 pots in first year
Expand product line on the basis of initial success
Make a pre-tax profit of 10 percent

At the first show, Pot Luck Studios sold over 7,000 pots, exceeding its targeted goal. Beginning with a limited range, it has since expanded its lines to include many colors and patterns, but it has stayed completely on track with a well-expressed vision its objective: selling to a particular market. In this case, the design element was the most vital ingredient to success. Early on, Skelton identified her market, designed her product for that market, and defined the future growth of her company.

While planning is vital, no plan is written in stone; your ability to be flexible and adapt to changing conditions, rewriting your plans as necessary, will help ensure future success. Mystic Woodwork in Warren, Maine, makes beautiful wooden household products, selling exclusively as a wholesale company at major gift shows. It evolved from a barely successful operation (participating in local craft fairs, hauling goods hundreds of miles for weekend shows, making scarcely enough money to cover costs) to a lucrative business concentrating instead on custom work and increasing their production for wholesale supply only.

Mystic Woodwork's original plan may have defined its product and market niche as craft fairs and retail sales, but in the implementation and assessment stage it underwent significant changes. At the outset, it wasn't in a position to produce the necessary quantities for wholesale, and it didn't have a clear enough understanding of the market. Only after doing the groundwork, including test marketing and retail selling, was it able to move on to wholesale marketing.

Control

Once you develop your business and have records to evaluate, you must take time to review the bigger picture. Assess the effectiveness of your strategy, using the information to reformulate and redirect your plan in the future. This is an ongoing task.

Ask yourself what's working. What needs changing? In today's highly competitive environment, you have to be constantly alert to new trends, fading styles, and new techniques. In short, you must be aware of the world around you. You cannot afford to rest on your past successes; you must constantly push the edges of your creativity in both management and design.

FINANCING

The financial side of a business is often the least attractive to artists and craftspeople. Yet money management is as essential to your endeavor as gasoline is to a car engine. Running out of gas at the wrong time leads to major headaches.

To structure the financial management of your enterprise, decide at what scale you wish to operate. Can you afford to start with a full tank of gas, or do you fill up partially? In other words, are your financial resources and your vision sufficient to set up a complete facility with all the manufacturing equipment you will need for future growth? Or, do you anticipate starting small and slowly building your business?

In our first example below, we are setting up an entire structure of operation at one time, so for the sake of convenience, we'll call this the *structural* model. In the structural model, all of the elements of a business are defined in terms of system requirements, similar to building an engine. For instance, if you plan to go into the metal-working business you would estimate the following:

Cost of shop tools:	$8,200
Space needed and cost (1000 square feet at $800 per month, requiring two months rent as security deposit):	$1,600
Preparation of the workshop:	$2,000

Setting up the workshop will require a capital outlay of $11,800 before you make any money. If you borrow the money, you need to assess your ability to make the monthly interest payments from your anticipated profits. If you personally guarantee a loan, which most banks require from small corporations, any inaccurate profit projections could lead to trouble.

A gradual, organic growth of a business is the more common approach for small-scale ventures, particularly in the early stages. In this second scenario, the *organic* model, you plow a portion of profits back into your business, reinvesting them to build up your equipment and inventory over time. Although this plan requires a lot of juggling of resources and sleepless nights when money is scarce, it will afford you greater flexibility when market changes and new opportunities present themselves. As you grow and develop different aims, you can make investments at the appropriate times and avoid overcommitting. The main advantages here are greater control and fewer debt obligations. The main disadvantage is that it takes a lot longer for the business to advance.

Using either of these financial models requires careful planning in order to maximize limited resources. In business and life, there is rarely enough money to do everything you would like, but if you're careful and know what you want, you can manage your finances for optimum results. Keep your overhead low and avoid being seduced by the illusion that a big workshop and a big truck with your name emblazoned on it mean success; stretch your resources, including staff, workshop, and office space, to the limit before making additional investments or financial commitments.

MANAGING YOUR CUSTOMER

When customers purchase your product, they are attracted to your vision and your aesthetic taste. To capitalize on that interest and maintain it, build your business one customer at a time. Once consumers part with their money to have one of your creations, it is up to you to follow up on the initial contact and develop a more permanent customer relationship. How you do this depends a lot on the context of the initial sale and the nature of your company. We'll cover the various ways to develop and maintain buyer connections in different markets more thoroughly in the next chapter, but the following examples should provide a few ways to build positive customer relations in different craft settings.

Retail Craft Fairs

Since the crowds are transient, it is difficult to turn retail craft show customers into repeat buyers. You can, however, recapture consumers throughout the year, or at the next show, if you develop a mailing list at the fairs. Leave a book or paper out to encourage people to leave their names and addresses. Try to find out if they come to a particular show on a regular basis, and put them on the mailing list. Mailings are very expensive, so a well-targeted list is vital. Eliminate people you think are not potential buyers.

After developing your list, send notification to people of your shows in their area. Depending on your craft, you might even offer a special promotional craft, such as a textile or leather bookmark, a pin, or a handmade paper product, to encourage their visit to your booth. There is inexpensive computer software that can help create selective mailings based on geographical location.

Wholesaling to Stores and Galleries

Building a relationship with retail buyers helps assure continuing orders from them. After making an initial wholesale trade show contact, you need to exert more energy to build personal contact. Convince buyers that you are serious about your business and that they can trust you to look after their interests.

To do this, you must be prepared; know the prices and the delivery times of your goods, and supply an easy-to-read wholesale price list and a bio sheet. Always be honest; if there are any problems with the production, quality, or timing of the order fulfillment, let the buyer know immediately. Be courteous and patient, and be available to answer their questions.

When you make an appointment to see buyers at their store or office, be on time. Afterward, follow up; continued communication is very important in developing relationships. You might send a card thanking the buyer for the initial meeting. After making shipments, call to ensure that there were no problems with the orders. Send photographs of new products and include pricing. Any additional information you can provide about your art shows, juried craft shows, and grants or awards will add to your marketability.

Strive to be well informed about market trends. Spend time visiting competing stores. Take time to listen to descriptions of the store's customers. Knowing how the buyers or store and gallery owners perceive their own clientele shows that you have their interests at heart and can customize your service.

THE MECHANICS OF SELLING

Creating a good first and continued impression with consumers is one of the most important marketing rules for a small company . Often the only contact you'll have with your customer is at a sales show, and in that very short amount of time, you have to create an impression of competence and trustworthiness.

Retail buyers who make a commitment to your crafts require pleasant service and reliability. If you turn up with a hastily assembled booth and minimal sales tools, you'll seem amateurish and undependable. If they feel that you can't deliver or that they'll receive shoddy merchandise, buyers won't place orders.

How do you gain the trust of your potential customer? There are many things you can do to show that you are professional and fully committed to your business. First, create a well-designed business card. You are an artist; this is a buyer's first introduction to you, and it should reflect your work. Print and copy shops offer various qualities of paper stock, and most are relatively inexpensive.

If you are working at a craft fair or trade show, keep your booth simple and direct. Buyers usually do not give more than a cursory glance when they first pass by, so you need to communicate what you do in a split second. They are besieged by merchandise, so your booth should give them strong visual signals about who you are and what you sell. Make a nice sign, preferably constructed from the materials in which you work. Position the best pieces at the front of the booth, keep related groupings together, and use larger pieces to attract attention. Keep as many things as you can at eye level, and don't crowd the floor and make it hard for people to walk into your booth. Mount pictures of your workshop or production facility in the booth or in a well-presented portfolio, and include a short biography of you and your company with your brochure, price list, or order form.

Business forms to record your order transactions are another vital tool for proper organization and presentation. All of the forms discussed in this section are available from any office supply company or copy shop. You can purchase them off the shelf or customize them for a very small fee. The customized versions look more professional, furthering the impression that you are a serious and reliable businessperson. Forms should have sequential numbering to track transactions easily.

Your order form can also serve as your invoice and packing list. Many buying organizations, however, have their own purchase order forms and prefer to use these. Try to match your shipping invoice and packing list to these forms as closely as possible; doing so will simplify the buyers' receiving of your order and shorten invoice payment times to you. Remember that the purchase order is a contract, and you should comply with the product and quantities ordered and the specified delivery time. Your invoice and purchase order should include the following basic information, in addition to the merchandise description and price:

- Your company name, address, and telephone number.
- The billing and shipping address of the customer.
- Date of order.
- Date of delivery.
- Description of goods ordered, including product and color.
- Price of goods ordered.
- Form of payment, such as "net 30 days" from the date of the invoice. If customers want to pay in 30 days, you should check their credit references. It is not unusual to request cash on delivery (COD) for a first order. If the purchase is on consignment, you should describe the terms of the contract clearly on the invoice. Consignment arrangements, including payment time, are negotiable, but whatever the agreement, be sure that you state the terms exactly on the purchase order. You can generally expect to be paid within 30 to 60 days after you make a sale.
- Statement that freight is to be paid by the customer from your shipping address.
- Statement regarding finance charges if the invoice is not paid within the terms of the contract. A 1.5 percent-per-month fee is a standard charge, although it is difficult to collect since buyers often just ignore finance charges and send payment without this fee.
- Description of return policy, giving a limited amount of time within which a customer can return the goods.

Depending on your filing system you'll need duplicate or triplicate copies of your purchase orders and invoices. The customer gets one at the time of sale, and you keep one. With a triplicate system, you can send the third copy as an invoice, packing slip, or a statement if buyers are late with payments. For retail sales at craft shows, duplicates are fine.

If there are any changes in the circumstances of their orders, you must notify your customers immediately because they have the right to refuse the goods with any change of the terms. If you are going to be late in delivery, or need to change a material, color, or price, you must let the buyers know and request approval for any new arrangement.

DISTRIBUTION AND PACKING

Setting up a packing and shipping center for wholesale distribution is fairly simple, but there are many things that can go wrong. The appearance of your shipping containers, and how well they're packed when they arrive, is an important indicator of professionalism and has an effect on confidence you instill in buyers' minds about shipping a quality product.

United Parcel Service (UPS) and Road Package Service pick up and deliver to any address in this country. Daily pick-up charges are under $5 per week plus shipping charges, and they bill weekly. Otherwise, you can call UPS when you're ready to ship, and they'll pick up your shipment and charge you per delivery. You'll need a scale (to give the package weight over the phone), tape, and packing materials to prepare your shipment. Both of these companies have size and weight restrictions, so if you have any larger pieces, you might need to use a trucking company. Look in your area telephone directory to find a local company with national network affiliations, rather than a large, national company; this way, if anything goes wrong, you'll usually get prompt service and accountability.

It is standard procedure to bill shipping charges to your customers. Some craftspeople also add a small fee for packing and handling such as $2.50 per box for smaller items and up to 15 percent of the total cost for pottery. You can also build these charges into the price of the goods; this lets you avoid questions later on, but may make your crafts seem more expensive at the point of sale. Whatever you decide, whether for retail or wholesale, your policies should not be a surprise to your customers; inform them of all charges at the time of the sale. On your order form, add a printed line saying "F.O.B. [fill in your city]". This means *freight on board,* which is another way of saying that customers pay the freight from your door to theirs.

Packaging fragile items is a big problem no matter which service you use. Boxes get thrown around, and packages break. It is best to double-box fragile pieces, with the item tightly packed in the smaller inside box and then nestled in two to three inches of shredded paper in the outer box. The secret to packing delicate pieces is to have pockets of air or space that will absorb any blows during shipping. If you pack something too tightly, the shock will simply be transferred through the packing materials into the piece, which will break.

Another way to pack a larger piece is to place it in bubble wrap and then put the whole thing in a bed of polystyrene or paper pulp "peanuts." One useful tip here is to put a layer of cardboard under the item to trap a layer of peanuts below it; otherwise, the item will settle down to the bottom of the box and may get broken.

Make sure you insure all packages so that you will be reimbursed for any breakage if you have to file a claim. With UPS you are automatically insured up to $100. Include the cost of insurance with your freight charges when you bill your customers.

Order packing materials such as labels, tape, and boxes through office supply stores or mail-order companies. Unless you have a special arrangement with a local supplier, you generally get better prices from the larger warehouse companies or discount office supply stores.

PRODUCTION FOR PROFIT

To move your business from occasional selling at craft shows into a profitable enterprise, you have to analyze your manufacturing process carefully. While developing a product line and making initial samples, be aware of your material costs and your targeted price points. It is difficult, however, to get a precise breakdown of the production costs until you are creating successful crafts on a regular basis.

As mentioned earlier, it is important to distinguish between pricing and costing. *Pricing* refers to defining the final retail price. *Costing* means the actual production costs—material, labor, and fixed expenses (overhead)—of your craft.

PRICING

As mentioned previously, there are two opposing forces acting on the final sale price of your goods: the price people are willing to pay versus your desired price, which is based on the cost of production plus anticipated profit.

Keep in mind that pricing goods for the market depends on various subjective factors: comparison with other products, added value to your product through improved design or construction, uniqueness and originality, and a complete merchandise line that adds worth. These external forces suggest what the market will pay for a particular item. If you create coffee mugs of a certain size and shape that the competition sells for $10, you might be able to sell yours for $18 because of excellent workmanship and presentation. But, you are still limited by consumer acceptance and perceived value. For example, you might not be able to sell the same mug for $25.

While market forces drive down the final selling price, your production costs raise the price, yet you need a decent return on your labor, as well as on the years and money invested in training and experimentation. The secret to profitable business production is to make an item with the highest perceived value for the lowest possible cost. By employing marketing strategies, you can increase the perceived value, and by analyzing and controlling costs, you will increase profits.

COSTING

When analyzing your costs, first calculate your fixed monthly expenses and then add a realistic profit that will enable you to live comfortably. Fixed costs are rent, electricity, telephone, interest payments on loans, and any other monthly bills. Allow for reinvestment in new capital stock, such as machinery and tools. This is the absolute minimum you need to cover your obligations and bring in the monthly profits that enable your business to continue. Other variables in your budget, such as advertising, travel, and your own salary, are more flexible and can depend on seasonal cash flow.

Below is an example of how you might break down your monthly expenses:

Rent	$800
Interest payments	$240
Utilities	$180
Travel expenses	$220
Advertising/promotion	$120
TOTAL	**$1,560**

In this example, you'd need to generate $1,560 per month to meet your fixed costs before you pay yourself any wages or invest in new equipment. Adding in the basic wage cost for a month and a small reinvestment sum, you get:

Wages at $10 per hour (40 hours per week for four weeks)	$1,600
Reinvestment	$ 200
TOTAL	**$1,800**

The total amount of money you need to generate every month then is $3,360 ($1,800 + $1,560). Most businesses have cycles of activity in which they are much busier than at other times; for craft fairs, summer is the main selling season. In a regular retail environment, or for wholesale, you'll be busiest in the fall and winter holiday seasons. If you have a budget for monthly expenses, you'll be better prepared for these seasonal fluctuations in income.

Where will all that money come from to keep you in business? Let's look more carefully at your production costs and capabilities to see how much you can make per item and whether you can sell enough to make a profit. To return to the coffee mug example, the market price of the cup is between $10 and $22. You can assume that people who come to craft shows or stores will be willing to pay more than customers of regular stores for the uniqueness of a handmade item. Although it is difficult to break down costs for such a small item, you could approximate the production costs as follows:

Materials

1.5 pounds of clay at $.25 per pound	$.37
Glazes	$.10
Electricity/gas for kiln (fixed costs)	$.60
TOTAL	**$1.07**

The cost of materials is very low in this case, the value being added by the input of your labor and skill. For argument's sake, we'll value your time at $10 per hour.

Time

Preparing 5 to 7 lbs. of clay (enough for 4 mugs)	10 minutes
Modeling cups	10 minutes
Preparing glazes	20 minutes
Storing, drying, and firing mug	20 minutes
TOTAL	**1 hour**

Since we valued your time and expertise at $10, the total cost of production is $11.07, only $1.07 of which is the cost for materials. If you sell your cup for $14, and it costs you $1.07 to make, you are making a profit of $12.93 per mug (selling price minus cost of production equals profit). To meet your basic monthly fixed expenses, which we estimated at $3,360 in the example, you need to sell 122 coffee mugs per month. The fixed monthly costs ($1560) divided by the profit-per-piece ($12.93) equals the necessary monthly production quantity (122 mugs).

You can put anything you make and sell after this toward your wages and profit, but you should make a similar calculation to see how much money you earn on the extra pieces. If you do profit profiles of each item in your line, you can target your production needs and make informed decisions about other aspects of your business. For example, if you don't have production capability that allows you to rent a space, you could consider sharing a workshop with someone or converting your garage into a studio. Armed with accurate information on production costs and profit-per-piece, you'll be in a better position to make intelligent business decisions.

There are also numerous other points that you should consider when costing your work:

- You must account for breakage and flawed products that you'll have to discard or sell at a discount. Add a reasonable amount such as 10 percent to your production goals to cover these losses. In the above scenario, you'd need to create and sell an extra 12 mugs, so your actual target quantity would be 134 mugs per month.
- Factor in product development time. Experiment on new designs and techniques. One reason people buy from a craftsperson is the originality and personality in their work. If you devote all your time to manufacturing, you will lose the very spark of your business. Plan for creative development when you make up your production schedules.
- Always be aware of the competition. While you do not want to overprice your work, underpricing can be equally damaging. Always keep in mind the ultimate retail price and work backward from that; you need to allow enough margin to make a profit and develop your operation, but you also want to maintain your reputation for fairness and quality.

IDENTIFYING RESOURCES

There are many elements that go into your final product. The more efficiently you can gather them together, the more cost-effective and profitable you'll be. To do this, examine the requirements of each component of your craft items.

To avoid over- or underpurchasing of raw materials, it is vital that you plan the necessary amounts for a specific product over a given time period. In our coffee-mug example, the raw ingredients did not account for the highest monetary cost. But if you run out of something at a crucial time in your production schedule and you need an express delivery of more material, it may add considerable expense to your craft. On the other hand, it is not very cost-efficient to have a huge stockpile of your basic materials. Overordering ties up valuable capital that you could employ elsewhere. You may have to pay for additional warehouse storage and, if not properly stored, there can be damage and waste.

To plan for timely availability of all of your materials, break down the components for each product and put them on a chart. An example of a bread box and bread board would look like this:

Product Materials

Bread box	4 feet of 2-×-8-inch pine
Bread board	2 feet of 2-×-6-inch oak

You could do this for each product in your line so that when you make up a production schedule you already know what your material needs are and you can readily calculate your total requirements. If you use a computer, basic spreadsheets are excellent for this purpose. Even if you're almost completely computer illiterate, you can learn to easily adapt these programs to your own needs. For complicated projects, you can purchase software management programs, but these tend to be expensive.

A timeline chart is useful for planning, particularly for very busy times, or for keeping strict deadlines. By starting with the delivery or completion dates and working backward, you can anticipate the steps required to finish the job on time, taking into account delivery times and production delays. For example, if you have a big delivery of bread boxes and bread boards scheduled to ship to a retailer by November 15 for the Christmas season, you can work backward from a November delivery date to arrange material purchasing and production schedules. This type of planning ensures timely shipments and happy customers. For a delivery of 200 pieces of each product, a timeline might look something like this:

August	September	October	November
order wood	cut out forms	glue and varnish	ship
prepare wood	hire extra help	sand and finish	
materials needed:	200 bread boxes =	800 feet of 2-×-8-inch pine 300 feet of $1/2$-inch edging	
	200 bread boards =	400 feet of 2-×-6-inch oak	

This type of chart will help with timely production and supplies. Next, you need to choose the right suppliers. Since the cheapest supplier is not always the best, you should consider other factors, in addition to basic cost, such as minimum quantities available, quality, location, freight, and reorder time. As your business grows, you'll need larger quantities. Can your current vendors meet your increased needs? You should always look at alternative sources to see what they can offer.

Your entire business will be defined by the material you work in. If you have a readily available and inexpensive source, you can increase your production and approach markets that need large quantities of lower-priced products. If you work in a rare and exotic wood, you'll have to concentrate on making a very well-designed product for a one-of-a-kind market. Because the availability, price, and quality of your materials will determine the production capacity, salaries, and skills of your labor force, you should put as much effort into the sourcing of supplies as you do into crafting your work.

To say that time is a valuable commodity is a gross understatement. As in the earlier, coffee-mug pricing instance, labor is usually the most expensive element in a handmade craft. Therefore, you need to evaluate your time with the same scrutiny with which you would analyze your pricing or raw material suppliers. For example, are you spending valuable time in one step of the production process that you could be using more effectively elsewhere—perhaps in the creative process? Break down all the manufacturing steps to their component parts and ascribe a time for their completion. Now, ask yourself the following:

- How much does it cost me to do this?
- Can I buy partly finished materials to eliminate one stage of production?
- Does it require my special skill and knowledge?
- Can someone else be taught to perform this task? Which parts of the production process can I delegate to others and which must I do myself? (For example, when making that coffee mug, is it the best use of your time to wedge and prepare the clay? You might consider buying prepared clay or hiring an apprentice to do this.)
- Do you to strive for a balance of your time between design and production?

As you look closely at what you do with your time, you may be surprised to find how much more efficiently you could be using it. This doesn't mean that you need to become an automaton who only lives to work. Heaven forbid that should happen! You chose this lifestyle to avoid being a cog in a machine. However, you do need to value your time because it is the most important resource you have. You might rearrange your studio and implement time-saving improvements, or delegate simple tasks, such as the packing and shipping of orders. As the artist, you should concentrate your time on the creative, skill-oriented tasks as much as possible. You might hire a staff to help with the mechanics of production, but be prepared to spend initial time training personnel and directing production.

Having employees can be costly and difficult to manage, but if you can find the right arrangement for your circumstances, you could liberate yourself considerably for more artistic endeavors. You'll be freer to experiment with new product designs. If you can afford it, look for an apprentice or a part-time worker who is interested in your craft and can help with the mundane production tasks, paperwork, and customer follow-up.

INVENTORY MANAGEMENT

No matter what the size of your operation, inventory management is another essential element of a profitable enterprise. If you have too much inventory, you risk tying up money. Having stock is not the same as money in the bank, and you assume the expense of storage space. In addition, if you finance your manufacturing with borrowed money, you incur interest payments on merchandise that isn't producing a profit.

To anticipate inventory needs, track the sales of each of your products over a period of time and make projections based on that information. There are several computer programs available that can help you manage sales and match inventory projections to your production schedule; one of the best and easiest to use is the Makers Automated Clerk from Industrious Software Solutions in Inglewood, California (telephone: 800-351-4225). This program links inventory to invoices and sales orders; as you invoice a customer, the software automatically subtracts the items from inventory. It also allows you to enter any "works in process" that you work into your production schedule, and it provides production recommendations to help you meet anticipated demand. The program costs about $900. You should investigate the benefits of this and similar software before you commit to the system and the expenditure.

Although you can track inventory without a computer, if you want to run an efficient business and maintain a competitive edge, you should learn to utilize the basic advantages of computer programs. To record sales without the use of a computer, you can start with index cards; every time you make a sale, you can mark it on an index card and eventually create a graph of the information at the end of a show or a selling season to give you a better idea of buying cycles. Keeping records manually or by computer will enable you to project forward to the next season and prepare the finished goods in advance.

A good method of ensuring adequate stock levels is to set minimum quantities on hand for all of your products. Mark these levels on the storage shelves or bins, and when the stock level falls below that point, replenish supplies.

No matter how systematized you become, there's no substitute for your own sense of the business and anticipated sales. Computer systems can't tell you about seasonal fluctuations or market trends. If you believe that something will sell well, based on your market research, follow your instincts and produce more if inventory is low. Conversely, if you think that something has played out its popularity, stop production and begin to design new products.

QUALITY CONTROL AND CONSISTENCY

The final test of your success is the product itself. If your crafts are flawed, no amount of sophisticated marketing, presentation, organization, or delivery will bring repeat orders. You'll waste time and money and lose valuable buyers, and this is a profession built on repeat customers. Don't underestimate the importance of trust between yourself and your customers; the worst thing you could do is destroy that trust by sending faulty products, because consumers will not return. It is far harder to win customers back than to win new customers.

There are some basic rules for ensuring good quality. To start, you must have high standards. Check every piece carefully, and don't sell anything that doesn't pass the most stringent quality assurance. As mentioned before, always be honest with your buyers; if you produce flawed items, sell them as seconds at a lower price. To help maintain a high quality level, standardize as many production procedures as you can without sacrificing the handmade quality of your work.

Also, have a sample piece, or a specifications sheet and a photograph, for *all* your products, not just the ones currently in your collection. Apart from providing a good record of your development, you can use this information to replicate the quality, color, and dimensions of a piece. This also makes it easier to delegate some of the production at a later date. Customers will tolerate a certain amount of variety in a handmade item; however, they still want the quality, strength, and consistency of a store-bought product.

NEW PRODUCT DEVELOPMENT

As explained previously, new product development is the lifeblood of any enterprise. It defines and expands personal vision and ensures future growth. As you adjust your direction, assess and reassess your product range. Develop a consistent line of best-sellers that are the basic stock of your business, but each season also refine your designs and prices to offer different choices and better merchandise presentation.

Interpreting the demands the market and marrying them to production and design capabilities is the essence of a successful craft business. Always leave time in your work week to experiment and develop new products. New ideas are everywhere. Look for inspiration away from your studio. Visit craft stores and shopping malls. Walk through trade shows. Read publications in your field to keep abreast of the current trends. Review major mail-order catalogs. Adapt machine-made, mass-marketed items to your craft style.

You can also learn from the past—take inspiration from old objects to add a historical perspective to your line. Refer to international and ethnic sources for inspiration, as well. Take training courses and workshops in your field; continuing education keeps you current and competitive.

MARKET
TYPES

To market, to market, to buy a fat pig,
Home again, home again, jiggerty-jig.
—*Anonymous nursery rhyme*

Sell when you can, you are not for all markets.
—*Shakespeare,* As You Like It

The old nursery rhyme conveys the ease with which a customer could buy goods in the marketplace. The buyer found an appealing product, bought it, and went home satisfied. By inference then, selling goods was probably also a simple task. You created a product and traveled to a central market to sell it or trade it for something you needed. If you had leftovers that didn't sell, you lowered your price. If you sold out, you went home and started the process again. It was simple.

The realities of selling are more complicated today. Now—both as artisans and consumers—we are bombarded with choices. Instead of one central marketplace, there are numerous alternatives. And, as Rosalind says in *As You Like It,* "You are not for all markets." As a craftsperson you need to understand the available options and find the niche into which your work fits. And, if you are serious about creating a successful crafts company, you must learn the fine art of crafting a business.

As with baking a cake, the basics are still part of the process: you obtain the ingredients, create a product, then bring it to market. But, you need the right mix—the proper proportions and the correct timing—to produce a successful result. One of the key ingredients to successful selling is finding the right markets in today's more competitive society.

You must also have a strategy that targets this appropriate audience. There is no right or wrong here—only the right strategy for you—but you must have a plan, do research, and study all the markets. Too many craftspeople seek only traditional markets, ones with which they are familiar. In an ever-enlarging world, you need to expand your horizons.

How do you reach the abundance of available markets, and how do you select the ones that are right for you? It is often a matter of experience, or perhaps even simple trial and error. You try one thing, you hear about another. To help determine where you belong, ask yourself all the questions put forth in the previous chapter about your goals, craft, target markets and customers, competition, prices, and production capacities. Do you cater to a high-end market, producing fewer, one-of-a-kind pieces, or do you concentrate on a lower-end, high-volume manufacturing? Do you want an upscale gallery to represent your work on commission? Can you afford to take that kind of long-range risk, or do you want to sell on a consistent basis to specialty markets? Are your prices competitive?

If you focus your attention on the right place for your work, you'll save both yourself and your buyers time, money, and effort. And, most importantly, you'll conserve your energy for your creative work.

This chapter lists and describes the many different markets. It covers wholesaling, retailing, and combined opportunities, and includes requirements and hints from professionals on their fields. Some information may be familiar to you, while some may seem surprisingly new. Following the descriptions are corresponding listings of businesses, organizations, or individuals to contact. Whichever venues you decide to enter, do your homework and find the right fit.

ART IN PUBLIC AND CORPORATE SPACES

Architects, interior designers, real-estate developers, corporations, and trade associations often select crafts to highlight their buildings or interiors. They offer excellent exposure for the artisans whose work they choose. Architects and designers usually seek one-of-a-kind pieces, or more expensive multiples, and they pay wholesale prices to the craftsperson. If you display work at major design centers, such as The Design Center in Washington, D.C., you have the opportunity for broad exposure to the design trade, and commissions can be lucrative.

Major corporations or banks and even smaller businesses often feature crafts in their lobbies and offices as a way to decorate their space. Occasionally, these crafts are displayed as sales exhibitions of one-of-a-kind art pieces.

In order to place work in the corporate marketplace, you may need the assistance of an art consultant, designer, or architect. They act as facilitators because it is often difficult to get an appointment with the appropriate art buyer. Corporate buys are usually one-time purchases, but art consultants keep slide inventories and may order new items from the same sources for other clients in the future. This is an opportunity for repeat patronage on expensive works. The art consultant either takes a commission or marks up the price of the piece accordingly.

If you sell to a decorator for a small project, you should expect to give a retail discount of 20 to 40 percent off your regular prices. Many larger projects, however, require custom orders, and the pricing for specially commissioned work is highly negotiable. Ask about the budget for a proposal to get an idea about possible fees. Don't be afraid to ask for payment in advance, or at least for a sizable deposit.

Placing work with any of these types of organizations can be highly prestigious, as well as profitable. The groups tend to be interrelated, so finding one will help you approach another. The following lists possible avenues for exposure to these groups.

- Use art consultants.
- Enter competitions, which are advertised in trade journals.
- Advertise in trade journals, such as *American Craft, Museum News,* or *Art Business News.*
- Become a member of the American Craft Association to keep abreast of industry news (toll free: 800-724-0859).
- Place your work in galleries that have established relations with designers, architects, and builders.
- List yourself in sourcebooks such as *Architectural Design Collaborators.*
- Join, or establish contacts with, numerous associations such as the American Institute of Architects, American Society of Interior Designers, International Board of Design, Institute of Business Designers, National Association of Home Builders, and Society for Environmental Graphic Design.
- Buy major directories or subscribe to newsletters that list major construction projects and public exhibition spaces, such as *Sales Prospector, Arts in America: Annual Guide to Galleries, Museums and Artists,* and *National Association of Artists' Organizations Directory.*
- Participate at association trade shows.

By consulting *The Encyclopedia of Associations* at your local library, you can discover organizations that you think might be the most appropriate for your work, and then call or write them for brochures describing their missions and objectives.

How do you get the attention of corporate art buyers? For many craftspeople this is terra incognita; however, if you are prepared, this can be an exciting and lucrative market.

"Nothing is impossible, if you do your homework, present yourself professionally, and develop a strategy," says Laura Kaufman, president of The Art Resource, Inc., a leading art dealership and consulting firm in Hollywood, Florida (305-432-9242), Washington, D.C., and Baltimore for more than ten years. As a first step, she suggests researching in your local public library to find out just who is actually buying art. By reviewing local and national business journals and newspapers, you can uncover key information including, she says, "Which industries are growing, which ones are making money. What the trends are. Who is moving, who is building a new building, which designer and/or architect is heading the project. And this will help you target your market."

The Art Resource represents hundreds of artists and craftspeople. It maintains in its offices an inventory of artwork and crafts, and a reference library of slides and photographs to service clients, who include corporations, interior designers, architects, developers, and private collectors. After a preliminary meeting, Kaufman determines clients' needs and works within their budgets to purchase works that are appropriate for their intended environments. The Art Resource and similar consulting firms represent an important link between craftspeople and hard-to-reach art buyers.

As Kaufman points out, "The corporate art buying market has changed significantly in the past five to 10 years. The glory days of spending money for major corporate art collections have dramatically declined. The trend is more toward decorating and adhering to budgets than forming a valuable art collection for prestige and investment value. Many companies have down-sized; they're still making lots of money, but they are reluctant to put their money in an art collection when they're laying people off. . . . They are more apt to question their acquisition costs than they were in the past."

Kaufman emphasizes that corporations still buy art and want quality, but they are more open to purchasing lesser known artists, whose prices are lower. This bodes well for craft designers. Once you identify the companies you want to sell to, the next step is to understand who selects the art, and this is not necessarily the CEO. Kaufman advises, "Find out who in the company is in charge [of buying art]. Some companies have in-house designers, while some leave it up to the building management company; others elect the secretary or office manager to do all the selecting, and several companies will choose art by committee. Many of these people will then hire either designers or art consultants to help them achieve their goals."

Although it is often difficult to get an appointment with these buyers, you can reach your targeted market. Kaufman suggests doing specific industry trade shows. Most major industries have their own associations and trade shows. If you want to sell to restaurants, doctors, nightclub owners, or others, find out when their associations meet, take a trade booth, and exhibit. If that's too costly the first time, try sharing booth space with other artists.

When you sell at a trade show, you must spend time on your presentation. If possible, leave space to walk around the booth. Try to have someone in the booth at all times, or leave a note saying when you will return. Buyers are too busy to try to find someone to answer questions, and they don't have the time for what they consider unprofessional behavior. When you get an order, give accurate lead times. If people place orders that they never receive, chances are they won't order from you again. As stated in the previous chapter, you can make mistakes, but you must communicate and advise about late delivery times and any other changes or information.

Presenting yourself, as well as your work, in a professional manner is important, too. According to Kaufman, "A warm smile and a friendly demeanor go a long way. Dressing appropriately is just as important; the old cliché of looking like an artist, whatever that means, doesn't usually work. Looking and acting professionally does." Your work presentation should include a résumé, portfolios, and photographs or a brochure. "Your portfolio tells people who you are and what you do," says Kaufman, who suggests having both a complete portfolio (containing a résumé, photographs of your work, award and exhibit notices, press releases, and, possibly, samples of the materials you use) and a short version (which includes a few photographs and a summary paragraph or two about yourself). The short portfolio gives buyers a quick look at your work to determine initial interest. For corporate clients photographs are better than slides.

"Another way to get noticed," says Kaufman, "is to get some press reporting on your work. One way to do this is to donate artwork to a charitable event [or organization]. This will also give you exposure to the corporate sponsors of the event. If you let the local press know that you made an art contribution, chances are they'll write something about it." You might also offer to hold an exhibit at a corporation, then call the local press and ask them to cover it as a feature story. Kaufman advises, "Never be afraid to ask [for additional press coverage]. You'd be surprised how much you can achieve just by asking."

The final step of your research includes understanding the appropriateness of your work with regard to the client's needs. If a company wants pottery for their reception areas, you need to offer a variety of works in a few sizes and price ranges to meet different budgets. High-tech firms might want contemporary crafts. Traditional pieces might be ideal for banks and law firms. Whatever the business, Kaufman advises that you be creative in your suggestions to each firm. Think conceptually; often the client wants a look, but doesn't know how to accomplish it. Set realistic goals for yourself. Keep the bigger picture in mind, but focus on the small steps—making phone calls and following up—that will allow you to make sales to the corporate art world.

The following listings provide the names, addresses, and telephone and fax numbers, when available, of architects, corporate art brokers, interior designers, and design centers throughout the country who are listed in The Crafts Center's database. You could also try contacting firms near you that aren't listed here.

ARCHITECTS

The American Institute of Architects (AIA) has offices throughout the country and they are listed here alphabetically by state. Contact them for names of affiliated architects.

AIA—Alabama
107 21st Street South
Birmingham, AL 35233
ph: (205) 322-4386
fax: (205) 328-1610

AIA—Arizona
802 North Fifth Avenue
Phoenix, AZ 85003
ph: (602) 257-1924
fax: (602) 257-9661

AIA—Arkansas
University Tower Building
1123 South University
Penthouse Suite
Little Rock, AR 72204
ph: (501) 663-8820
fax: (501) 663-9148

AIA—California
1303 J Street, Suite 200
Sacramento, CA 95814
ph: (916) 448-9082
fax: (916) 442-5356

130 Sutter Street, 6th floor
San Francisco, CA 94104
ph: (415) 362-7397
fax: (415) 362-4802

AIA—Colorado
1526 15th Street
Denver, CO 80202
ph: (303) 831-6183
fax: (303) 831-8833

AIA—Connecticut
87 Willow Street
New Haven, CT 06511
ph: (203) 865-2195
fax: (203) 562-5378

AIA—District of Columbia
1777 Church Street N.W.
Washington, DC 20036
ph: (202) 667-1798
fax: (202) 667-4327

AIA—Florida
104 East Jefferson Street
Tallahassee, FL 32301
ph: (904) 222-7590
fax: (904) 224-8048

AIA—Guam
P. O. Box 24392
GMF, Guam 96921
ph: (671) 649-3242

AIA—Idaho
405 South Eighth Street, Suite 365
Boise, ID 83702
ph: (208) 345-3072
fax: (208) 343-8046

AIA—Illinois
520 South Second Street, Suite 802
Springfield, IL 62701
ph: (217) 522-2309
fax: (217) 522-5370

AIA—Indiana
47 South Pennsylvania Street
Indianapolis, IN 46204
ph: (317) 634-6993
fax: (317) 266-0515

AIA—Iowa
1000 Walnut Street, Suite 101
Des Moines, IA 50309
ph: (515) 244-7505
fax: (515) 244-5347

AIA—Kansas
700 Jackson Street, Suite 209
Topeka, KS 66603
ph: (913) 357-5308
fax: (913) 357-6450

AIA—Kentucky
209 East High Street
Lexington, KY 40507
ph: (606) 233-7671
fax: (606) 233-1716

AIA—Louisiana
521 America Street
Baton Rouge, LA 70802
ph: (504) 387-5579
fax: (504) 387-2743

AIA—Maine
3 Sylvan Way
Manchester, ME 04351
ph: (207) 623-1218
fax: same

AIA—Maryland
111/2 West Chase Street
Baltimore, MD 21201
ph: (410) 625-2585
fax: (410) 727-4620

AIA—Massachusetts
52 Broad Street
Boston, MA 02109
ph: (617) 951-1433
fax: (617) 951-0845

AIA—Michigan
553 East Jefferson Street
Detroit, MI 48226
ph: (313) 965-4100
fax: (313) 965-1501

AIA—Minnesota
International Market Square
275 Market Street, Suite 54
Minneapolis, MN 55405
ph: (612) 338-6763
fax: (612) 338-7981

AIA—Mississippi
812 North President Street
Jackson, MS 39202
ph: (601) 948-6735
fax: (601) 352-4384

AIA—Missouri
204-A East High Street
Jefferson City, MO 65101
ph: (314) 635-8555
fax: (314) 636-5783

AIA—Montana
P. O. Box 20996
Billings, MT 59104
ph: (406) 259-7300
fax: (406) 259-4211

AIA—Nebraska
University of Nebraska-Lincoln
P. O. Box 80045
Lincoln, NE 68501
ph: (402) 472-1456
fax: (402) 472-3806

AIA—Nevada
University of Nevada-Las Vegas
Houssels House
Las Vegas, NV 89154
ph: (702) 895-0936
fax: (702) 895-4417

AIA—New Hampshire
P. O. Box 247
Concord, NH 03302
ph: (603) 226-4550
fax: same

AIA—New Mexico
111 Carlisle S.E., Suite 5
Albuquerque, NM 87106
ph: (505) 255-2170
fax: (505) 255-2157

AIA—New York
235 Lark Street
Albany, NY 12210
ph: (518) 449-3334
fax: (518) 436-8176

200 Lexington Avenue, 6th floor
New York, NY 10016
ph: (212) 683-0023
fax: (212) 696-5022

AIA—North Carolina
115 West Morgan Street
Raleigh, NC 27601
ph: (919) 833-6656
fax: (919) 833-2015

AIA—North Dakota
P. O. Box 1403
Fargo, ND 58107
ph: (701) 235-4918
fax: (701) 293-1353

AIA—Ohio
17 South High Street, 12th floor
Columbus, OH 43215
ph: (614) 221-0338
fax: (614) 221-1989

AIA—Oklahoma
304 N.W. 13th Street, Suite 100
Oklahoma City, OK 73103
ph: (405) 235-3712
fax: (405) 235-5205

AIA—Oregon
1207 Southwest Sixth Avenue
Portland, OR 97204
ph: (503) 223-2330
fax: (503) 228-4529

AIA—Pennsylvania
117 South 17th Street
Philadelphia, PA 19103
ph: (215) 569-3186
fax: (215) 569-9226

AIA—Rhode Island
P. O. Box 40206
Providence, RI 02940
ph: (401) 272-6418
fax: (401) 943-8489

AIA—South Carolina
1522 Richland Street
Columbia, SC 29201
ph: (803) 252-6050
fax: (803) 256-0546

AIA—South Dakota
P. O. Box 1596
Sioux Falls, SD 57101
ph: (605) 334-2422
fax: (605) 332-8902

AIA—Tennessee
102 Woodmont Boulevard, Suite 360
Nashville, TN 37305
ph: (615) 298-1250
fax: (615) 298-9858

AIA—Texas
114 West Seventh Street
Austin, TX 78701
ph: (512) 478-7386
fax: (512) 478-0528

AIA—Utah
75 East Broadway
Salt Lake City, UT 84111
ph: (801) 532-1727
fax: (801) 532-4576

AIA—Vermont
Rural Delivery 1
P. O. Box 67
Waitsfield, VT 05673
ph: (802) 496-3761
fax: (802) 496-5124

AIA—Virginia
15 South Fifth Street
Richmond, VA 23219
ph: (804) 644-3051
fax: (804) 643-4607

AIA—Washington
1110 Capitol Way South
Capitol Court, Suite 237
Olympia, WA 98501
ph: (206) 943-6012
fax: (206) 352-1870

AIA—West Virginia
P. O. Box 813
Charleston, WV 25323
ph: (304) 344-9872
fax: (304) 343-0205

AIA—Wisconsin
321 South Hamilton Street
Madison, WI 53703
ph: (608) 257-8077
fax: (608) 257-0242

The following architects are listed
alphabetically by business name. You
can also check your local directories
for names of other architects.

Architects Public Strat Association
150 West State Street
Trenton, NJ 08608

Gauge Corporation
1304 Hilltop Avenue
Wilmington, DE 19809

Herman Stoller Coliver Architects
66 Grace Street
San Francisco, CA 94103
ph: (415) 552-9210

Innerspace Design
133 East de la Guerra, Suite 180
Santa Barbara, CA 93101
ph: (805) 966-7786

Washington Design Collaborative –
Studio Design
1508 19th Street N.W.
Washington, DC 20036
ph: (202) 667-6133

William Turnbull Associates
Architects and Planners
Pier 1 1/2
The Embarcadero
San Francisco, CA 94111
ph: (415) 986-3642
fax: (415) 986-4778

CORPORATE ART BROKERS

Alter/Associates
122 Cary Avenue
Highland Park, IL 60035
ph: (708) 433-1229
fax: (312) 236-1365

American Art Resources
7026 Old Katy Road, Suite 26
Houston, TX 77024
ph: (713) 282-0204
fax: (713) 863-1041

Art Advisory Services
25 Maravista Court
Tiburon, CA 94920
ph: (415) 435-0721

The Art Bank
3028 North Whitehall Road
Norristown, PA 19403
ph: (215) 539-2265
fax: same

Art Consulting Services
3148 Plainfield N.E., Suite 140
Grand Rapids, MI 49505
ph: (616) 361-9172
fax: same

Art Esprit
6629 Majorca Lane
East Phoenix, AZ 85016
ph: (602) 274-8589
fax: (602) 266-0338

The Art Exchange
539 East Town Street
Columbus, OH 43215
ph: (614) 464-4611
fax: (614) 464-4619

Artfinds
1125 West Fifth Avenue
Eugene, OR 97402
ph: (503) 344-0071
fax: (503) 344-0870

Artist Showcase
1625 Larimer Street, Suite 601
Denver, CO 80202
ph: (303) 825-1955
fax: (303) 571-1007

Art Management & Planning
1060 Wynkroop Street, Suite 1060
Denver, CO 80202
ph: (303) 446-8325
fax: (303) 446-8326

The Art Resource
2916 Cabin Creek Drive
Burtonsville, MD 20866
ph: (301) 989-9589
fax: (301) 989-9760

The Art Source
1326 Asbury Avenue
Evanston, IL 60201
ph: (708) 328-2728
fax: (708) 328-5407

Artsource Consultants
509 West Whitaker Mill Road,
Suite 105
Raleigh, NC 27608
ph: (919) 833-0013
fax: (919) 833-8641

Art Source L.A.
1416 Sixth Street
Santa Monica, CA 90401
ph: (310) 917-6688
fax: (310) 917-6685

ArtSouth
4401 Cresson Street
Philadelphia, PA 19127
ph: (215) 482-4500
fax: (215) 482-4572

Audrey Owen Contemporary Sculpture
1200 North Lake Shore Drive
Chicago, IL 60610
ph: (312) 664-0474

Blue Sky Art Consultants
3955 Bigelow Boulevard, Suite 803
Pittsburgh, PA 15213
ph: (412) 682-7050
fax: (412) 682-6315

Boston Corporate Art
470 Atlantic Avenue
Boston, MA 02210
ph: (617) 426-8880

Carol A. Dabb Art Consultants
41 Sunkist Lane
Los Altos, CA 94022
ph: (415) 941-1907
fax: (415) 948-4019

Carol Simonson Portfolio
2320 Newton Avenue South
Minneapolis, MN 55405
ph: (612) 374-5704

Carolyn S. Husemoller Fine Arts
P. O. Box 933
Barrington, IL 60011
ph: (708) 526-3444
fax: (708) 526-5271

Cathy Baum & Associates Art Advisors
384 Stevick Drive
Atherton, CA 94027
ph: (415) 854-5668
fax: (415) 854-8522

Contemporary Art Advisors
245 Unquowa Road, Suite 110
Fairfield, CT 06430
ph: (203) 259-6333

Corporate Art Associates
2665 South Bayshore Drive
Miami, FL 33133
ph: (305) 871-0005

Corporate Art Associates Limited
270 Lafayette Street, Suite 402
New York, NY 10012
ph: (212) 941-9685
fax: (212) 941-4780

Corporate Art Design
P. O. Box 19432
Portland, OR 97219
ph: (503) 246-1648

Corporate Art Directions
41 East 57th Street, 8th floor
New York, NY 10022
ph: (212) 355-5370
fax: (212) 758-6332

Corporate Art Services
19581 Topeka Lane
Huntington Beach, CA 92646
ph: (714) 963-3071

Corporate Art Source
5950 Carmichael Place, Suite 105
Montgomery, AL 36117
ph: (205) 271-3772
fax: (205) 244-9588

Corporate Art Specialists
2220 Colorado Avenue Building 4,
Suite 400
Santa Monica, CA 90404
ph: (310) 828-3964

Corporate Artworks
1300 Remington Road, Suite H
Schaumburg, IL 60173
ph: (708) 843-3636
fax: (708)-843-8047

Corporate Fine Art
6273 Variel Avenue, Suite A
Woodlands Hills, CA 91367
ph: (818) 884-8574

Corporate Investment Art
5046 West Pico Boulevard
Los Angeles, CA 90019
ph: (213) 965-9470
fax: (213) 965-9032

Corporate Portfolio
244 Morningside Drive S.E.
Grand Rapids, MI 49506
ph: (619) 949-4730

Corporations and Arts Organizations
1349 Lexington Avenue
New York, NY 10128
ph: (212) 722-0417

Debra Rhodes Fine Art Services
226 Mountain Avenue
Summit, NJ 07901
ph: (908) 273-8976

Dorsey Barr Contemporary Art
Consultant
333 18th Street
Santa Monica, CA 90402
ph: (310) 393-3345

E. C. May & Company
201 King Street, Suite 3-A
Alexandria, VA 22314
ph: (703) 683-4170
fax: (703) 683-4398

Elinor Woron-Associates,
Art Advisors
1 Longfellow Place, Suite 3410
Boston, MA 02114
ph: (617) 367-9191

Franzoni International
2160 Fleur de Lis Court
Arlington, TX 76012
ph: (807) 265-6175

Gagnaire & Goode
P. O. Box 820515
Dallas, TX 75382
ph: (214) 343-8558
fax: (214) 341-6842

Galman Lepow Associates
1879 Old Cuthbert Road, Suite 12
Cherry Hill, NJ 08034
ph: (609) 354-0771

G. J. Cloninger & Company
Art Consultants
39 East Hanover Avenue
Morris Plains, NJ 07950
ph: (201) 540-1195
fax: (201) 538-7667

Graphic Resources Corporate
Art Service
465 Lakeside Place
Highland Park, IL 60035
ph: (703) 433-3688
fax: (703) 433-3628

Harleen and Allen Fine Arts
427 Bryant Street
San Francisco, CA 94107
ph: (415) 777-0920

Jan Price Art Associates
7013 Woodchuck Hill Road
Fayetteville, NY 13066
ph: (315) 446-4722

Kittrell/Riffkind Art Glass
12215 Coit Road, Suite 163
Dallas, TX 75251
ph: (214) 239-7957

Leader Associates
7 Nottingham Road
Wayne, NJ 07470
ph: (201) 696-1836
fax: same

Lyman Art Advisory
325 West Huron, Suite 470
Chicago, IL 60610
ph: (312) 751-2985
fax: (312) 751-2987

McGrath & Braun Art Consultants
12 Albion Street
Denver, CO 80220
ph: (303) 893-0449
fax: (303) 893-8130

Medici Corporation
68 North Second Street
Philadelphia, PA 19106
ph: (215) 627-8109

Nussbaum McElwain Art
Advisory Service
5615 Pershing Avenue, Suite 24
St. Louis, MO 63112
ph: (314) 361-3701
fax: (314) 361-3702

Sardi Associates
68 Commerce Drive
East Farmingdale, NY 11735
ph: (516) 753-0451

Sculpture Placement
P. O. Box 9709
Washington, DC 20016
ph: (202) 362-9310
fax: (202) 944-4416

Shutler/ Ziv Art Group
3119 West Post Road
Las Vegas, NV 89118
ph: (702) 896-2218
fax: (702) 896-3488

Stevens Design Associates
3600 Kingbury Avenue
Fort Worth, TX 76118
ph: (817) 589-7101
fax: (817) 590-0970

Suzy R. Locke & Associates
4254 Piedmont Avenue
Oakland, CA 94611
ph: (510) 547-5455
fax: (510) 547-5495

Szoke Koo Associates
591 Broadway
New York, NY 10012
ph: (212) 219-8355
fax: (212) 966-6034

Visual Art Access
225B Anita Place
Santa Fe, NM 87501
ph: (505) 820-0121
fax: (505) 820-0038

Volkman/Berdow Associates
345 East 86th Street
New York, NY 10028
ph: (212) 831-6489

Walls Alive, Corporate Art Consultants
1754 Junction Avenue
San Jose, CA 95112
ph: (408) 436-8131
fax: (408) 436-8137

Weller Cwalinski Art Consultants
4114 Dunlavi
Houston, TX 77006
ph: (713) 522-4034
fax: same

INTERIOR DESIGNERS AND DESIGN CENTERS

Allan Shavitz Associates
336 North Charles Street
Baltimore, MD 21201
ph: (410) 837-1560

American Society of Interior Designers
23811 Aliso Creek Road, Suite 124-B
Laguna Beach, CA 92656
ph: (714) 643-1549

American Society of Interior Designers
440 East Holt Avenue
Pomona, CA 91767
ph: (415) 626-2743

American Society of Interior Designers
1024 22nd Street
Sacramento, CA 95816
ph: (916) 446-7984

American Society of Interior Designers
4010 Morena Boulevard, Suite 246
San Diego, CA 92117
ph: (619) 270-7510

American Society of Interior Designers
Two Henry Adams Street, Suite 301
San Francisco, CA 91767
ph: (415) 626-2743

American Society of Interior Designers
8687 Melrose Avenue, Suite BM-52
West Hollywood, CA 90069
ph: (310) 659-8998

American Society of Interior Designers
1801 Wynkoop Street, Suite C-11
Denver, CO 80202
PH: (303) 292-2024

American Society of Interior Designers
1855 Griffin Street, Suite 485-B
Dania, FL 33044
ph: (305) 926-7555

American Society of Interior Designers
P. O. Box 187
Davidson, NC 28036
ph: (704) 892-3346

Artcraft Collection
8605 Stevenson Road
Stevenson, MD 21153
ph: (410) 653-2168

Baut Studios
1095 Main Street
Swoyersville, PA 18704
ph: (717) 288-1431
fax: (717) 288-0380

Betsy Summer Interior
1027 Duchess Drive
McLean, VA 22102
ph: (703) 790-0174

Betty Schulman Interiors
32 Cascade Road
West Hartford, CT 06117
ph: (203) 523-1630

Blackwood Creative Design
90 Seagrove Loop
Lincoln City, OR 97367
ph: (503) 994-9043

Color Trends
5129 Ballard Avenue N.W.
Seattle, WA 98107
ph: (206) 789-1065
fax: (206) 783-9676

Contract Design Center
600 Townsend Street
San Francisco, CA 94103
ph: (415) 864-8541

Creative Interior Design
39120 Argonaut Way, Suite 175
Fremont, CA 94538
ph: (510) 657-5606

David A. Hanks and Associates
200 Park Avenue South, Suite 1406
New York, NY 10003
ph: (212) 674-7726

Decor Unlimited
409 Wyntrelea Drive
Bryn Mawr, PA 19010
ph: (215) 527-8096

Design Center
5104 Kavanaugh
Little Rock, AR 72207
ph: (501) 664-7148

Design Center Northwest
5701 Sixth Avenue South
Seattle, WA 98108
ph: (206) 762-1200

Distinctive Design
5040 Lake Elmo Avenue North
Lake Elmo, MN 55042
ph: (612) 430-1268
fax: (612) 430-0956

Edith Whitman Interiors
21 Old Avon Village
Route 44
Avon, CT 06001
ph: (203) 677-5000

Kathleen Sullivan Elliott
26 Flanagan Drive
Framingham, MA 01701
ph: (617) 788-0736

Fran Burbary Interior Design
2575 South Syracuse Way, Suite K-104
Denver, CO 80231
ph: (303) 368-1020

Freeman Decorating Company
6300 Stapleton Drive
Denver, CO 80216
ph: (303) 329-3442

Gail Adams Interiors
110 East San Miguel
Phoenix, AZ 85012
ph: (602) 274-0074

Genesis Interior Design
301 South Central Avenue
Marshfield, WI 54449
ph: (715) 387-0340

Grange Furniture
1400 Turtle Creek Boulevard, Suite 106
Dallas, TX 75207
ph: (214) 744-9007

Home Furnishings Design Studio
47 Union Street, Suite 203
Montclair, NJ 07042
ph: (201) 746-5132
fax: same

Interiors and Extras
324 Metairie Road
Metairie, LA 70005
ph: (504) 835-9902
fax: (504) 835-9913

Jane Piper Reid and Company
1000 Leonora Avenue, Suite 301
Seattle, WA 98121
ph: (206) 621-9290

Janet K. Higgins Interiors
1666 Castle Hill Road
Walnut Creek, CA 94595
ph: (510) 934-1666

La Follette Designs
701 Dexter Avenue North, Suite 307
Seattle, WA 98109
ph: (206) 284-2500

Lemarie Interieurs
P. O. Box 583
Belair, MD 21014
ph: (410) 379-4664
fax: (410) 838-3616

Lorraine Schill Interiors
9025 Sierra Valley Lane
Loomis, CA 94650
ph: (916) 652-3178

Matches at Miley
300 D Street S.W., Suite 440
Washington, DC 20024
ph: (202) 863-0333
fax: (202) 63-0336

Natalie Craig Interior Design
39120 Argonaut Way, Suite 175
Fremont, CA 94538
ph: (510) 657-5606
fax: (510) 656-4969

Pacific Design Center
8687 Melrose Avenue
West Hollywood, CA 90069
ph: (213) 657-0800
fax: (213) 652-8576

Provost Design
221 Pine Street
Florence, MA 01060
ph: (413) 585-1515

Sadlers Home Furnishings
161 South Klevin Street
Anchorage, AK 99508
ph: (907) 272-5800

S.G. Interiors
P. O. Box 766
Dickson's Mill Road
New Vernon, NJ 07976
ph: (201) 822-8236
fax: (201) 593-9275

Sheila Meyers Interior Design
129 Summer Village Drive
Annapolis, MD 21401
ph: (410) 974-6095

Showplace Square
Two Henry Adams Street
San Francisco, CA 94103
ph: (415) 864-1500

Steven Earl Showroom
520 South Findlay
Seattle, WA 98108
ph: (206) 767-7220

Kerry Touchette
1730 Corcoran Street N.W.
Washington, DC 20009
ph: (202) 667-3249

TR Designs
4943 Elm Street
Bethesda, MD 20814

Washington Design Center
300 D Street S.W.
Washington, DC 20024
ph: (202) 554-5053

BOUTIQUES AND CRAFT SHOPS

These are retail stores that cater to specific clients. Individually owned, concessioned out, or operated as business partnerships, these stores may be free-standing or located in shopping malls or special environments such as airports, hospitals, hotels, universities, or tourist centers. Even when store owners or buyers run more than one shop, their craft purchases are conservative. They look for unique items that augment their store atmosphere or personal vision.

Some store owners are dedicated to promoting American crafts only, while others also stock imported crafts and other gifts. Some buy crafts produced in a broad range of mediums, but others specialize. They may also want to buy on consignment so that they can rotate their stock with each season. Buys—especially first-time buys—are usually limited in quantity.

Deborah Farber-Isaacson, co-owner of Mindscape Gallery in Evanston, Illinois, which is the largest consignment gallery in the country, describes the four different markets that Mindscape caters to: "We have the same four that we opened with in 1973—gifts, home furnishings, serious collectors, and wearable art. The gift business is our bread and butter. It has seen us through bizarre economic times. When all else fails—no matter what the economic climate—people still have to get that Mother's Day gift." Gifts in this category, bought year after year, range from $25 to $300.

In contrast, customer purchases of home furnishings tend to be one-time buys. Once they fill the space in their home, customers are finished buying. "The serious collector, on the other hand," says Farber-Isaacson, "has been nurtured and educated and has spent years collecting—making decisions to gather certain things. They are less tied into home furnishings. They say, 'I'll find a spot for it.' They come with a shopping list of particular artists or a series by an artist."

Jewelry and other wearable art such as vests, men's ties, opera capes, and handloomed sweaters are consistently popular. "People are always looking to make themselves feel attractive," says Farber-Isaacson. "They want to look a certain way or convey a certain message. There's that theory—a women cannot conceivably own too much jewelry."

Mindscape purchases most of its crafts on consignment, and the price range is about 15 to several thousand dollars. The gallery limits wholesale buying to lower-end production in the gift-item range of $10 to $200. Whether bought outright or on consignment, everything is juried, and artists can call or write to request a jury package, which explains the procedures and policies (see page 83 for address). Generally, Mindscape requires five slides of one type of work, and they take 60 days to respond.

Farber-Isaacson offers this advice to potential craft sellers, "Act like true professionals. Know how to set up price structure, send invoices, keep copies, and send supportive materials. We've gotten drawings on envelopes with notes asking 'Do you like my style?' or 'Do you want to carry my work?' Every month there's one or two. This is a turnoff; the assumption is that they need to get out and have a little experience. Our job is not to provide business training, but to evaluate if we have a market for our clientele."

She also recommends the following:

- Take a crash course in business procedure.
- Don't overcommit—there's a painful gap between what's promised and what's delivered, even among skilled craftspeople.
- Don't try to make money by adding high shipping charges—readjust your wholesale price based on supply and demand instead of making up the difference with ridiculous freight costs.
- Include an artist statement explaining why you are making something and why it's of interest. It adds credibility to the value of an object.

The following list was pulled from The Crafts Center database, but you can consult your local phone directory for more listings.

BOUTIQUES AND CRAFT SHOPS

Alaska

The Artworks
3677 College Road, Suite 3
Fairbanks, AK 99709
ph: (907) 479-2563

Beads and Things
537 Second Avenue
Fairbanks, AK 99701
ph: (907) 456-2323

Chilkat Valley Arts
P. O. Box 145
Haines, AK 99827
ph: (907) 766-2990

Kiko B Fibearts
8 Carlyle Way
Fairbanks, AK 99709
ph: (907) 456-2202

Neat Stuff
P. O. Box 6955
Ketchikan, AK 99901
ph: (907) 225-2895

Objects of Bright Pride
65 South Franklin Street
Juneau, AK 99801
ph: (907) 586-4969

Taheela
605 A Street
Anchorage, AK 99501
ph: (907) 272-5829

Arizona

Aguajito Del Sol
Tlaquepaque 103-A
P. O. Box 1607
Sedona, AZ 86336
ph: (602) 282-5258

Desert Moon
2785 West 89A
Sedona, AZ 86336
ph: (602) 204-1195

ERTCO
P. O. Box 1970
Sedona, AZ 86336
ph: (602) 282-4945

Every Blooming Thing, Inc.
2010 East University Drive
Tempe, AZ 85281
ph: (602) 921-1196

Galeria Mesa
155 North Center
Mesa, AZ 85201
ph: (602) 644-2242

Gifted Hands
P. O. Box 1388
Sedona, AZ 86339
ph: (602) 282-4822

Glendale Public Library Store
5959 West Brown Street
Glendale, AZ 85302
ph: (602) 435-4972

Pearson & Company
7022 East Main Street
Scottsdale, AZ 85251
ph: (602) 840-6447

Sky Fire
P. O. Box 95
Jerome, AZ 86331
ph: (602) 634-8081
fax: same

Arkansas
Artisan Source
HCR 78
P. O. Box 64
Alco, AR 72610
ph: (501) 746-4650
fax: (501) 746-4793

Crazy Bone Gallery
37 Spring Street
Eureka Springs, AR 72632
ph: (501) 253-6600

California
Aesthetic Collection, Inc.
1060 17th Street
San Diego, CA 92101
ph: (619) 238-1860

All Creatures Great and Small
3510 Thorndale Road
Pasadena, CA 91107
ph: (818) 792-7387

All That Glitters
625 Second Street, Suite 302
San Francisco, CA 94107
ph: (415) 243-0131

American Indian Contemporary Arts
685 Market Street, Suite 250
San Francisco, CA 94105
ph: (415) 495-7600
fax: (415) 495-7781

American Indian Store
1095 South Magnolia Avenue
El Cajon, CA 92020
ph: (619) 588-5352

American Panache
31430 Broad Beach Road
Malibu, CA 90265

Angie & Company
360 Titleist Court
San Jose, CA 95127
ph: (408) 323-9220

The Architect's Interior
300 North Santa Cruz Avenue
Los Gatos, CA 95030
ph: (408) 354-1020

The Art Company
25 West Gutierrez Street
Santa Barbara, CA 93101
ph: (805) 963-1157

The Artery
207 G Street
Davis, CA 95616
ph: (916) 758-8330

The Artful Eye
1333A Lincoln Avenue
Calistoga, CA 94515
ph: (707) 942-4743

Artifact
17 Stockton Street
San Francisco, CA 94108
ph: (415) 788-9375

Artifacts Gallery
3024 Fillmore Street
San Francisco, CA 94123
ph: (415) 922-8465

Artisance
278 Beach Street
Laguna Beach, CA 92651
ph: (714) 494-0687

Art Options
319 South Robertson Boulevard
Los Angeles, CA 90048
ph: (310) 392-9099

Art Options
372 Hayes Street
San Francisco, CA 94102
ph: (415) 567-8535

The Art Works
340 Westbourne Street
La Jolla, CA 92037
ph: (619) 459-7688

Art World Design
18337 Sherman Way
Reseda, CA 91335
ph: (818) 774-3620

Bazar Del Mundo
2754 Calhoun Street
San Diego, CA 92110
ph: (619) 296-3161

Beadwork
10895 Pico Boulevard
Los Angeles, CA 90064
ph: (310) 313-0430

Bell'occhio
8 Brady Street
San Francisco, CA 94103
ph: (415) 864-4048

Blaker Art Studio
2001 Kingsley Street
Santa Cruz, CA 95062
ph: (408) 479-0906

Bronze Plus, Inc.
6790 Depot Street
Sebastopol, CA 95472
ph: (707) 829-5480

CA Contemporary Crafts
Association
P. O. Box 2060
Sausalito, CA 94966
ph: (415) 927-3158

Celebrate Life
28 East Colorado Boulevard
Pasadena, CA 91105
ph: (818) 585-0690

Chapson Artsvision
750 Union Street
San Francisco, CA 94123
ph: (415) 292-6560

Chapson Artsvision Limited
Two Henry Adams Street
San Francisco, CA 94103
ph: (415) 863-2117

Chez Mac
812 Post Street
San Francisco, CA 94109
ph: (415) 775-2515

Christine of Santa Fe
220 Forest Avenue
Laguna Beach, CA 92651
ph: (714) 494-3610

Closets & Cloths
617 Blue Spruce Drive
Danville, CA 94506

Conifer Crent Company
P. O. Box 4057
Richmond, CA 74804
ph: (510) 527-8222

Contemporary Center
2630 West Sepulveda Boulevard
Torrance, CA 90505
ph: (310) 539-1933

Craft Palace
3808 Fanbrough Drive
Bakersfield, CA 93304
ph: (805) 833-1775

Craftsman's Guild
300 De Haro Street, Suite 342
San Francisco, CA 94103
ph: (415) 431-5425

The Crate – American Handcrafts
1200 K Street
9 Hyatt Regency Plaza
Sacramento, CA 95814
ph: (916) 441-4136

Crock-R-Box
El Paseo Village
73-425 El Paseo
Palm Desert, CA 92260
ph: (619) 568-6688

Crystal Moon
P. O. Box 580
Belmont, CA 94002
ph: (415) 595-4144

Crystal Reflection
150 Park Lane
Brisbane, CA 94005
ph: (415) 468-2520
fax: (415) 468-2554

Cullum and Sena
45 Polk Street
San Francisco, CA 94102
ph: (415) 863-5300

A Definite Maybe
10701 Wilshire Boulevard, Apt. 1506
Los Angeles, CA 90024
ph: (310) 826-5119

De Novo
250 University Avenue
Palo Alto, CA 94301
ph: (415) 327-1256

Discoveries Contemporary Craft
17350 17th Street, Suite E
Tustin, CA 92680
ph: (714) 544-6206

Dolce Vita
2907 Pasatiempo Lane
Sacramento, CA 95821
ph: (916) 482-8045

Earthworks
290 Main Street
Los Altos, CA 94022
ph: (415) 948-5141

Eastern Sierra Trading Company
P. O. Box 731
Bridgeport, CA 93517
ph: (619) 932-7231

Elements
911 Marquerita Avenue
Santa Monica, CA 90402
ph: (310) 450-8867

Ethnic Arts
1314 Tenth Street
Berkeley, CA 94710
ph: (510) 527-5270

Ferrari of Carmel
San Carlos Fifth and Sixth
P. O. Box 3273
Carmel, CA 93921
ph: (408) 624-9677

Fine Woodworking of Carmel
San Carlos and Mission
Carmel, CA 93921
ph: (408) 622-9663

Following Sea
8522 Beverly Boulevard
Los Angeles, CA 90048
ph: (213) 659-0592

Fox On The Green
254 Main Street
Salinas, CA 93901

Garden of Beaden
P. O. Box 1535
Redway, CA 95540
ph: (707) 923-9120

Georgeo's Collection
416 North Rodeo Drive
Beverly Hills, CA 90210
ph: (310) 275-7967

Georgeo's Collection
269 Forest Avenue
Laguna Beach, CA 92651
ph: (714) 497-0907

Golden Tulip
464 First Street, Suite E
Sonoma, CA 95476
ph: (707) 938-3624

Good Day Sunshine
29 East Napa Street
Sonoma, CA 95476
ph: (707) 938-4001

Graystone Jewelers
Second & F Streets
Eureka, CA 95501
ph: (707) 442-1232

Handworks
Dolores & Sixth Avenue
Carmel, CA 93921
ph: (408) 624-6000

Human Arts
310 East Ojai Avenue
Ojai, CA 93023
ph: (805) 646-1525

Humboldt's Finest
417 Second Street
Eureka, CA 95501
ph: (707) 443-1258

Images of the North
1782 Union Street
San Francisco, CA 94123
ph: (415) 673-1273

Interia
11404 Sorrento Valley Road
San Diego, CA 92121
ph: (619) 455-7177

Japonesque
824 Montgomery Street
San Francisco, CA 94133
ph: (415) 398-8577
fax: (415) 391-3530

Judith Litvich Contemporary Arts
Two Henry Adams Street, Suite M-69
San Francisco, CA 94103
ph: (415) 863-3329

Kimberley's
25601 Pine Creek Lane
Wilmington, CA 90744
ph: (310) 835-4169

La De Da!
240 Lincoln Center
Stockton, CA 95207
ph: (209) 474-6688
fax: (209) 474-2256

Left Coast
539 East Villa Street, Suite 29
Pasadena, CA 91101

The Limn Company
457 Pacific Avenue
San Francisco, CA 94133
ph: (415) 986-3884

The Los Angeles Art Exchange
2451 Broadway
Santa Monica, CA 90404
ph: (310) 828-6866

Los Gatos Company
17 North Santa Cruz Avenue
Los Gatos, CA 95030
ph: (408) 354-2433

Made In Mendocino
P. O. Box 510
Hopland, CA 95449
ph: (707) 744-1300

Mad River Company
1624 Lowell Street
Eureka, CA 95501
ph: (707) 442-5520

Main Street Jewelers
125 North Main Street
Lakeport, CA 95453

Mandel & Company
8687 Melrose Avenue
Los Angeles, CA 90069
ph: (310) 652-5025

Marcella Noon Imports
101 Henry Adams Street, Suite 423
San Francisco, CA 94103
ph: (415) 255-8485

May Company
6160 Laurel Canyon Boulevard
North Hollywood, CA 91606
ph: (818) 509-5226

McHenry Mansion Gift Store
906 15th Street
P. O. Box 642
Modesto, CA 95353
ph: (209) 577-5367

The Melting Pot
Main at Lansing Streets
P. O. Box 845
Mendocino, CA 95460
ph: (707) 937-0173

Missouri Trader
123 East Channel Islands Boulevard
Hollywood, CA 93041
ph: (213) 465-4066

Misty Meadows
18411 Hatteras Street, Apt. 247
Tarzana, CA 91356

Modern Living
8125 Melrose Avenue
Los Angeles, CA 90046
ph: (213) 655-3898

The Oak Tree
546 Old Mammoth Road
Mammoth Lakes, CA 93546
ph: (619) 935-4032

On The Vine
P. O. Box 284
St. Helena, CA 94574
ph: (707) 963-2209

Out of Hands
1303 Castro Street
San Francisco, CA 94114
ph: (415) 826-3885

Palm Springs Desert Museum
101 North Museum Drive
Palm Springs, CA 92262
ph: (619) 325-7186

A Passing Glimpse
9219 West Pico Boulevard
Los Angeles, CA 90035

Periwinkle Prints & Gifts
88 Eureka Square
Pacifica, CA 94044
ph: (415) 359-4236

Petri's
675 Bridgeway
Sausalito, CA 94965
ph: (415) 332-2225

Piecemakers
1720 Adams Avenue
Costa Mesa, CA 40216
ph: (714) 641-3112

Pinnacle Grouse
127 Forest Street
Boulder Creek, CA 95006
ph: (408) 338-3563

Plums
5096 North Palm Avenue
Fresno, CA 93704
ph: (209) 237-1822

Power Sewing
185 Fifth Avenue
San Francisco, CA 94118
ph: (415) 386-0400

The Quest
777 Bridgeway
Sausalito, CA 94965
ph: (415) 332-6832

RAKU Ceramics Collection
6540 Washington Street
Yountville, CA 94599
ph: (707) 944-9424
fax: (707) 944-2501

Rosemary's Garden
132 North Main Street
Sebastopol, CA 95472
ph: (707) 829-2539

Santa Barbara Style & Design
137 East De La Guerra Street
Santa Barbara, CA 93101
ph: (805) 965-6291

Satori Fine Herbals
1803 Mission Street, Suite 589
Santa Cruz, CA 95060
ph: (408) 475-6154

Sculpture To Wear
9638 Brighton Way
Beverly Hills, CA 90210
ph: (310) 277-2542

Shibui House
630 Cliff Drive
Aptos, CA 95003
ph: (408) 688-7195

Snakes and Beads
P. O. Box 230967
Encinitas, CA 92023

South Bay Bronze
P. O. Box 3254
San Jose, CA 93428
ph: (805) 927-1800

Spirals
367 University Avenue
Palo Alto, CA 94301
ph: (415) 324-1155

Stillwater's
1228 Main Street
St. Helena, CA 94574
ph: (707) 745-0254

Studio 41
739 First Street
Benicia, CA 94574
ph: (707) 745-0254

Terrain
165 Jessie Street, Suite 2
San Francisco, CA 94105
ph: (415) 543-0656

Ulrich Creative Arts
P. O. Box 684
Ventura, CA 93002
ph: (805) 643-4160

Union Street Goldsmiths
1909 Union Street
San Francisco, CA 94123
ph: (415) 776-8048
fax: (415) 776-1557

Various & Sundries
411 San Anselmo Avenue
San Anselmo, CA 94960
ph: (415) 454-1442

Verdi
723 Bridgeway
Sausalito, CA 94965
ph: (415) 331-3009

Viewpoints Art
315 State Street
Los Altos, CA 94022
ph: (415) 941-5789

Village Art
121 West Branch Street
Arroyo Grande, CA 93420
ph: (805) 489-3587

Village Artisans
2315 Honolulu Avenue
Montrose, CA 91020
ph: (818) 957-3228

Village Artistry Gallery
Dolores Between Ocean & Seventh
P. O. Box 5493
Carmel, CA 93921
ph: (408) 624-7628

Village Spinning and Weaving Shop
425-B Alisal Road
Solvang, CA 93463
ph: (805) 686-1192

Vizions Artwear
644 Santa Cruz Avenue
Menlo Park, CA 94025
ph: (415) 321-1100

The Wild Oat
Sonoma County Museum
425 Seventh Street
Santa Rosa, CA 95401
ph: (707) 579-1500

Colorado

Artisan Center
2757 East Third Avenue
Denver, CO 80206
ph: (303) 333-1201

Art West Designs
8743 West Floyd Avenue
Denver, CO 80227
ph: (303) 986-1439

Carson Group Limited
1734 Wazee Street
Denver, CO 80202
ph: (303) 297-8585

Commonwheel Artist Co-op
102 Canon Avenue
Manitou Springs, CO 80829
ph: (719) 685-1008

Eccentricity
2440 East Third Avenue
Denver, CO 80206
ph: (303) 388-8877

In Touch Imports
701 Grand Avenue
Glenwood Springs, CO 81601
ph: (970) 945-1468
fax: same

Pismo
2727 East Third Avenue
Denver, CO 80206
ph: (303) 333-7724

Sangre de Cristo Arts Center
210 North Santa Fe
Pueblo, CO 81003
ph: (719) 543-0130
fax: (719) 543-0134

Shanahan Collections
595 South Broadway, Suite 100S
Denver, CO 80209
ph: (303) 778-7088

Show of Hands
2610 East Third Avenue
Denver, CO 80206
ph: (303) 399-0201
fax: same

Squashblossom
98 Gore Creek Drive
Vail, CO 81657
ph: (970) 476-3129

Steamboat Art Company
903 Lincoln Avenue
Steamboat Springs, CO 80487
ph: (970) 879-3383

Tapestry
2859 East Third Avenue
Denver, CO 80206
ph: (303) 393-0535

Traders of the Lost Art
1429 Pearl Street
Boulder, CO 80302
ph: (303) 440-9664

Connecticut
American Hand
125 Post Road
Westport, CT 06880
ph: (203) 226-8883

Artistic Surroundings
40 1/2 Padanaram Road
Danbury, CT 06811
ph: (203) 798-0361

Church Street Trading Company
19 Church Street
New Milford, CT 06776
ph: (203) 355-2790

Company of Craftsmen
43 West Main Street
Mystic, CT 06355
ph: (203) 536-4189

Cottage Crafts of Barkhamsted
292 New Hartford Road
Winsted, CT 06098
ph: (203) 379-2411

A Different Drum
45 Welles Street, Suite A
Glastonbury, CT 06033
ph: (203) 659-4407

The Elements
14 Liberty Way
Greenwich, CT 06830
ph: (203) 661-0014

Foreign Cargo
Main Street
Kent, CT 06757
ph: (203) 927-3900

Glebe House Shop
Hollow Road
P. O. Box 245
Woodbury, CT 06798
ph: (203) 263-2855

Hummingbird
9 Main Street
East Haddam, CT 06423
ph: (203) 873-3780

Laughing Coyote Kaleidoscope
25 Upper Butcher Road
Vernon-Rockville, CT 06066
ph: (203) 875-5098

Silvermine Guild Arts Center
1037 Silvermine Road
New Canaan, CT 06840
ph: (203) 966-5618
fax: (203) 966-9700

A Touch Of Glass
P. O. Box 433
North Moodus Road
Moodus, CT 06469
ph: (203) 873-9709

Wooden Leather
760 Main Street
Plantsville, CT 06479
ph: (860) 628-4579

Delaware
Artisans III
100 West Ninth Street
Wilmington, DE 19801
ph: (302) 656-7370

Craft Collection
129-D Rehoboth Avenue
Rehoboth Beach, DE 19971
ph: (302) 227-3640

The Stepping Stone
107 West Market Street
Lewes, DE 19958
ph: (302) 645-1254

District of Columbia
Africamania
1621 Wisconsin Avenue, NW
Washington, DC 20007
ph: (202) 342-2427

American Hand Plus
2906 M Street Northwest
Washington, DC 20007
ph: (202) 965-3273

Appalachian Spring
50 Massachusetts Avenue N.E.
Washington, DC 20002
ph: (202) 682-0505

Appalachian Spring
3240 Prospect Street N.W.
Washington, DC 20007
ph: (202) 342-5578

Artifactory
641 Indiana Avenue N.W.
Washington, DC 20004
ph: (202) 393-2727

Beadazzled
1522 Connecticut Avenue N.W.
Washington, DC 20036
ph: (202) 265-2323

Contrast
50 Massachusetts Avenue N.E.
Washington, DC 20002
ph: (202) 371-0566

Cotton Warehouse
416 Seventh Street N.W.
Washington, DC 20001
ph: (202) 232-3535

The Farrell Collection
2633 Connecticut Avenue N.W.
Washington, DC 20008
ph: (202) 483-8334

Gazelle Gallery
5335 Wisconsin Avenue N.W.
Washington, DC 20015
ph: (202) 686-5656

Indian Craft Shop
U.S. Department of Interior
1849 C Street N.W., Room 1023
Washington, DC 20240
ph: (202) 737-4381

The Kellogg Collection
3424 Wisconsin Avenue N.W.
Washington, DC 20016
ph: (202) 363-6878

Kobos
2444 18th Street N.W.
Washington, DC 20009
ph: (202) 332-9580

Magical Animal
342 12th Street S.E.
Washington, DC 20003
ph: (202) 337-4476

Moon, Blossoms and Snow
225 Pennsylvania Avenue S.E.
Washington, DC 20003
ph: (202) 543-8181
fax: same

Rooms with a View
3240 P Street N.W.
Washington, DC 20007
ph: (202) 625-0610

Santa Fe Style
1413 Wisconsin Avenue N.W.
Washington, DC 20007
ph: (202) 333-3747

Shaune Bazner Accessories
5117 MacArthur Boulevard N.W.
Washington, DC 20016
ph: (202) 362-2042

Sign of the Times Cultural
Workshop and Gallery
605 56th Street N.E.
Washington, DC 20019
ph: (202) 399-3400
fax: (202) 399-5460

Toast and Strawberries
1608 Connecticut Avenue N.W.
Washington, DC 20036
ph: (202) 234-2424

Uptown Arts
3236 P Street N.W.
Washington, DC 20007
ph: (202) 337-0600

Florida
Ahava
414 Plaza Real
Boca Raton, FL 33432
ph: (407) 393-5001

American Craftworks
5050 Town Center Circle, Suite 219
Boca Raton, FL 33486
ph: (407) 362-4220

Artcetera
640 East Atlantic Cave
Delray Beach, FL 33483
ph: (407) 279-9939

Art Glass Environments
174 Northwest 13th Street
Boca Raton, FL 33432
ph: (407) 391-7310

Blue Berry Hill
119 South Indiana Drive
Englewood, FL 34223
ph: (813) 475-1183

Brooke Pottery
223 North Kentucky Avenue
Lakeland, FL 33801
ph: (813) 688-6844

Cain Studios
619 South Main Street
Gainesville, FL 32601
ph: (904) 377-7657
fax: (904) 377-7038

Dream Weaver
36664 St. Armands
Sarasota, FL 34236
ph: (813) 388-1118

Elements of Design
5802 Sunset Drive
South Miami, FL 33143
ph: (305) 666-5639

Exit Art
The Centre
5380 Gulf Of Mexico Drive
Longboat Key, FL 34228
ph: (813) 383-4099

Florida Craftsmen
501 Central Avenues
St. Petersburg, FL 33701
ph: (813) 821-7391
fax: (813) 822-4294

Harper Company
4 Via Parigi
Palm Beach, FL 33480
ph: (305) 655-8490

Heartworks
820 Lomax Street
Jacksonville, FL 32204
ph: (904) 355-6210

Helium
760 Ocean Drive
Miami, FL 33139
ph: (305) 538-4111

Mielkes Mud
4361 Northwest 32nd Street
Fort Lauderdale, FL 33319
ph: (305) 231-8371

Mount Mananas
1102-A Duval Street
Key West, FL 33040
ph: (305) 743-5779

Nature's Gallery
22 Northeast 11th Street
Gainesville, FL 32601

Overwhelmed
445 Plaza Real
Mizner Park
Boca Raton, FL 33432
ph: (407) 368-0078

Picture this USA
4216 Lakewood Drive
Seffner, FL 33584
ph: (813) 948-1895

Plantation Potters
521 Fleming Street
Key West, FL 33040
ph: (305) 294-3143

The Rain Barrel
86700 Overseas Highway
Islamorada, FL 33026
ph: (305) 852-3084

SG Collection Art Plus
4534 Cocoplum Way
Delray Beach, FL 33445
ph: (407) 637-8899

Spectrum of American Artists
3101 PGA Boulevard B-117
Palm Beach Gardens, FL 33410
ph: (407) 622-2527

State of Origin Gifts
8106 Woodlawn Circle South
Ellenton, FL 34222
ph: (813) 722-2888

Treehouse Gift Shop
630 Tarpon Bay Road,
Suite 10
Sanibel, FL 33957
ph: (813) 472-1850

Visual Arts Center
19 East Fourth Street
Panama City, FL 32401
ph: (904) 769-4454

Georgia
Adventures
2525 Auburn Avenue
Colombus, GA 31906
ph: (706) 563-3553

By Hand South
112 East Ponce De Leon Avenue
Decatur, GA 30030
ph: (404) 378-0118

The Creative Mark
130 West Washington Street
Madison, GA 30650
ph: (404) 342-2153

Illumina
3500 Peachtree Road Northeast,
Suite 24-A
Atlanta, GA 30326
ph: (404) 233-3010

Junkman's Daughter's Brother
160 East Clayton Street
Athens, GA 30601
ph: (706) 543-4454

Local Color
4 Misty Ridge Manor
Atlanta, GA 30327
ph: (404) 441-9191

Southern Accessories Today
Atlanta Merchandise Mart,
Suite 12-A2
Atlanta, GA 30303
ph: (404) 581-0811

Hawaii
David T. Islands of Excellence
3408 Franis Street
Honolulu, HI 96815
ph: (808) 737-6488

Dreams of Paradise
308 Kamehameha Avenue,
Suite 106
Hilo, HI 96720
ph: (808) 935-5670

The Following Sea
4211 Wajalae Avenue
Honolulu, HI 96814
ph: (808) 537-4181

Raku International
917 Halekauwila Street
Honolulu, HI 96814
ph: (808) 537-4181

Illinois
Adesso
600 Central Avenue
Highland Park, IL 60035
ph: (708) 433-8525

Art and Artisans
108 South Michigan Avenue
Chicago, IL 60603
ph: (312) 855-9220

Art Concepts
2411 Macarthur Boulevard
Springfield, IL 62704
ph: (217) 793-1600

Art Effect
641 West Armitage
Chicago, IL 60614
ph: (312) 664-0997

Artists' Cove
27 North Grove Avenue
Elgin, IL 60120
ph: (708) 695-2683

Art Scape
1625 North Alpine Road
Rockford, IL 61107

Callard & Osgood
1611 Merchandise Mart
Chicago, IL 60654
ph: (312) 670-3640

City Woods
658 Central Avenue
Highland Park, IL 60035
ph: (708) 432-9393

Cornucopia Naturals
2400 East Main Street, Suite 285
St. Charles, IL 60174
ph: (208) 858-2600

Crossroads
906 Crest Lane Drive
Normal, IL 61761
ph: (309) 827-0121

Gallery Art to Wear
431 Lakeside Terrace
Glencoe, IL 60022
ph: (708) 835-2666
fax: (708) 835-2696

Gimcracks
1513 Sherman Avenue
Evanston, IL 60201
ph: (708) 475-0900

Green Planet
484 North Main Street
Glen Ellyn, IL 60137
ph: (708) 858-9593

Heltzer Design
4853 North Ravenswood Avenue
Chicago, IL 60640
ph: (312) 561-5612

Klein Art Works
400 North Morgan Street
Chicago, IL 60622
ph: (312) 243-0400

Mandel & Company
1600 Merchandise Mart
Chicago, IL 60654
ph: (312) 644-8242

Mindscape Gallery
1506 Sherman Avenue
Evanston, IL 60201
ph: (708) 864-2660
fax: (708) 864-2815

Motif
1101 West Webster Avenue
Chicago, IL 60614
ph: (312) 880-9900

Perlman Fine Jewelry
1322 Springhill Mall
Dundee, IL 60118

Pieces
644 Central
Highland Park, IL 60035
ph: (708) 432-2131

Prairie Peacock
53 South Seminary Street
Galesburg, IL 61401
ph: (309) 342-4900

Prestige Art Plus
8800 Gross Point Road
Skokie, IL 60077
ph: (708) 966-4020

Sea Captain's Lady
17 West State Street
Geneva, IL 60134
ph: (708) 232-7570
fax: (708) 232-7594

Southern Illinois Arts and Crafts
Marketplace at Rend Lake
P. O. Box 69
Whittington, IL 62897
ph: (618) 629-2220

Special Effects Interiors
405 Lake Cook Road
Deerfield, IL 60015
ph: (708) 480-1973

Swank
401 North Milwaukee Avenue
Chicago, IL 60610
ph: (312) 942-0444

Textile Art Centre
916 West Diversey Parkway
Chicago, IL 60614
ph: (312) 929-5655

Unique Accents
3137 Dundee Road
Northbrook, IL 60062
ph: (708) 205-9400

A Unique Presence
2121 North Clybourn Avenue
Chicago, IL 60614
ph: (312) 929-4292

Whimsky
3234 North Southport Avenue
Chicago, IL 60657
ph: (312) 665-1760

Indiana
Artifacts
6327 Guilford
Indianapolis, IN 46220
ph: (317) 255-1178

Artisans
72 West Mulberry Street
P. O. Box 222
Kokomo, IN 46901
ph: (317) 452-5505

Cactus Flower
322 East Kirkwood
Bloomington, IN 47408
ph: (812) 333-8279

Chatauqua of Arts
119 West Main Street
Madison, IN 47225
ph: (812) 265-5080

Earthly Designs
8701 Keystone Crossing
Indianapolis, IN 46240
ph: (317) 580-1861

Folk Art Imports
6503 North Carrollton Avenue
Indianapolis, IN 46220
ph: (317) 257-7602

Patrick King Contemporary Art
1726 East 86th Street
Indianapolis, IN 46240
ph: (317) 634-4101

Perennial Designs
120 North Walnut
Bloomington, IN 47404
ph: (812) 332-3551

Iowa
Agora Artisans Marketplace
308 West Water Street
Decorah, IA 52101
ph: (319) 382-8786

Artists Concepts
7 Longview KNLS Northeast
Iowa City, IA 52240
ph: (319) 337-2361

From Gifted Hands
400 Main (on the Park)
Ames, IA 50010
ph: (515) 232-5656

The Lagniappe
114 Fifth Street
West Des Moines, IA 50265
ph: (515) 277-0047

Kansas
Granny Square
1011 West Douglas
Wichita, KS 67213
ph: (316) 263-8733

Parman Brothers
P. O. Box 7
Johnson, KS 67855
ph: (516) 492-6282

Santa Fe Connection
4563 Indian Creek Parkway
Shawnee Mission, KS 66207
ph: (913) 897-2275

Silver Works and More
715 Massachusetts
Lawrence, KS 66044
ph: (913) 842-1460

Stoney Broke
2810 West 53rd Street
Fairway, KS 66205
ph: (913) 432-3700

Kentucky
Appalachian Fireside
182 Main Street
Berea, KY 40403
ph: (606) 986-9013

Artique
410 West Vine Civic Center Shops
Lexington, KY 40507
ph: (606) 233-1774
fax: (606) 231-1794

Basket Barn
5267 North Dixie
Elizabeth Town, KY 42701
ph: (502) 737-9499

Baskets and Things
136 Miller Lane
London, KY 40741
ph: (606) 864-7767

Brockman Weavers
4401 Highway 30 West
Annville, KY 40402
ph: (606) 364-5457

Churchill Weavers
P. O. Box 30
Berea, KY 40403
ph: (606) 986-3126
fax: (606) 986-2861

Completely Kentucky
235 West Broadway Street
Frankfort, KY 40601
ph: (502) 223-5240

Contemporary Artifacts
128 North Broadway Street
Berea, KY 40403
ph: (606) 986-1096

Country by Liz
10978 State Route 69 North
Dundee, KY 42338
ph: (502) 276-5018

Kentucky Hills Industries
P. O. Box 186
Pine Knot, KY 42635
ph: (606) 354-2813

Morris Fork Crafts
930 Morris Fork Road
Boonville, KY 41314
ph: (606) 398-2194

The Nash Collection
843 Lane Allen Road
Lexington, KY 40504
ph: (606) 276-0116

Southern Secrets
P. O. Box 1402
Owensboro, KY 42302
ph: (502) 685-1910

Louisiana
Ariodante Contemporary Craft
535 Jula Street
New Orleans, LA 70130
ph: (504) 524-3233

Artists Alliance (mailing address)
P. O. Box 4006
Lafayette, LA 70502
(store address)
125 West Vermilion Street
Lafayette, LA 70501
ph: (318) 233-7518

Dyed in the World
P. O. Box 498
Crowley, LA 70527
ph: (318) 783-6485

Maine
Benson's Fiber & Wood
59 Mountain Street
Camden, ME 04843
ph: (207) 236-6564

Blacks Handweaving Shop
597 Main Street
West Barnstable, ME 02668
ph: (508) 362-3955

Clipper Trade Maine
110 Front Street
Bath, ME 04530
ph: (207) 442-8671

Coyote Moon
54 Main Street
Belfast, ME
ph: (207) 338-5659

Earthly Delights
81 Water Street
Hallowell, ME 04347
ph: (207) 622-9801

Edgecomb Potters
Route 27
P. O. 2104
Edgecomb, ME 04556
ph: (207) 882-6802

Emphasis on Maine
36 Main Street
Bridgeton, ME 04009
ph: (207) 647-2161

Green Head Forge
Old Quarry Road
Stonington, ME 04681
ph: (207) 367-2632

Longacre Enterprises
Old Eastport Road
P. O. Box 196
Perry, ME 04667
ph: (207) 853-2762

Maine Cottage Furniture
Lower Falls Landing
Yarmouth, ME 04096
ph: (207) 846-0602

Material Objects
500 Congress Street
Portland, ME 04101
ph: (207) 774-1241

Plum Dandy
Goose Rocks Road
P. O. Box 161
Kennebunkport, ME 04046
ph: (207) 967-3463

Maryland

Ahni and Company
2014 Renard Court
Annapolis, MD 21401
ph: (410) 266-8089

Appalachiana
10400 Old Georgetown Road
Bethesda, MD 20814

Artisans Collection
11216 Old Carriage Road
Glen Arm, MD 21057
ph: (301) 661-1118

Bamboozled!
4929 St. Elmo Avenue
Bethesda, MD 20814
ph: (301) 907-9020

The Brassworks
1641 Thames Street
Baltimore, MD 21231
ph: (301) 327-7280

Calico Cat
2137 Gwynn Oak Avenue
Baltimore, MD 21207
ph: (410) 944-2450

Cathy Hart Pottery Studio
Mill Centre Studio 221
Baltimore, MD 21211
ph: (301) 467-4911

Cattails and Dragonfly
8565 Horseshoe Lane
Potomac, MD 20854
ph: (301) 983-2167

Chesapeake East
General Delivery
Upper Fairmount, MD 21867
ph: (301) 543-8175

Craft Concepts
Green Spring Station
Lutherville, MD 21093
ph: (410) 823-2533

Crazy Mountain Antiques
14708 Dumbarton Drive
Upper Marlboro, MD 20772

The Finer Side
209B North Boulevard
Salisbury, MD 21801
ph: (410) 749-4081

Finewares
7042 Carroll Avenue
Silver Spring, MD 20912
ph: (301) 270-3138

Forest Glen Country Store
6 Post Office Road
Silver Spring, MD 20910
ph: (301) 585-0303

Gazelle Gallery
5300 Falls Road
Baltimore, MD 21210
ph: (301) 433-3305

Glass Fantasies
209 East Diamond Street
Gaithersburg, MD 20877
ph: (301) 258-0841

Harmony in Living
5333 Hollow Stone Circle
Baltimore, MD 21237
ph: (410) 931-1017

Jurus
5618 Newbury Street
Baltimore, MD 21209
ph: (410) 542-5227

Main Street Memories
14801 Main Street
Upper Marlboro, MD 20772
ph: (301) 627-8962

New Images
919 Reisterstown Road
Baltimore, MD 21208
ph: (410) 486-0155

One Step Up
4705 Miller Avenue
Bethesda, MD 20814
ph: (301) 656-2550

Pieces of Olde
P. O. Box 65130
Baltimore, MD 21209
ph: (410) 366-4949

Presence
7720 Woodmont Avenue
Bethesda, MD 20814
ph: (301) 986-4710

Rainbow Shoppe
600 Memorial Avenue
Cumberland, MD 21502
ph: (301) 777-5795

Stoneware Shop
232 East Patrick Street
Frederick, MD 21701
ph: (301) 662-9427

The Store
24 Village Square
Village of Cross Keys
Baltimore, MD 21210
ph: (410) 323-2350
fax: same

Tin Rooster
P. O. Box 8
Manchester, MD 21102
ph: (410) 239-6155

Tomlinson Craft Collection
711 West 40th Street
Baltimore, MD 21211
ph: (410) 338-1572

Wear It Well
4816 Bethesda Avenue
Bethesda, MD 20814
ph: (301) 652-3713

Zyzyx
1809 Reisterstown Road
Baltimore, MD 21208
ph: (410) 486-9785

Massachusetts
Alianza
154 Newbury Street
Boston, MA 02116
ph: (617) 262-2385

Artful Image
161 Walden Street
Concord, MA 01742
ph: (508) 371-2353

Bens
19 Main Street
Amesbury, MA 01913
ph: (508) 388-0471

Bramhall & Dunn
Main Street
P. O. Box 923
Vineyard Haven, MA 02568
ph: (508) 693-6437

Busy Beaver Gift Shop
7 Brockton Avenue
Abington, MA 02351
ph: (617) 878-4041

Casa de Moda
272 Cabot Street
Beverly, MA 01915
ph: (508) 922-8100
fax: (508) 922-1445

Concord Spice and Grain
93 Thoreau Street
Concord, MA 01742
ph: (508) 369-1535

Country Roads
81 Walnut Street
Arlington, MA 01770
ph: (617) 646-7260

The Crafty Yankee
1838 Massachusetts Avenue
Lexington, MA 02173
ph: (617) 863-1219

Danco Furniture
Routes 5 & 10
West Hatfield, MA 01088
ph: (413) 247-5681

Decor International
141 Newbury Street
Boston, MA 02116
ph: (617) 262-1529

Divinity's Splendour Glow
311 Broadway
Arlington, MA 02174
ph: (617) 648-7100

Falconer's
492 Main Street
Chatham, MA 02633
ph: (508) 945-2867

Fire Opal
7 Pond Street
Jamaica Plain, MA 02130
ph: (617) 524-0262

Flowers Etcetera
2 Surro Drive
Framingham, MA 01701
ph: (508) 877-6364

The Gifted Hand
32 Church Street
Wellesley, MA 02181
ph: (617) 235-7171

Gilda's
101 Union Street
Newton, MA 02159
ph: (617) 964-7199

Glad Rags
76 Church Street
Lenox, MA 01240
ph: (413) 637-0088

Grey Goose
95 Chapel Street
Needham, MA 02192
ph: (617) 449-8441

Half Moon Harry
19 Bearskin Neck
Rockport, MA 01966
ph: (508) 546-6601

Handworks
157 Great Road, Suite 2-A
Acton, MA 01720
ph: (508) 263-7107

Handworks
10 South Road
Rockport, MA 01966
ph: (508) 546-6200

Hibiscus
114 Main Street
Gloucester, MA 01930
ph: (508) 286-3848

Impulse
188 Commercial Street
Provincetown, MA 02657
ph: (508) 487-1154

Iris
1782 Massachusetts Avenue
Cambridge, MA 02140
ph: (617) 661-1192

Jubilation
91 Union Street
Picadilly Station
Newton, MA 02116
ph: (617) 266-6665

Knock on Wood
126 Tiffany Road
Norwell, MA 02061
ph: (617) 826-9502

Laughing Bear
P. O. Box 717
Oak Bluffs, MA 02557
ph: (508) 693-9342

Limited Editions
176 Walnut Street
Newton Highlands, MA 02161
ph: (617) 965-5474

Mobilia
358 Huron Avenue
Cambridge, MA 02138
ph: (617) 876-2109

Neal Rosenblum Goldsmiths
287 Park Avenue
Worcester, MA 01609
ph: (508) 755-4244

Nothing Too Common
1502 Highland Avenue
Needham, MA 02192

Oriel
17 College Street
South Hadley, MA 01075
ph: (413) 532-6469

Peacework Gallery and Crafts
263 Main Street
Northampton, MA 01060
ph: (413) 586-7033

Perceptions
67 Main Street
Concord, MA 01742
ph: (508) 369-6797

Primitive Artisan
40 Pecks Road
Pittsfield, MA 01201
ph: (413) 443-4777

Quadrum
The Mall At Chestnut Hill
Chestnut Hill, MA 02167
ph: (617) 262-9601

Salmon Falls Artisans Showroom
Ashfield Road
P. O. Box 17
Shelburne Falls, MA 01370
ph: (413) 625-9833

Scottish Designer House
160 Gilbertville Road
Ware, MA 01082
ph: (413) 967-9901

Signature
P. O. Box 2307
10 Steeple Street
Mashpee, MA 02649
ph: (508) 539-0045
fax: (508) 539-0509

Silverscape Designs
264 North Pleasant Street
Amherst, MA 01002
ph: (413) 253-3324

Sioux Eagle Designs
80 Main Street
P. O. Box 1352
Vineyard Haven, MA 02568
ph: (508) 693-6537

The Spectrum of American
Craftsmen and Artists
369 Old Kings Highway
Brewster, MA 02631
ph: (508) 385-3322
fax: (508) 385-2897

Vaillancourt Folk Art
145 Armsby Road
Sutton, MA 01590
ph: (508) 865-9183
fax: (508) 865-4140

Whippoorwill Crafts
126 Faneuil Hall Marketplace
Boston, MA 02109
ph: (617) 523-5149

Michigan
Birmingham Beads
154 West Maple Road
Birmingham, MI 48009
ph: (313) 644-7609

Boyer Glassworks
207 North State Street
Harborsprings, MI 49740
ph: (616) 526-6359

Collected Works
317 South Main Street
Ann Arbor, MI 48104
ph: (313) 955-4222
fax: same

Deco Art
815 First Street
Menominee, MI 49858
ph: (906) 863-3300

For Love Nor Money
314 East Lake Street
Petoskey, MI 49770
ph: (616) 348-3075

Friends Furnishings & Designs
126 Main Centre
Northville, MI 48167
ph: (313) 380-6930

Garden House Interiors
9426 Birch Run Road
Birch Run, MI 48415
ph: (517) 624-9649

Glen Arbor City Limits
P. O. Box 444
Glen Arbor, MI 49636

Good Goods
106 Mason Street
Saugatuck, MI 49453
ph: (616) 857-1557

The Great Frame-Up
2876 Washtenaw Road
Ypsilanti, MI 48197
ph: (313) 434-8556

Handiworks
5260 Helena Street
Alden, MI 49612
ph: (616) 331-6787

Hollander's
2727 Lillian Road
Ann Arbor, MI 48104
ph: (313) 741-7531

Horrock's
7420 West Saginaw Highway
Lansing, MI 48917
ph: (517) 323-3782
fax: same

Huzza
136 East Main Street
Harbor Springs, MI 49740
ph: (616) 526-2128

Kali's East
108 Division Street
East Lansing, MI 48823
ph: (517) 337-3220

Kennedy's
661 Croswell Avenue S.E.
Grand Rapids, MI 49506

Lakeside Studio
15251 Lakeshore Road
Lakeside, MI 49116
ph: (616) 469-1377

Mattie Flynn
1033 East Fulton Street
Grand Rapids, MI 49503
ph: (616) 454-8775

Milieu
20 South Main
Clarkston, MI 48346
ph: (313) 625-7617

Northern Possessions
222 Park Avenue
Petoskey, MI 49770
ph: (616) 348-3344

Objects of Art
6243 Orchard Lake Road
West Bloomfield, MI 48332
ph: (810) 539-3332
fax: (810) 539-0851

Out On A Limb
109 Phillips Street
P. O. Box 232
Lake Leelanau, MI 49653
ph: (616) 256-7205

The Peaceable Kingdom
210 S Main Street
Ann Arbor, MI 48104
ph: (313) 668-7886

The Penniman Showcase
827 Penniman Avenue
Plymouth, MI 48170
ph: (313) 455-5531

Revolution
23257 Woodward Avenue
Ferndale, MI 48220
ph: (810) 541-3444

The Secret Garden
10206 Front Street
P. O. Box 31
Empire, MI 49630
ph: (616) 326-5428

Urban Architecture
5 East Kirby Street
Detroit, MI 48202
ph: (313) 873-2707

Village Green
715 South Saginaw
Midland, MI 48640
ph: (517) 631-2500

The Wetsman Collection
132 North Woodward Avenue
Birmingham, MI 48009
ph: (810) 645-6212

Minnesota
The Bibelot Shops
1082 Grand Avenue
St. Paul, MN 55105
ph: (612) 222-0321

Celebration Designs
1089 Grand Avenue
St. Paul, MN 55105
ph: (612) 690-4344

Coat of Many Colors
1666 Grand Avenue
St. Paul, MN 55105
ph: (612) 690-5255

The Crate
3001 Hennepin Avenue South
Minneapolis, MN 55408
ph: (612) 823-4777

Distinctive Design
5040 Lake Elmo Avenue North
Lake Elmo, MN 55042
ph: (612) 430-1268
fax: (612) 430-0956

Gabberts Furniture
3501 West 69th Street
Minneapolis, MN 55435
ph: (612) 927-1500

The Gathering
850 Grand Avenue
St. Paul, MN 55105
ph: (612) 290-2939

Glasspectacle
14791 Square Lake TRL North
Stillwater, MN 55032
ph: (612) 439-0757

Northern Clay Center
2375 University Avenue West
St. Paul, MN 55114
ph: (612) 642-1735

Out of the Ordinary
8800 Highway Seven
St. Louis Park, MN 43054

Three Rooms Up
3515 West 69th Street
Edina, MN 55435
ph: (612) 926-1774

The Woodworker Store
12801 Industrial Boulevard
Rogers, MN 55374
ph: (612) 428-3200

Mississippi
Chimneyville Crafts
1150 Lakeland Drive
Jackson, MS 39213
ph: (601) 988-9253

Earth Traders
1060 East County Line Road
Ridgeland, MS 39157
ph: (601) 957-2343

Hillyer House
207 East Scenic Drive
Pass Christian, MS 39571
ph: (601) 452-4810

Missouri
B. Z. Wagman Art
15 Dromara Road
St. Louis, MO 63124

Coyote's Paw Gallery
6388 Delmar Boulevard
St. Louis, MO 63130
ph: (314) 721-7576
fax: (314) 721-7576

The Craft Alliance
6640 Delmar Boulevard
St. Louis, MO 63130
ph: (314) 725-1177

Hella's Art To Wear & Fibers
9769 Clayton Road
St. Louis, MO 63124
ph: (314) 997-9696

Interwoven Designs
4400 Laclede Avenue
St. Louis, MO 63108
ph: (314) 531-6200

Kimmswick Pottery
P. O. Box 25
Kimmswick, MO 63053
ph: (314) 464-3041

New Accents
33 Beacon Hill Lane
St. Louis, MO 63141

Style Works
6934 Dartmouth Avenue
St. Louis, MO 63130
ph: (314) 531-3900

Terra Cotta Creations
Route 2
P. O. Box 1605
Nixa, MO 65714
ph: (417) 725-1108

Montana
Artifacts
403 North Ninth Street
Livingston, MT 28209
ph: (406) 586-3755

Artifacts Gallery
308 East Main Street
Bozeman, MT 59715
ph: (406) 586-3755

Artistic Touch
209 Central Avenue
Whitefish, MT 59937
ph: (406) 862-4813

Furniture
17 Main Street
Kalispell, MT 59901
ph: (406) 756-8555

The Squirrel Nest
1332 Lewis Avenue
Billings, MT 59102
ph: (406) 259-5461

Tipi Gift Shop
Rural Route 62
P. O. Box 3110-E
Livingston, MT 59047
ph: (406) 222-8575

Nebraska
The Acreage Emporium
6000 South 56th Street
Lincoln, NE 68516
ph: (402) 423-4344

Honeysuckle Crafts
Rural Route 3
P. O. Box 150
Cambridge, NE 69022
ph: (308) 697-4408

Souq, Limited
1018 Howard Street
Omaha, NE 68102
ph: (402) 342-2972
fax: (402) 345-1762

University Place Art Center
2601 North 48th Street
Lincoln, NE 68504
ph: (402) 466-8692

New Hampshire
Artisans Group
General Delivery
P. O. Box 1039
Dublin, NH 03444
ph: (603) 563-8782

Craftings
72 Hanover Street
Manchester, NH 03101
ph: (603) 623-4108

Fair Skies
129 Market Street
Portsmouth, NH 03801
ph: (603) 431-1663

Isis & Rasputin
P. O. Box 1872
Concord, NH 03302

Two Moon Traders
270 Louden Road
Concord, NH 03301
ph: (603) 226-3920

Wild Carrot
Main Street
P. O. Box 2126
North Conway, NH 03860
ph: (603) 356-3398

New Jersey
Animal Imagery
P. O. Box 159
Madison, NJ 07940
ph: (201) 377-5541

Arcadia
10 Bridge Street
Frenchtown, NJ 08825
ph: (908) 996-7570

Art Directions
38 Wilcox Drive
Mountain Lakes, NJ 07046
ph: (201) 263-1420

Artforms
16 Monmouth Street
Red Bank, NJ 07701
ph: (908) 530-4330

Artisan Alcove
523 LaFayette Street
Cape May, NJ 08204
ph: (609) 898-0202

The Bea Hive
472 Cedar Lane
Teaneck, NJ 07666
ph: (201) 836-1366

Blooms
98 Albany Street
New Brunswick, NJ 08901
ph: (908) 246-0818

Blue Turtle
14 Prospect Street
Madison, NJ 07940
ph: (201) 377-0980

Chester Crafts
30 Main Street
Chester, NJ 07930
ph: (908) 879-2900

Contrasts
49 Broad Street
Red Bank, NJ 07701
ph: (908) 741-9177

Cottage Crafts
43 Main Street
Route 520
Holmdel, NJ 07733
ph: (201) 946-3229

Crafty Editions
595 Mountain Avenue
Berkeley Heights, NJ 07922
ph: (908) 665-0939

Dashing Designs
295 West Marlton Pike
Cherry Hill, NJ 08002
ph: (609) 428-4022

Design Quest
3 Grand Avenue
Englewood, NJ 07631
ph: (201) 568-7001

Dexterity
26 Church Street
Montclair, NJ 07042
ph: (201) 746-5370

Earthly Pleasures
610 North Maple Avenue
Ho Ho Kus, NJ 07423
ph: (201) 444-4834

East West Connection
274 Route 31
Lebanon, NJ 08833
ph: (908) 713-9655

Goldsmiths
26 North Union Station
Lambertville, NJ 08530
ph: (609) 398-4590

Grey Dove
159 South Livingston Avenue
Livingston, NJ 07039
ph: (201) 994-2266

Kimberly Designs
1111 Park Avenue
Plainfield, NJ 07060
ph: (201) 561-5344

La Gallerie Du Vitrail
70 Tanner Street, Suite 2
Haddonfield, NJ 08033
ph: (609) 428-6712

Limited Editions
2200 Long Beach Boulevard
Surf City, NJ 08008
ph: (609) 494-0527

Margaret's Craft Shop
413 Raritan Avenue
Highland Park, NJ 08904
ph: (908) 247-2210

McCulloh Sampler
58 English Plaza
Red Bank, NJ 07940
ph: (908) 758-8518

McNally Instruments
11 Long View Road
Rockaway, NJ 07866
ph: (201) 983-9153

New Jersey Designer Crafts
65 Church Street
New Brunswick, NJ 08901
ph: (908) 246-4066
fax: (908) 247-4005

Panich
26 North Dean Street
Englewood, NJ 07631
ph: (201) 871-7446

Peters Valley Craft Center
19 Kuhn Road
Layton, NJ 07851
ph: (201) 948-5200
fax: (201) 948-0011

Potpourri
204 Main Street
Hackettstown, NJ 07840
ph: (201) 852-9552

Pottery International
28 Park Place On The Green
Morristown, NJ 07960
ph: (201) 538-1919

The Quest
38 Main Street
Chester, NJ 07930
ph: (908) 879-8144

Room With A View
433 Francine Drive
Cherry Hill, NJ 08003
ph: (609) 354-1737

Signature Designs
5 West Main Street
Moorestown, NJ 08057
ph: (609) 778-8657

Song of the Sea
32 West 32nd Street, Suite 7
Beach Haven, NJ 08008
ph: (609) 492-5053

Strafford Designs
140 Carlough Road
Saddle River, NJ 07458
ph: (201) 934-6053

True Colors
Road 3
P. O. Box 91
Pittstown, NJ 08867
ph: (908) 879-4288

New Mexico
All the World's Children
105 East Marcy Street
Santa Fe, NM 87501
ph: (505) 983-7855

Form & Function
328 Guadalupe Street
Santa Fe, NM 87501
ph: (505) 984-8226

Handwoven Originals
211 Old Santa Fe Trail
Santa Fe, NM 87501
ph: (505) 982-4118

Mabel's West
201 Canyon Road
Santa Fe, NM 87501
ph: (505) 986-9105

Origins
135 West San Francisco Street
Santa Fe, NM 87501
ph: (505) 988-2323

Ornament of Santa Fe
209 West San Francisco Street
Santa Fe, NM 87501
ph: (505) 983-9399

Post Western
201 Galileo Street
Santa Fe, NM 87501
ph: (505) 984-9195

Pueblo of Zuni Arts and Crafts
P. O. Box 425
Zuni, NM 87327
ph: (505) 782-4481

Quilts
625 Canyon Road
Santa Fe, NM 87501
ph: (505) 988-5888

Santa Fe East
200 Old Santa Fe Trail
Santa Fe, NM 87501
ph: (505) 988-3103

Sky's The Limit
1031 Mechem Drive
Ruidoso, NM 88345
ph: (505) 257-7705

Textile Arts
1571 Canyon Road
Santa Fe, NM 87501
ph: (505) 983-9780

Tinworker
1027 Houghton Street
Santa Fe, NM 87501
ph: (505) 983-8850

New York
Adirondack Artwork
Route 3 Main Street
Natural Bridge, NY 13665
ph: (315) 644-4645

After The Rain
149 Mercer Street
New York, NY 10012
ph: (212) 431-1044

Alphabets
115 Avenue A
New York, NY 10009
ph: (212) 475-7250
fax: (212) 473-6342

An American Craftsman
P. O. Box 480
Slate Hill, NY 10973
ph: (914) 355-2400

Anthony Garden Boutique
1190 Lexington Avenue
New York, NY 10028

Archetype
115 Mercer Street
New York, NY 10012
ph: (212) 334-0100

Archimage
668 Monroe Avenue
Rochester, NY 14607
ph: (716) 271-2789

Arrangements
172 Merrick Road
Merrick, NY 10012
ph: (516) 334-0100

Artisans International
89 Main Street
West Hampton Beach, NY 11978
ph: (516) 288-2222

Artium
730 Fifth Avenue, Suite 1710
New York, NY 10001
ph: (212) 333-5800

Audets
363 East Avenue
Rochester, NY 14604
ph: (716) 325-4880
fax: (716) 325-4173

Basic Blue
Kings Highway
P. O. Box 59
Sugar Loaf, NY 10981
ph: (914) 469-9208

Bayberry
Montauk Highway
P. O. Box 718
Amagansett, NY 11930
ph: (516) 267-3000

Bellardo
100 Christopher Street
New York, NY 10014
ph: (212) 675-2668

Benjane Arts
P. O. Box 298
West Hempstead, NY 11552
ph: (516) 483-1330
fax: (516) 739-2716

The Bindle
7070 Cedar Bay Road
Fayetteville, NY 13066
ph: (315) 445-5629

The Booktique
Stony Point Conference Center
Stony Point, NY 10980
ph: (914) 786-5674

Carriage House Studio
79 Guernsey Street
Brooklyn, NY 11222
ph: (617) 629-2337

Ceramics and More
197 Hawkins Street
City Island, NY 10464
ph: (718) 885-0319

Cimarron
64 South Broadway
Nyack, NY 10960

The Clay Pot
162 Seventh Avenue
Brooklyn, NY 11215
ph: (718) 788-6564
fax: (718) 965-1138

Common Ground
19 Greenwich Avenue
New York, NY 10014
ph: (212) 989-4178

Contemporary Primitive
P. O. Box 469
Beacon, NY 12508
ph: (914) 831-2200

Country Gear
General Delivery
Bridgehampton, NY 11932
ph: (516) 537-1032

The Craft Barn
30 Wheller Road
P. O. Box 577
Florida, NY 10921
ph: (914) 651-7949

Craft Company Number Six
785 University Avenue
Rochester, NY 14607
ph: (716) 473-3413

Craft Market Place
35 King Street
Chappaqua, NY 10514
ph: (914) 238-1454

The Craftsmen
Route 9 South Road
Poughkeepsie, NY 12601
ph: (914) 454-2336

Crafts People
424 Spill Way
West Hurley, NY 12491
ph: (914) 331-3859

The Creator's Hands
336 Arnett Boulevard
Rochester, NY 14619
ph: (716) 235-8550

Cross Harris Fine Crafts
979 Third Avenue
New York, NY 10022
ph: (212) 888-7878

Designer Studio
492 Broadway
Saratoga Springs, NY 12866
ph: (518) 584-0987

Design Plus
853 Broadway, Suite 1607
New York, NY 10003
ph: (212) 477-8811

Diana's Boutique
P. O. Box 621
Canandaigua, NY 14424
ph: (716) 394-9450

Enchanted Forest
85 Mercer Street
New York, NY 10012
ph: (212) 431-1045

Entree Libre
Galerie Contemporaine
110 Wooster Street
New York, NY 10012
ph: (212) 431-5279

Eureka Crafts
210 Walton Street
Syracuse, NY 13202
ph: (315) 471-4601

Fabulous Furniture
Route 28
Boiceville, NY 12412
ph: (914) 657-6317

Felissimo
10 West 56th Street
New York, NY 10019
ph: (212) 247-5656

Foreign Wide
3 North Front Street
New Paltz, NY 12561
ph: (914) 255-8822

Forge River Decoys
197 Longfellow Drive
Mistic Beach, NY 11951
ph: (516) 399-4539

Gallimaufry
1 Croton Point Avenue
Croton-on-Hudson, NY 10520
ph: (914) 271-3110
fax: (914) 271-1106

Gargoyles
138 West 25th Street
New York, NY 10001
ph: (212) 255-0135

Gift Cupboard
104 Lafayette Avenue
Suffern, NY 10901
ph: (914) 357-8200

Gift Horse
600 Routes 44-55
Highland, NY 12528
ph: (914) 691-6434

Good Company General Store
715 Monroe Avenue
Rochester, NY 14607
ph: (716) 244-5719

Hand of the Craftsman
58 South Broadway
Nyack, NY 10960
ph: (914) 358-3366

Hummingbird Designs
29 Third Street
Troy, NY 12180
ph: (518) 272-1807

Hummingbird Jewelers
14 East Market Street
Rhinebeck, NY 12572
ph: (914) 876-4585

Hyacinth Contemporary Crafts
4004 Bell Boulevard
Bayside, NY 11361
ph: (718) 224-9228

Important American Craft
70 Riverside Drive
New York, NY 10024
ph: (212) 496-1804

The Interart Center
167 Spring Street, 2nd floor
New York, NY 10012
ph: (212) 431-7500

The Jewelry Project
59 West 71st Street, 9-A
New York, NY 10023

Leo Kaplan Modern
965 Madison Avenue
New York, NY 10011
ph: (212) 535-0240

Liberty Crafts
13 South Broadway
Nyack, NY 10960
ph: (914) 358-3864

Modern Stone Age
111 Greene Street
New York, NY 10012
ph: (212) 966-2570

Mohawk Impressions
P. O. Box 20
Mohawk Nation
Hogansburg, NY 13655
ph: (518) 358-2467

Moose River Trading Company
419 Mandeville Street
Utica, NY 13502
ph: (315) 732-2900

Native Peoples Arts and Craftshop
210 Fabius Street
P. O. Box 851
Syracuse, NY 13201
ph: (315) 432-0450

North River Pottery
107 Hall Street
Brooklyn, NY 11205
ph: (718) 636-8608

Objects of Bright Pride
455-A Columbus Avenue
New York, NY 10024
ph: (212) 721-4579

Offerings
59 Katonah Avenue
Katonah, NY 10514
ph: (914) 232-9643

One of a Kind
978 Broadway
Thornwood, NY 10594
ph: (914) 769-5777

Peipers and Kojen
1023 Lexington Avenue
New York, NY 10021
ph: (212) 744-1047

People's Pottery
158 The Commons
Ithaca, NY 14850
ph: (607) 273-0938

Southwest Studio Connection
65 Main Street
South Hampton, NY 11968
ph: (516) 283-9649

Spectrum
165 East 33rd Street
New York, NY 10016
ph: (212) 447-6385

Sunstone
Rural Delivery 4
P. O. Box 700-A
Cooperstown, NY 13326
ph: (607) 547-8207

Symmetry
348 Broadway
Saratoga Springs, NY 12866
ph: (518) 584-5090

A Thousand Cranes
29 Harrison Street
New York, NY 10013
ph: (212) 233-4439

Town and Country Linen
295 Fifth Avenue
New York, NY 10016
ph: (212) 889-7911

Trackside Emporium
14 East Broadway
Port Jefferson, NY 11777
ph: (516) 473-8222

Tricia's Jewelry
P. O. Box 557
Hyde Park, NY 10543
ph: (914) 698-6618

Turbulence
812 Broadway
New York, NY 10003
ph: (212) 598-9030

Tuskewe Krafts
2089 Upper Mountain Road
Sanborn, NY 14132
ph: (716) 297-1821

Vitrix Hot Glass Studio
77 West Market Street
Corning, NY 14830
ph: (607) 936-8707

Wares For Art
421 Hudson Street, Apt. 220
New York, NY 10014
ph: (212) 989-7845

Whispering Thunder Crafts
P. O. Box 44
Lowville, NY 13367
ph: (315) 376-2997

Winston & Company
97-A Seventh Avenue
Brooklyn, NY 11215
ph: (718) 638-7942

Winter Sun
10 East Market Street
Rhinebeck, NY 12572
ph: (914) 876-3555

Woodstock Guild
34 Tinker Street
Woodstock, NY 12498
ph: (914) 679-2079

Zona
97 Greene Street
New York, NY 10012
ph: (212) 925-6750

North Carolina

Art
502 Pollock Street
New Bern, NC 28562
ph: (919) 636-2120

Artifacts
2908 Selwyn Avenue
Charlotte, NC 28209
ph: (704) 358-8910
fax: (704) 375-8911

Art on the Wall
16 Wall Street
Asheville, NC 28801
ph: (704) 251-1229

Bellagio
5 Biltmore Plaza
Asheville, NC 28803
ph: (704) 277-8100

Bizarre Duck Bazaar
16 Wall Street
Asheville, NC 28801

Blue Spiral
38 Biltmore Avenue
Asheville, NC 28801
ph: (704) 251-0202

Browning Artwork
P. O. Box 275
Highway 12
Frisco, NC 27936
ph: (919) 995-5538

Cameron's
University Mall
University of North Carolina
Chapel Hill, NC 27514
ph: (919) 942-5554

The Center Shop
750 Marguerite Drive
Winston-Salem, NC 27106
ph: (910) 725-1904

City Gardener
3510 Wade Avenue
Raleigh, NC 27605
ph: (919) 821-2718

Continuity
P. O. Box 999
Maggie Valley, NC 28751
ph: (704) 926-0333

Fine Line
304 South Stratford Road
Winston-Salem, NC 27103
ph: (919) 723-8066

Folk Art Center
Milepost 382
Blue Ridge Parkway
Asheville, NC 28815
ph: (704) 298-7928

Gallery of the Mountains
P. O. Box 8283
290 Macon Avenue
Asheville, NC 28814
ph: (704) 254-2068

Just a Bunch of Baskets
109 Wing Road
Bakersville, NC 28705
ph: (704) 688-2399

La Cache
217 Reynold Village
Winston-Salem, NC 27106
ph: (910) 727-1515

Lick Log Mill Store
Dillard Road
Highlands, NC 28741
ph: (704) 526-3934

Little Mountain Pottery
Route 2
Peniel Road
P. O. Box 60
Tryon, NC 28782
ph: (704) 894-8091

Maco Crafts Association
652 Georgia Highway
Franklin, NC 28734
ph: (704) 524-7878

Morning Star Gallery
503 State Street Station
Greensboro, NC 27405
ph: (910) 272-4733

The Picture House
1520 East Fourth Street
Charlotte, NC 28204
ph: (704) 333-8235

Piedmont Craftsmen
1204 Reynolda Road
Winston-Salem, NC 27104
ph: (910) 725-1516
fax: (910) 722-6038

Southern Expressions
2157 New Hendersonville Highway
Pisgah Forest, NC 28768
ph: (704) 884-6242

T. Williamson Interiors
530 Causeway Drive
Wrightsville Beach, NC 28480
ph: (910) 256-3256
fax: (919) 256-9617

North Dakota
The Art Connection
624 Main Avenue
Fargo, ND 58103
ph: (701) 237-6655

Artmain
13 South Main Street
Minot, ND 58701
ph: (701) 838-4747

Browning Arts
22 North Fourth Street
Grand Forks, ND 58203
ph: (701) 746-5090

Wright Made Products
415 17th Avenue South
Grand Forks, ND 58201
ph: (701) 772-6554

Ohio
Art at the Powerhouse
2000 Sycamore Street
Nautica Complex
Cleveland, OH 44113
ph: (216) 696-1942

Artisans All
111 Pearel Road
Brunswick, OH 44212
ph: (216) 225-1118

Aurum and Argent Studio
5723 Main Street
Sylvania, OH 43560
ph: (419) 241-8941

Benchworks
2563 North High Street
Columbus, OH 43202
ph: (614) 263-2111

Cargo Net
General Delivery
P. O. Box 369
Put In Bay, OH 43456
ph: (419) 285-4231

Colacelli
Franklin Park Mall
Toledo, OH 43623
ph: (419) 473-0835

Designs of All Times
28001 Chagrin Boulevard
Cleveland, OH 44122
ph: (216) 831-3010

Jeweler and Metalsmiths
140 Manning Drive
Berea, OH 44017
ph: (216) 234-4877

Mud Mothers Pottery
241 South Court
Medina, OH 44256
ph: (216) 722-8065

Muriel Meray Studio Shop
537 East Maple Street
North Canton, OH 44720
ph: (216) 494-3736

Murray Hill Art & Crafts
2181 Murray Hill Road
Cleveland, OH 44106
ph: (216) 231-2010

Ohio Signatures
13101 Shaker Square
Cleveland, OH 44120
ph: (216) 561-5665

Out of the Ordinary
55-R West Main Street
New Albany, OH 43054
ph: (614) 855-3807

Rainbowers
7720 Olde Eight Road
Hudson, OH 44236
ph: (216) 467-0259

Sandusky Cultural Center
2130 Hayes Avenue
Sandusky, OH 44870
ph: (419) 625-8097

The Sculpture Center
12206 Euclid Avenue
Cleveland, OH 44106
ph: (216) 229-6527

Silver Llama
4786 Dresler Road
Canton, OH 44718
ph: (216) 493-6650

Something Different
3427 Memphis Avenue
Cleveland, OH 44109
ph: (216) 398-0472

Son of a Son of a Cobbler
2212 North High Street
Columbus, OH 43201
ph: (614) 294-2716

Trillium House
P. O. Box 25
Winesburg, OH 44690
ph: (216) 359-5978

Village Artisans Cooperative
220 Xenia Avenue
Yellow Springs, OH 45387
ph: (513) 767-1209

Whitten Studio
1180 County Road 30-A
Ashland, OH 44805
ph: (419) 368-8366

Oklahoma
Buffalo Sun
P. O. Box 1556
Miami, OK 74355
ph: (918) 542-8870

The Gift Place
329 South Main
Eufaula, OK 74432
ph: (918) 689-3158

Mister Indians
1000 South Main
Sapulpa, OK 74066
ph: (918) 224-6511

Oklahoma Indian Arts and
Crafts Cooperative
P. O. Box 966
Anadarko, OK 73005
ph: (405) 247-3486

Tah-Mels
P. O. Box 1123
Tahlequah, OK 74465
ph: (918) 456-5451

Oregon
Artist Brushes
13195 Southwest Glenn Court
Beaverton, OR 97008
ph: (503) 643-4548

Ginny's Ear-Nest
2707 Southeast 35th Place
Portland, OR 97202
ph: (503) 231-8744

Itchy Fingers
513 Northwest 23rd Avenue
Portland, OR 97210
ph: (503) 222-5237

The Real Mother Goose
901 Southwest Yamhill
Portland, OR 97205
ph: (503) 223-9510

Saxons
3138 North Highway 97
Bend, OR 97701
ph: (503) 389-6655

Toad Hall
237 West Third Street
Yachatz, OR 97498
ph: (503) 547-4044

Twist
30 Northwest Westover Road
Portland, OR 97210
ph: (503) 224-0334

Pennsylvania
Accents & Images
General Delivery
P. O. Box 18931
Lahaska, PA 18931
ph: (215) 794-7660

A-Mano
128 South Main Street
New Hope, PA 18938
ph: (215) 862-5122

Ambitious Endeavours
11 Union Avenue
Bala Cynwyd, PA 19004
ph: (610) 667-7377

Art Accents
350 Montgomery Avenue
Merion Station, PA 19066
ph: (215) 664-4444

Artisans Three
The Village Center
Spring House, PA 19477
ph: (215) 643-4504

Best Friends
4329 Main Street
Philadelphia, PA 19127
ph: (215) 487-1250

Campbell Studios
228 Church Street
Cambridge Springs, PA 16403
ph: (814) 398-2148
fax: (814) 398-8844

Cat's Paw Gallery
31 Race Street
Jim Thorpe, PA 18229
ph: (717) 325-4041

Clay Place
5416 Walnut Street
Pittsburgh, PA 15232
ph: (412) 682-3737

The Clay Studio
139 North Second Street
Philadelphia, PA 19106
ph: (215) 925-3453

Country Classics
36 East Germantown Pike
Norristown, PA 19401
ph: (215) 275-3666

The Country Studio
590 Georgetown Road
Hadley, PA 16130
ph: (412) 253-2493

Creative Hands
Peddlers Village
Lahaska, PA 18931
ph: (215) 794-7012

Discoveries
P. O. Box 1552
Reading, PA 19603
ph: (610) 372-2595

Dotty's Things
24 Merion Lane
Hummelstown, PA 17036
ph: (717) 566-6047

Earthworks
227 Haverford Avenue
Narbeth, PA 19072
ph: (215) 667-1143

End Result
109 South Allen
State College, PA 16801
ph: (814) 237-9657

The Fabric Workshop
1100 Vine Street, 13th floor
Philadelphia, PA 19107
ph: (215) 922-7303

Garland of Letters
527 South Street
Philadelphia, PA 19147
ph: (215) 923-5946

Gunlefingers
303 West State Street
Media, PA 19063

Handwoven on Carson
2013 East Carson Street
Pittsburgh, PA 15203
ph: (412) 488-0112

Inklinations
1947 West Strasburg Road
Coatesville, PA 19320
ph: (610) 486-6311

John Vahanian Studios
1501 State Street
Erie, PA 16501
ph: (814) 453-7947

Kangagura
339 South Street
Philadelphia, PA 19147
ph: (215) 440-9106

Lannon's
1007 Lancaster Avenue
Bryn Mawr, PA 19010
ph: (215) 440-7136

Larimore Furniture
160 North Third Street
Philadelphia, PA 19010
ph: (215) 440-7136

Lipman Designer Productions
437 North Lombard Street
Dallastown, PA 17313
ph: (717) 244-8438

Marsha Child Contemporary
P. O. Box 0364
Solebury, PA 18963
ph: (215) 297-0414

Media Pottery
303 West State Street
Media, PA 19063
ph: (610) 891-1899

Metalworks Contemporary
532 South Fourth Street
Philadelphia, PA 19147
ph: (215) 625-2640

The Otter Creek Store
106 South Diamond Street
Mercer, PA 16137
ph: (412) 662-2830

Pine Haven Village
Rural Delivery 2
P. O. Box 63
Somerset, PA 15501
ph: (814) 445-3457

Savoir Faire
837 West Rolling Road
Springfield, PA 19064
ph: (215) 544-8998

Shakti
311 Market Street
Kingston, PA 18704
ph: (717) 283-4247

Show Of Hands
1006 Pine Street
Philadelphia, PA 19107
ph: (215) 592-4010

Something Special
153 Main Street
Bradford, PA 16701
ph: (814) 368-6011

Starr Pottery
754 Abbottstown Pike
Hanover, PA 17331
ph: (717) 632-0027

Strawberry & Company
79 West King Street
Lancaster, PA 17603
ph: (717) 392-5345

Studio in Swarthmore
14 Park Avenue
Swarthmore, PA 19081
ph: (610) 543-5779

Sundance
P. O. Box 311
Lahaska, PA 18931
ph: (215) 794-8871

Topeo
35 North Main Street
New Hope, PA 18938
ph: (610) 862-2750

Touches
225 South 15th Street
Philadelphia, PA 19102
ph: (215) 546-1221

Turtledove
4373 Main Street
Philadelphia, PA 19127
ph: (215) 487-7350

Waterlou Gardens
136 Lancaster Avenue
Devon, PA 19333
ph: (610) 293-0800

The Weaver
P. O. Box 80
Smicksburg, PA 16256
ph: (814) 257-8891

Woodburners
Market and Broad Streets
Hatfield, PA 19440
ph: (215) 362-2443
fax: (215) 362-3732

Puerto Rico
Maryanne's Caribbean Gift Shop
136 Northeast Road
Ramey, PR 00604
ph: (809) 890-3801

Rhode Island
Comina
245 South Main Street
Providence, RI 02903
ph: (401) 273-4522

Copacetic Rudely Elegant Jewelry
65 Weybosset Street
Providence, RI 02903
ph: (401) 273-0470

Green Ink
17 Brown Street
Wickford, RI 02852
ph: (401) 294-6266

Mackenzie – Dove Dawn Kitompani
P. O. Box 741
Hope Valley, RI 02832

The Opulent Owl
295 South Main Street
Providence, RI 02903
ph: (401) 521-6698

Ramson House Antiques
86 Franklin Street
Newport, RI 02840
ph: (401) 847-0555

Spectrum of American Artists
306 Thames Street
Newport, RI 02840
ph: (401) 847-4477

Thames Glass
688 Thames Street
Newport, RI 02840
ph: (401) 846-0576

South Carolina

Artists Parlor
126 Laurens Street Northwest
Aiken, SC 29801
ph: (803) 648-4639

Bohemian
2112 Devine Street
Columbia, SC 29205
ph: (803) 256-0629

East of Eden
218 King Street
Charleston, SC 29401
ph: (803) 237-4888

Nina Liu & Friends
24 State Street
Charleston, SC 29401
ph: (803) 722-2724

Whimsical Woman
1836 Ashley River Road, Suite 109
Charleston, SC 29407

South Dakota

Prairie People Handicraft Market
Route 1
P. O. Box 33
Armour, SD 57313
ph: (605) 724-2404

Tipi Shop
P. O. Box 1542
Rapid City, SD 57709
ph: (605) 343-8128

Tennessee

American Artisan
4231 Harding Road
Nashville, TN 37205
ph: (615) 298-4691
fax: (615) 298-4604

Americana Sampler
P. O. Box 160020
Nashville, TN 37216
ph: (615) 227-2080

The Browsery
424 Rivermont Drive
Clarksville, TN 37043
ph: (615) 552-2733

Crescent Moon
The Peabody Hotel
149 Union Avenue
Memphis, TN 38103
ph: (901) 526-9110
fax: (901) 757-5310

Hanson Artsource
5607 Kingston Pike
Knoxville, TN 37919
ph: (615) 584-6097

Jonesborough Art Glass
101 East Main Street
Jonesborough, TN 37659
ph: (615) 753-5401

Scarlett Begonia
2805 West End Avenue
Nashville, TN 37203
ph: (615) 329-1272

Window on Main Street
1845 Laurel Ridge Drive
Nashville, TN 37215
ph: (615) 251-0097

Texas

Acquisatory
3016 Greenville Avenue
Dallas, TX 75206

Alabama-Choushatta
Tribal Enterprise
Route 3
P. O. Box 640
Livingston, TX 77351
ph: (409) 563-4391
fax: (409) 563-2186

Apple Corps
2324 University Boulevard
Houston, TX 77005
ph: (713) 524-2221

Art Group
1119 North Windomere Avenue
Dallas, TX 75208
ph: (214) 942-0258

Artsource
3800 North Mesa, Suite 6-B
El Paso, TX 79902
ph: (915) 532-0887

Avanti
2716 Greenville Avenue
Dallas, TX 75206
ph: (214) 824-0260

Blue Hand
2323 University Boulevard
Houston, TX 77005
ph: (713) 666-2583

Clarksville Pottery
4001 North Lamar Boulevard, Suite 200
Austin, TX 78756
ph: (512) 478-9079
fax: (512) 454-8991

Clarksville Pottery 2
Arboretum Market
9722 Great Hills
Austin, TX 78759
ph: (512) 794-8580

Cowgirls and Flowers
508 Walsh
Austin, TX 78703
ph: (512) 478-4626

Culler Concepts
1347 Cedar Hill Avenue
Dallas, TX 75208
ph: (214) 942-1646

Gardens
1818 West 35th Street
Austin, TX 78703
ph: (512) 451-5490

High Gloss
515 Hedwig Street
Houston, TX 77024
ph: (713) 961-7868

Hummingbird Originals
4319 Camp Bowie Boulevard
Fort Worth, TX 76107
ph: (817) 732-1549

La Dean
5308 Birchman
Fort Worth, TX 76107
ph: (817) 731-3595

Legacy's
1846 Rose Mead Parkway,
Suite 148
Carrollton, TX 75007

The Ole Moon
3016 Greenville Avenue
Dallas, TX 75206
ph: (214) 827-9921

Positive Images
1118 West Sixth Street
Austin, TX 78703
ph: (512) 472-1831

The Preston Collection
305 Preston Royal
Dallas, TX 75230
ph: (214) 373-6065

Quaint Corner
4026 Westheimer
Houston, TX 77027
ph: (713) 961-4898
fax: (713) 961-5668

Shades of Old
P. O. Box 630
Grapeland, TX 75844
ph: (512) 858-1629

Southwest Crafts Center
300 Augusta Avenue
San Antonio, TX 78205
ph: (512) 224-1848

The Village Weavers
418 La Villita Street
San Antonio, TX 78205
ph: (210) 222-0776

Visions
2019 Montana Avenue
El Paso, TX 79903
ph: (915) 532-4148
fax: same

Vermont
Cornwall Crafts
Road 4
P. O. Box 450
Middlebury, VT 05753
ph: (802) 462-2438

Frog Hollow Craft Center
1 Mill Street
Middlebury, VT 05753
ph: (802) 388-3177

Golden Rings and Silver Things
33 Airport Parkway
South Burlington, VT 05403

Hawkins House
262 North Street
Bennington, VT 05201
ph: (802) 447-1171

Illuminee du Monde
P. O. Box 304
28 Rockydale Road
Bristol, VT 05443
ph: (802) 453-3952

Motley and Friends
67 Central Street
Woodstock, VT 05091
ph: (802) 457-5151

Mountain High American Craft
The Market Place
Ludlow, VT 05149
ph: (802) 228-5216

Natural Provisions
93 Portland Street
St. Johnsbury, VT 05819
ph: (802) 748-3587

Silver Forest of Vermont
P. O. Box 515
Bellows Falls, VT 05101
ph: (802) 463-2144
fax: (802) 463-3996

Simon Pearce Glass
General Delivery
Quechee, VT 05059
ph: (802) 295-2711

Stone Soldier Pottery
P. O. Box 286
Jacksonville, VT 05342
ph: (802) 368-7077
fax: (802) 368-2634

Unicorn
15 Central Street
Woodstock, VT 05091
ph: (802) 457-2480
fax: (802) 457-3133

Vermont Artisan Designs
115 Main Street
Brattleboro, VT 05301
ph: (802) 257-7044

Virginia
Akkarai
4703 Tara Drive
Fairfax, VA 22032
ph: (703) 764-2042

American Artisan
201 King Street
Alexandria, VA 22314
ph: (703) 548-3431

Art and Soul
1127 King Street
Alexandria, VA 22314
ph: (703) 549-4881

Artisan's Studio
105 Hanover Avenue
Ashland, VA 23005
ph: (804) 798-3321

Artisans United Craft Gallery
4022 Hummer Road
Annandale, VA 22003
ph: (703) 941-0202

Banana Tree
1223 King Street
Alexandria, VA 22314
ph: (703) 836-4317

Breit Functional Crafts
1701 Colley Avenue
Norfolk, VA 23517
ph: (804) 640-1012

Cave House Craft Shop
279 East Main Street
Abingdon, VA 24210
ph: (540) 628-7721

d'Art Center
125 College Place
Norfolk, VA 23510
ph: (804) 625-4211
fax: (804) 625-0670

Ebashae
309 Mill Street
Occaquan, VA 22125
ph: (703) 491-5984

Elder Crafters of Alexandria
405 Cameron Street
Alexandria, VA 22314
ph: (703) 683-4338

Fantasies
21 Nelson Street West
Lexington, VA 24450

Fiber Designs
1509 South Randolph Street
Arlington, VA 22204
ph: (703) 548-1461

Galaxy Trading Company
P. O. Box 1099
Galax, VA 24333
ph: (540) 236-8287

High Cotton
4028 H Cox Road
Glen Allen, VA 23060
ph: (804) 747-9996

Limeton Pottery
10 Buck Mountain Road
Bentonville, VA 22610
ph: (540) 636-8666

McGregor's Garden Shop
Arlington Forest Shopping Center
Route 50 and Park Drive
Arlington, VA 22203
ph: (703) 528-8773

On the Hill Cultural Art Center
Yorktown Arts Foundation
121 Alexander Hamilton Boulevard
Yorktown, VA 23690
ph: (804) 898-3076

River of High Banks Craft Shop
Rural Route 2
P. O. Box 270
West Point, VA 23181
ph: (804) 769-4711

Silver Phoenix
2946-D Chain Bridge Road
Oakton, VA 22124
ph: (703) 385-8839

Simply Country
733 Eldern Street
Herndon, VA 22070
ph: (703) 435-9500

Strawberry
217 East Main Street
Charlottesville, VA 22901
ph: (804) 979-0179

Toano Toy Works
P. O. Box 193
Toano, VA 23168
ph: (804) 566-0171

Unique Handcrafts and Gifts
213 King Street
Alexandria, VA 22314
ph: (703) 836-6686

Vista Fine Crafts
P. O. Box 2034
5 West Washington Street
Middleburg, VA 22117
ph: (540) 687-3317

Woodmont Weavers
2422 North Fillmore Street
Arlington, VA 22207
ph: (703) 358-6343
fax: (703) 524-1393

Washington
The Collection
118 South Washington Street
Pioneer Square
Seattle, WA 98104
ph: (206) 682-6181

Earthenworks
P. O. Box 702
La Conner, WA 98257
ph: (206) 466-4422

Facere Jewelry Art
1420 Fifth Avenue, Suite 108
Seattle, WA 98101
ph: (206) 624-6768

Flying Shuttle
607 First Street
Seattle, WA 98104
ph: (206) 343-9762

Gardens Of Art
2900 Sylvan Street
Bellingham, WA 98226
ph: (206) 671-1069

Glasshouse Art Glass
Pioneer Square
311 Occidental Avenue
Seattle, WA 98104
ph: (206) 682-9939

Highly Strung
4222 East Madison Street
Seattle, WA 98112
ph: (206) 328-1045

Jasminka
3820 North 26
Tacoma, WA 98407
ph: (206) 752-8700

Martha E. Harris Flowers
4733 University Village Place N.E.
Seattle, WA 98105
ph: (206) 527-1820

Marvel on Madison
69 Madison Avenue
Seattle, WA
ph: (206) 282-8282

Melange
120 Lakeside Avenue
Seattle, WA 98122
ph: (206) 322-1341

Mesolini & Amici
77 1/2 South Main Street
Seattle, WA 98104
ph: (206) 587-0275

Northwest Craft Center and Gallery
Seattle Center
Seattle, WA 98109
ph: (206) 728-1555

Northwest Discovery
142 Bellevue Square
Bellevue, WA 98004
ph: (206) 454-1676

Northwind Trading Company
P. O. Box 217
Anacortes, WA 98221
ph: (206) 293-6404

Page and Thorbeck Studio
604 North 34th Street
Seattle, WA 98103
ph: (206) 632-6178

Serendipity
909 Commercial Avenue
Anacortes, WA 98221

Shaiman Studio
1415 Second Avenue , Suite 1405
Seattle, WA 98101
ph: (206) 624-1986

Spokane Pottery
2906 South Lamonte Street
Spokane, WA 99203

Tin-Na-Tit Kin-Ne-Ki Indian
Arts and Crafts
P. O. Box 1057
Republic, WA 99166
ph: (509) 775-3077

Toppers
1260 Carillon PT
Kirkland, WA 98033
ph: (206) 889-9311

Turnipseed Brothers
33400 Eighth Avenue, Suite 117
Federal Way, WA 98003
ph: (206) 952-9300

West Virginia
The Art Store
1013 Bridge Road
Charleston, WV 25314
ph: (304) 345-1038

Cornucopia
912 Bridge Road
Charleston, WV 25314
ph: (304) 342-7148
fax: (304) 342-7133

Kris Kringle's
526 Brookdale Avenue
Martinsburg, WV 25401
ph: (304) 274-1228

Little Kanawha Crafts House
113 Ann Street
Parkersburg, WV 26101
ph: (304) 485-3149
fax: (304) 485-5526

Mountain Trading Company
1526 Autumn Road
Charleston, WV 25314

Quilts Unlimited
203 East Washington Street
Lewisburg, WV 24901
ph: (304) 647-4208

Wisconsin
Ironwood
3435 Junction Road
Egg Harbor, WI 54209
ph: (414) 823-2418

Lil General
233 West Center Street
Milwaukee, WI 53212
ph: (414) 374-3473

North West Discovery
142 Bellevue Mall
Bellevue, WI 98004
ph: (414) 454-1676

Rhapsody
2844 University Avenue
Madison, WI 53705
ph: (608) 231-3556

Rockdale Union Stoneware
1858 Artisan Road
P. O. Box 231
Edgerton, WI 53534
ph: (608) 884-9483
fax: (608) 884-7800

Small Potatoes
1151 East Johnson Street
Madison, WI 53703
ph: (608) 256-6646

Umbrella Group
403 Farwell Drive
Madison, WI 53704
ph: (608) 244-7120

Wa-Swa-Gon Arts and Crafts
P. O. Box 477
Lac du Flambeau, WI 54538
ph: (715) 588-9030

BUYING OFFICES, DEPARTMENT STORES, CHAINS, AND SPECIALTY RETAILERS

Linked by a parent organization, such as Associated Merchandising Corporation (AMC), major department stores establish buying offices domestically and overseas to consolidate buying opportunities. For example, AMC is an association of over 700 stores; buyer representatives alert the member stores when they discover craft producers who can supply quantity. The buyers then make a conglomerate purchase and provide the merchandise to member stores. This often involves bulk orders, on which price breaks are expected. This is also a convenience for department-store promotions. As the supplier, your ability to handle production of large quantities is critical here.

Department stores offer broad selections of retail goods. Typically, companies have many branch stores, often clustered in a specific region in the United States. Usually, one buyer has purchasing responsibility for a department or department grouping (such as Children's or Housewares) within the store. Buyers tend to follow seasonal and market trends, and they can usually be very demanding. They have a rigid budget and buying schedule; and, they can issue purchase orders with long lead times, yet still adhere to a strict cancellation policy. Buying for special storewide promotions, they sometimes focus on sales presentations that feature a specific country or region. For example, they might highlight crafts by theme or geographic area and buy both large quantities of duplicate items and one-of-a-kind pieces. The exposure is prestigious, but the danger is that these may be one-time buys with no reorder the following year. Department stores are also notoriously slow payers.

Chains are department stores, such as J. C. Penney, Sears, and Montgomery Ward, that usually have 1,000 or more locations all around the country. They have central buying offices that make high-volume purchases at the most economical prices. Their image is less exclusive and less expensive than one-location department stores. Chains occasionally buy crafts for in-store promotions, but craftspeople must be able to supply quantity.

Specialty retailers are stores that cater to special interest markets, such as gardening, food, kitchen accessories, clothes for certain age groups, ethnic accessories, and so on. This is often referred to as *niche marketing*. Specialty stores carry a narrower selection of merchandise than traditional department stores, and they can be single-location shops or numerous branch locations in major cities. They may even send out seasonal catalogs to their own customer mailing list.

Specialty stores such as Pier 1 Imports, Crate and Barrel, and Williams-Sonoma often use crafts to complement their offering of mass-produced merchandise. They will stock items geared to the special interests of their customers, and then look for craft suppliers or artisans to add accent pieces or other custom work. An example of one such store is Felissimo in New York City. "We create a unique shopping environment that is very artful in design," says Rona Tison, Felissimo's executive vice president. "We want to inspire a lifestyle with an eclectic mix of merchandise, incorporating old and new, in an environment that stimulates the senses. At Felissimo, we want to give the customers a sense of tranquillity so they can disassociate themselves from the chaotic city."

Felissimo inhabits a neoclassical, turn-of-the-century townhouse. With hospitality as a goal, Felissimo commissioned Clodagh, a minimalist designer, to refurbish the building. Clodagh blended the historic architecture into his design, which reflects the feeling of home, warmth, and serenity. A retreat from city stress, the Felissimo "home" incorporates a living room, dining room, bedroom, dressing room, garden area with fountains, tea salon, library, and art space. For the interior, the decorator employed various artists to create a soothing atmosphere to enhance the products and the shopping experience.

In keeping with its dedication to the arts, Felissimo has an open-vendor day once a month. By word-of-mouth, this popular day draws numerous craft designers, who wander in and present their products to be evaluated on a first-come, first-serve basis. Buyers work with craftspeople and suggest ideas; they cultivate relationships with the artists they commission, and inspire the artists to create special pieces that fit the space in the store. Felissimo also has in-house promotions and meet-the-artist events, and in conjunction with the New York Foundation of the Arts, the store holds a competition, gives awards, and sells many of its artists' work. Often, the buyers continue successful relationships with these craftspeople on new projects.

Like Felissimo, most specialty retailers create a unique environment based on the store owner's vision. Each store is highly personalized, and craft purchases reflect the owner's tastes and aesthetics. Buyers look for merchandise that reflects the overall store atmosphere. They make many of their purchases at wholesale trade shows, but they are always searching for that next new item. To attract their attention, you need to have a feeling for the store and its customers. What is appropriate for one store may not feel right to another, even if you think your work belongs in both.

The best way to gain a sense of the store environment is simply to visit different shops. On your visits, stand back and just observe. Get a feeling for the place. Look at the lighting, fixtures, signage, and visual props. Notice how things are displayed. Wander around and look at the actual products. What crafts are featured? What are the price ranges? How much floor space is devoted to textiles, ceramics, jewelry, wood, glass, and so on? Is this the ambiance in which you would like to see your work? How closely do the crafts in stock resemble yours? Would yours fit in yet be different? You should also observe the customers. What attracts them? What do they merely glance at, and what do they actually buy?

If this is a store that interests you, the next step is to understand its buying policy. First, you need to get the buyer's name; often, just greeting a sales person and asking, "Who does the buying?" will get you this and perhaps other useful information. If they don't know who is responsible for buying, they can give you a corporate telephone number (or you can get it from directory assistance). Just ask for the buying office when you call.

Find out if the buyer makes appointments and prefers to see photographs, slides, or actual work. Don't send unsolicited samples; buyers everywhere are overwhelmed with them. If a sample wasn't requested, it is likely to remain unopened for a long time. If you make an appointment, bring work that reflects the store's mission as you understand it. Don't try to show everything you make, but bring a portfolio in case the buyer wants to view your complete line.

Don't be discouraged if buyers say your work is not right for their store; they usually know at a glance what is appropriate for their look and price range. Just try a different shop. This department-store listing was culled from The Crafts Center's database, but you may know of other stores to contact.

DEPARTMENT STORES
AND CHAINS

Associated Merchandising
Corporation
1440 Broadway
New York, NY 10018
ph: (212) 596-4000

Bloomingdale's
1000 Third Avenue
New York, NY 10022
ph: (212) 705-2000

The Body Shop
3207 M Street N.W.
Washington, DC 20007
ph: (202) 298-7353

The Bon
Pine and Third Avenue
Seattle, WA 98181
ph: (206) 344-3121

Buffum's
P. O. Box 967
Montebello, CA 90640
ph: (310) 432-7000

Crate and Barrel
646 North Michigan Avenue
Chicago, IL 60611
ph: (312) 787-5900

Davidson's
3700 Atlanta Highway
Athens, GA 30610
ph: (404) 353-4985

Hecht's
Ballston Shopping Center
Arlington, VA 22203
ph: (703) 628-6661

John Wanamaker's
1300 Market Streets
Philadelphia, PA 19107
ph: (215) 422-2000

Macy's
Herald Square
151 West 34th Street
New York, NY 10001
ph: (212) 695-4400

Marshall Field and Company
111 North State Street
Chicago, IL 60690
ph: (312) 781-1000

Neiman Marcus
1618 Main Street
Dallas, TX 75201
ph: (214) 573-5994
fax: (214) 573-6142

Nordstrom's
1501 Fifth Avenue
Seattle, WA 98101
ph: (206) 628-2111

Pier 1 Imports
4477 Connecticut Avenue N.W.
Washington, DC 20008
ph: (202) 362-4080

Saks Fifth Avenue
611 Fifth Avenue
New York, NY 10022
ph: (212) 753-4000

Sylvester Company
Main Street
P. O. Box 2069
Sag Harbor, NY 11963
ph: (516) 725-5012
fax: (516) 425-5020

Williams-Sonoma
100 North Point
San Francisco, CA 94133
ph: (415) 421-7900

CATALOGS AND SPECIAL MAGAZINES

Mail-order in the United States is a $60-billion-a-year business. Many department stores, specialty shops, and museum stores send out mail-order catalogs as a separate, additional business, or as an advertisement to enhance their product offering and bring customers into their stores. Other catalogs are retail mail-order businesses only with no store outlets. Catalogs often target a special market segment, such as gardening, home furnishings, ready-to-wear, and kitchen accessories. And, in this vein, many magazines also put out special issues devoted primarily to crafts.

When selecting crafts for inclusion in their catalogs, the catalog buyers' primary concerns are the ability of craftspeople to supply consistent quality and sufficient quantity. The appeal of having unique, exclusive items not found in other mail-order catalogs also motivates buyers in their craft selections. Your ability to customize your crafts (in color or design) for, or to provide them exclusively to, a particular catalog will make your product line more attractive to catalog buyers. Catalog houses merchandise their mailings by item, page, theme, or color, and every product must carry its weight. Buyers are always interested in depth of production (ability to supply large quantities of a single item) and narrow selection, in contrast to store buyers who merchandise according to shop themes and want less quantity but broad choices.

"Customers vote with their purchases," says John Giesecke, vice president and chief operating officer of *Art and Artifact* and *What on Earth* catalogs (see following listings for addresses). The perennial question in the retail mail-order business is, Which comes first—the mailing list or the product? Two schools of thought reflect slightly different approaches to merchandising a retail trade catalog. On the one hand, some catalog merchants make a supreme effort to know their customers, doing extensive surveys and learning everything about their audience. The other type of merchant cares more about the item experience—i.e., what sells.

Giesecke subscribes to the latter theory: "This is an item business driven by previous successes, market trends, and consumer demand. The item has to stand on its own." *Art and Artifact* is a culturally based catalog that features different ethnic merchandise from around the world. Its buyers are always looking to discover the next hot craft product. Although they have tried marketing Native American crafts, their catalog successes have come largely with items from countries other than the United States. Still, if their buyers found the right fit they would test other crafts.

Other catalogs such as *Sundance* have great successes with indigenous American crafts. Mary Whitesides, merchandise and design consultant for *Sundance,* works with many American craft artists to promote their products. She chooses crafts that complement the "lifestyle feel" that her catalog offers. Founded by actor Robert Redford, the *Sundance* catalog conveys the overall philosophy of the Sundance arts community. A natural part of its mission is to help people who make things by hand. Although it isn't possible to carry a completely handmade selection, the catalog does attempt to show as many crafts as is economically feasible. About 40 percent of the catalog is craft related, offering home furnishings and personal fashion items.

"Products that have a hands-on approach have a different feeling," says Whitesides. "Craftspeople always want to change something. While variations can be explained in copy and won't disappoint people, artisans have to produce the same product over and over. They have to want to work this way. For example, one craftsperson was making handmade pottery mugs with petroglyph designs for us. He agreed to make them, but they began to take up all of his time." This experience can be frustrating to an artist who wants to be creative. She also adds that this business is "fast-turnover, high-quantity oriented and is diametrically opposed to carrying crafts."

Catalog companies look at the income-per-square-inch and the dollar amount that a product brings in. If an item sells well, it will be included in future catalogs, so the opportunity for repeat business exists. However, if a product doesn't bring in enough volume, it won't get a second chance. Whitesides suggests thinking about this business by putting it into two categories: easy-to-produce items that the catalog can use as a base for income and wants to repeat; and separate, one-of-a-kind items that the catalog can use creatively to enhance the look of a catalog page.

Whitesides develops strong artist relationships and works closely on each craft project, often designing something together with the artisan. The artist has to understand her vision and interpret it for the catalog. For example, she worked with one craftsperson (who made wall sculptures and angels out of old car parts) to develop a unique catalog product. The creative aspect for the artist is the initial interpretation of the catalog vision, even though the final piece of art will be duplicated to accommodate quantity requirements.

Like Giesecke, Whitesides also believes that the business is item driven, and she fits her selections onto themed catalog pages. Therefore, when she promotes a craft in the catalog, she emphasizes the need for a story. She wants to know, for example, how the artist was inspired, whether there is a family meaning, and if the item was made from recycled material.

The catalog industry does a lot of testing, and its buyers find product at all the major trade shows, including craft fairs. (Buyers for *Art and Artifact,* for example, find 98 percent of their product at trade shows and prefer not to have office appointments.) If you don't show at the fairs, catalog buyers generally prefer photographs, but all catalog houses have different needs and requirements. It is best to first request a catalog to see if your work would complement the current merchandise in both price and quality, and then inquire by telephone about the buying procedures and whom to contact. Learn as much as you can about the catalog before approaching the buyers. They're busy, and it is difficult for them to assess your product's viability in their catalog over the phone without seeing a picture. Note that these buyers select products primarily on visual criteria.

A major consideration for any catalog buyer is your ability to supply quantity. And because customers want exactly what they see on the page, consistent quality and looks are also important buying factors. Of course, slight variations in handmade objects are acceptable and can be explained in descriptive catalog copy.

Generally, buyers look for products that fit their catalog image and price range, but each catalog is different and caters to different audiences. Make sure you understand the market before you try to sell to it.

Another similar craft venue is the special magazine. Occasionally, magazines will produce special issues devoted to crafts. For instance, *Better Homes and Gardens* produces *Crafts Showcase,* which has the format of a magazine, with informative articles, but offers pictures, prices, and descriptions of items throughout like a catalog.

"We call it a 'magalog,'" says *Crafts Showcase* editor Matthew Jones. "It brings people to additional markets, reaching a wide audiences of craft shoppers and home decorators." Published quarterly, each issue offers crafts from domestic artisans. Included are wearable art, home and fashion accessories, jewelry, and various one-of-a-kind items, along with artist names and addresses for direct retail orders or wholesale inquiries. *Better Homes and Gardens* sends information to each craftsperson regarding upcoming themes for each issue, and craftspeople are free to change their products to match the next issue. Their holiday "magalog" is their most popular one.

Look for these and other journals on the newsstands, especially around holiday time. Invest in a few copies or try to find them at the library. Check the editorial masthead page for telephone numbers and statement of policy, or phone the editorial offices to inquire about the procedures for inclusion in their magazine. *Crafts Showcase,* for example, requests samples and then does all its own photography of accepted crafts.

CATALOGS

Americraft
P. O. Box 814
Wendell, MA 01379
ph: (800) 866-2723

Anyone Can Whistle
323 Wall Street
Kingston, NY 12401
ph: (914) 331-7728
fax: (914) 339-3301

Appalachian Crafts
P. O. Box 104
Irvine, KY 40336
ph: (606) 723-4678

Arawjo Baskets
P. O. Box 477
Bushkill, PA 18324
ph: (717) 588-6957

Art and Artifact
2451 East Enterprise Parkway
Twinsburg, OH 44087
ph: (216) 963-6554
fax: (216) 963-5987

Art Expressions
5904 North College Avenue
Indianapolis, IN 46220
ph: (317) 257-5448

Art in the Dark
Galerie 500 Collection
500 Ninth Street S.E.
Washington, DC 20003
ph: (202) 543-9200

Artisans
9337-B Katy Freeway, Suite 333
Houston, TX 77024
ph: (800) 566-2787

The Bead Museum
140 South Montezuma Street
Prescott, AZ 86303
ph: (520) 445-2431
fax: same

The Clay Pot
162 Seventh Avenue
Brooklyn, NY 11215
ph: (718) 788-6564
fax: (718) 965-1138

Coldwater Creek
1123 Lake Street
Sandpoint, ID 83864
ph: (208) 263-2266

Cottage Country Baskets
64346 Arrowhead Road
Cambridge, OH 43725
ph: (614) 439-4610
fax: same

Curiosity Kits
P. O. Box 811
Cockeysville, MD 21030
ph: (800) 584-5487
fax: (410) 584-1247

Deva Lifewear
P. O. Box 668
Ranson, WV 25438-0668
ph: (304) 728-6790
fax: (304) 725-9429

Earth Care
555 Leslie Street
Ukiah, CA 95482
ph: (800) 347-0070
fax: (707) 468-9486

Good Green Fun
P. O. Box 27
Miami, FL 33257
ph: (800) 684-8882
fax: (305) 663-0605
http://www.gate.net/good-green-fun/

Grand Teton Natural History
Association
P. O. Box 170
Moose, WY 83012
ph: (307) 739-3404
fax: (307) 739-3438

Hanna Andersson
1010 Northwest Flanders
Portland, OR 97209

The J. Peterman Company
1318 Russell Cave Road
Lexington, KY 40505
ph: (800) 231-7341
fax: (800) 346-3081

Kentucky Hills Industries
P. O. Box 186
Pine Knot, KY 42635
ph: (606) 354-2813

Lark Books
50 College Street
Asheville, NC 28801
ph: (800) 284-3388
fax: (704) 253-7952

Lincoln County Heritage Trust
P. O. Box 98
Lincoln, NM 88338
ph: (505) 653-4445

Meadow Mountain Designs
380 Tolman Road
Warren, ME 04864
ph: (207) 594-9231
fax: (207) 596-7371

Mister Indians
1000 South Main
Sapulpa, OK 74066
ph: (918) 224-6511

Red Rose Collection
P. O. Box 280140
San Francisco, CA 94128
ph: (800) 451-5683

The River Farm
Route 1
P. O. Box 401
Timberville, VA 22853
ph: (540) 740-3314

River Oaks Leather
P. O. Box 767
Capitan, NM 88316
ph: (505) 354-2676

Save the Children
54 Wilton Road
Westport, CT 06880
ph: (800) 243-5075
fax: (203) 221-4205

Smith & Hawken
25 Corte Madera
Mill Valley, CA 94941
ph: (415) 383-4415

Smithsonian Retail Division
600 Maryland Avenue S.W.,
Suite 295-B
Washington, DC 20024
ph: (202) 287-3563
fax: (202) 287-3080

The Southwest Indian Foundation
P. O. Box 86
Gallup, NM 87302
ph: (505) 863-4037
fax: (505) 863-2760

Spiegel
3500 Lacey Road
Downer Grove, IL 60515
ph: (708) 769-2591

Stone Soldier Pottery
P. O. Box 286
Jacksonville, VT 05342
ph: (802) 368-7077
fax: (802) 368-2634

Sundance Catalog
1909 South, Suite 4250
Salt Lake City, UT 84104
ph: (801) 973-2711
fax: (801) 973-4949

SunFeather Herbal Soap Company
1551 State Highway 72
Potsdam, NY 13676
ph: (315) 265-3648
fax: (315) 265-2902

Textile Museum Catalog
2320 S Street N.W.
Washington, DC 20008
ph: (202) 667-0441
fax: (202) 483-0994

Times Circle East
30 East 65th Street, #13A
New York, NY 10021

Vaillancourt Folk Art
145 Armsby Road
Sutton, MA 01590
ph: (508) 865-9183
fax: (508) 865-4140

Village Spinning and
Weaving Shop
425-B Alisal Road
Solvang, CA 93463
ph: (805) 686-1192

Walker Metalsmiths
1 Main Street
P. O. Box 706
Andover, NY 14806
ph: (607) 478-8868

What on Earth
2451 East Enterprise Parkway
Twinsburg, OH 44087
ph: (216) 963-6554

Wireless
1000 West Gate Drive
St. Paul, MN 55114
ph: (612) 659-3600

SPECIAL MAGAZINES

Americana
29 West 38th Street
New York, NY 10022
ph: (212) 398-1550
fax: (212) 840-6790

American Ceramics
9 East 45th Street
New York, NY 10017
ph: (212) 661-4397

American Craft
72 Spring Street
New York, NY 10012
ph: (212) 274-0630
fax: (212) 274-0650

American Indian Art Magazine
7314 East Osborne Drive
Scottsdale, AZ 85251
ph: (602) 994-5445

Americanstyle
3000 Chestnut Avenue,
Suite 304
Baltimore, MD 21211

Arts and Crafts Catalyst
1101 Marshall Richardson Road
P. O. Box 159
Bogalusa, LA 70429

Arts Indiana
47 South Pennsylvania Avenue,
Suite 701
Indianapolis, IN 46204
ph: (317) 632-7894

The Bead Directory
P. O. Box 10103
Oakland, CA 94610
ph: (510) 452-0836

*Better Homes and Gardens Craft
Showcase*
P. O. Box 400422
Des Moines, IA 50340
ph: (800) 846-4004

Buckeye Artisan
P. O. Box 954
Westerville, OH 43081

The California Craft Connection
DeMortmain Publishing
P. O. Box 280
Pine Grove, CA 95665

Catalog Age
6 River Bend
911 Hope Street, Building Six
Stamford, CT 06907
ph: (203) 358-9900

Ceramic Scope Buyers' Guide
P. O. Box 1992
Wilmington, DE 19899
ph: (800) 777-7098

Ceramics Monthly
1609 Northwest Boulevard
P. O. Box 12788
Columbus, OH 43212
ph: (614) 488-8236
fax: (614) 488-4561

Craft and Needlework Age
225 Gordons Corner Plaza
P. O. Box 420
Manalapan, NJ 07726
ph: (908) 536-3758

The Craft Digest
P. O. Box 155
New Britain, CT 06050
ph: (203) 225-8875

Craftmaster Enterprises
P. O. Box 39429
Downey, CA 90241
ph: (310) 869-5882

Craft Show Bulletin
P. O. Box 1914
Westfield, MA 01086

Crochet World
306 East Parr Road
Berne, IN 46711
ph: (219) 589-8874

Designers World Magazine
3255 Wilshire Boulevard
Los Angeles, CA 90010
ph: (213) 657-8231
fax: (213) 657-3673

Doll Reader Magazine
13106 Winchester Road S.W.,
Suite 102
LaVale, MD 21502
ph: (301) 729-6145

Fabric and Fiber Sourcebook
P. O. Box 49770
Austin, TX 78765
ph: (512) 343-6112
fax: same

Fairs and Festivals
Arts Extension Service
Division of Continuing Education
University of Massachusetts
Amherst, MA 01003
ph: (413) 545-2360

Fairs Unlimited
16410 San Carlos Boulevard,
Suite 465
Fort Myers, FL 33908

Fiberarts
50 College Street
Asheville, NC 28801
ph: (704) 253-0467
fax: (704) 253-7952

Fiberworks Publications
P. O. Box 49770
Austin, TX 78765
ph: (512) 343-6112
fax: same

Fine Woodworking
The Taunton Press
P. O. Box 5506
Newtown, CT 06470
ph: (203) 426-8171
fax: (203) 426-3434

Glass Art
P. O. Box 260377
Highlands Ranch, CO 80126
ph: (303) 791-8998
fax: (303) 791-7739

Glass Art Society Journal
20300 North Greenway Street
Southfield, MI 48076
ph: (313) 357-0783

Glass Magazine
647 Fulton Street
Brooklyn, NY 11217
ph: (718) 625-3685

Handmade Accents
P. O. Box 210
Honaker, VA 24260

Hand Papermaking
P. O. Box 77027
Washington, DC 20013
ph: (301) 587-3635

Hands On Guide
255 Cranston Crest, Suite N
Escondido, CA 92025
ph: (619) 747-8206

Hobby House Press
P. O. Box 600
Grantsville, MD 21536
ph: (301) 895-3792

Indian Arts and Crafts
United States Department of the
Interior, Suite 4004
Washington, DC 20240
ph: (202) 208-3773
fax: (202) 208-5196

Island Craft Bulletin
J. E. Tamura and Company
110-D Lellehua Road
Wahlawa, HI 96786

Kaleidoscope
P. O. Box 22642
Kansas City, MO 64113
ph: (800) 888-7422

Lapidary Journal
60 Chestnut Avenue,
Suite 201
Devon, PA 19323
ph: (610) 293-1112
fax: (610) 293-1717

Leather Crafters Journal
331 Annette Court
Rhinelander, WI 54501
ph: (715) 362-5393

Life Style Crafts
1665 West Fifth Avenue
Columbus, OH 43212
ph: (614) 486-7119

Maine Craft Fairs
State House Station 25
55 Capitol Street
Augusta, ME 04333
ph: (207) 289-2724
fax: (207) 289-2861

Manufacturing Jewelers Silversmiths
One State Street, Suite 6
Providence, RI 02908
ph: (401) 274-3840

Metalsmith
5009 Londonderry Drive
Tampa, FL 33647
ph: (813) 977-5326
fax: (813) 977-8462

Michigan Art Fairs
Executive Plaza
1200 Sixth Avenue
Detroit, MI 48226
ph: (313) 256-3735
fax: (313) 256-3781

Minnesota Art Fairs
2400 Third Avenue South
Minneapolis, MN 55404
ph: (612) 870-3200

Missouri Art and Craft Fairs
6640 Delmar Boulevard
St. Louis, MO 63130
ph: (314) 725-1177

Missouri Show News
Crafts Unlimited
P. O. Box 308
Cuba, MO 65453

Museum Store
501 South Cherry Street,
Suite 460
Denver, CO 80222
ph: (303) 329-6968

Native American Directory
P. O. Box 1030
San Carlos, AZ 85550

Needle Arts Magazine
335 West Broadway, Suite 100
Louisville, KY 40202
ph: (502) 589-6956

New Hampshire Craft Fair Directory
Mutton Road
P. O. Box 241-B
Webster, NH 03303

Ohio Festivals and Competitions
727 East Main Street
Columbus, OH 43205
ph: (614) 466-2613
fax: (614) 466-4494

Oklahoma Arts and Crafts Review
601 Lynn Drive
El Reno, OK 73036
ph: (405) 262-8666

Oklahoma Fairs and Festivals
P. O. Box 52001
Oklahoma City, OK 73152
ph: (405) 521-2931
fax: (405) 521-6418

Rocky Mountain Bead Society News
727 10th Street
Boulder, CO 80302

Shopping for Crafts in the USA
21 South Elting Corner Road
Highland, NY 12528
ph: (914) 883-6100
fax: (914) 883-6130

South Dakota Art Fairs and Festivals
230 South Phillips Avenue, Suite 204
Sioux Falls, SD 57102
ph: (605) 399-6646

Southern Living
2100 Lakeshore Drive
Birmingham, AL 35209
ph: (205) 877-6000
fax: (205) 877-6700

Southwest Crafts
707 Kautz Road
St. Charles, IL 60174
ph: (708) 377-8000

Southwest Museum News
234 Museum Drive
Los Angeles, CA 90041
ph: (213) 221-2164
fax: (213) 224-8223

Stain Glass
Frasco Lane
Norwood, NJ 07648

Sunshine Artists
2600 Temple Drive
Winter Park, FL 32789
ph: (407) 539-1399

Tennessee Fairs and Festivals Directory
320 Sixth Avenue North, Suite 100
Nashville, TN 37219
ph: (615) 741-1701

Wasatch Front Craft Guide
P. O. Box 5
Bountiful, UT 84010
ph: (801) 292-4469

Woodworker's Business News
5604 Alameda Place N.E.
Albuquerque, NM 87113

The Woodworkers' Journal
1 News Plaza
Peoria, IL 61643
ph: (309) 682-6626

MUSEUM GIFT SHOPS AND OTHER
CULTURAL AND NONPROFIT STORES

Most American museums and related nonprofit organizations, such as cultural centers, naturalist parks, zoos, gardens, and aquariums, have gift shops. Products sold vary with the museums' collections and exhibitions, and can include gifts, books, toys, jewelry, crafts, stationery products, desk and home accessories, and souvenirs. Many museums want small quantities of handmade crafts for their stores, while a few major museums stock large quantities for their shops and catalogs. It is a prestigious market for your crafts.

To sell to any museum store, your work should relate to a museum's permanent collection or any special traveling exhibits. Shops in natural history and cultural museums are good markets for indigenous crafts. Museums focusing on regional history may be well suited for local handcrafts. But, even an air-and-space museum that focuses primarily on science might indulge and stock creative crafts in its gift shop. This could be just the place for your small, whimsical sculptures depicting imaginative flying machines made from recycled bicycle parts. Knowing that an organization's educational and cultural missions dictate its store merchandise will help you target your sales efforts to the appropriate shop.

Museums often coordinate special or traveling exhibitions that generate interest in crafts from one specific country or about a particular theme. A museum store may even create a special-exhibition shop to sell these craft items. As a result, buyers look for products that come with background information about the crafts, the artisan, or the creative process. They need to be able to tell their customers, either with words or visuals (such as photographs or videos), how something is made. Since consumers love to see the artist at work, you might suggest a "meet-the-artist day" if you sell to a local museum.

"I want to know where the craft came from and who made it," says Elysa Blacker, Senior Buyer for the Smithsonian Institution Museum Shops. "A nice card with each piece makes a difference." She buys crafts, gifts, and jewelry for about 25 shops in 12 Smithsonian museums and for numerous special-exhibition sites. Crafts play an important part of the merchandise mix for these stores. Beyond the basic criteria of education and relatedness to the permanent collection, museum store buyers look for groupings of product lines that tell a story.

Blacker suggests pricing your craft lines to fit the way buyers purchase. "A craftsperson may show two things with a similar look, but for technical reasons [that customers cannot see], the prices are slightly different. It's as if someone taught them how to cost out each item but never stand back and look at things as a group." To remedy this pricing situation, she often asks craftspeople to average their prices, because it is easier to buy and think of an entire group at different price points that will appeal to various customers. "You want to try to have the group make sense. You don't want to have five styles that are 50 cents apart."

Most museum-store buyers make outright purchases. Occasionally they will take products on consignment, which is usually a 60:40 (artist:shop) or 50:50 agreement.

They often use this arrangement for larger or more expensive pieces and may also want to try this when they are unsure about carrying merchandise that is above their normal customer price points.

Contacting buyers in nonprofit organizations is often a complex and confusing process. It is not unusual for the larger organizations to have several buyers, those for different categories of merchandise and also those for their retail stores, catalogs, and wholesale trade market. Typical museum-store buyers handle multiple job functions, and their department is usually understaffed. Additional buyer duties in a small museum can include managing the store, and hiring, among other responsibilities. In the gift shops of larger museums, administrative work and stocking for special exhibits consume more time.

Buyers are difficult to reach and they travel frequently. Anything you can do to save them time is welcome. The best way to start is by sending pictures, information, and wholesale prices, and then calling to schedule an appointment. If you send unsolicited samples, be prepared to wait, possibly several months, for a response. If you want your unsolicited samples or slides back, include return postage and packaging.

Before sending slides or calling a buyer to introduce your product, visit the shop where you think your crafts belong. If distance makes a trip impractical, request a guidebook, shop catalog, or brochure to determine if your work is right for the shop. Often, a call to the receptionist at the buying office can be informative and provide you with enough detail to determine if a return call to the buyer is worthwhile. In a complex organization, this can also enable you to find out which buyer to contact. When you choose a museum or other nonprofit institution to approach, ask yourself these questions:

- Does your work relate to the organization's collection?
- Is your work similar to what the shop currently carries?
- Would your line look different to potential museum shoppers yet be compatible with what the store offers?
- What distinguishes your line from others?
- Who are the customers?
- Are your prices in the appropriate range for the shop?
- Do you have descriptive material about your craft technique that you can provide the shop?
- Do you like the shop displays, and would you like to have your crafts represented there?

Orders from museum stores may be small initially; however, museum-store buyers often reorder over time. They also look for crafts that can enhance a shop's normal merchandise mix for special shows. And, because museums have changing exhibits and bring in traveling shows, there are selling possibilities for additional museum venues beyond the main store.

Whether your regular line is appropriate for a particular museum or not, try building a product-development relationship with the buyers. With so many museum-store clones, actual museum stores have a clear need to recapture their marketing edge. Buyers always search for exclusive products to distinguish their offering. Working with them on product development projects—for example, adaptations of, or works inspired by, pieces in the collections—can help museum stores stay competitive and also open new opportunities for you.

The museums and cultural organizations listed are those in The Crafts Center's database. You could also try approaching buyers from other museums not mentioned here.

**MUSEUMS AND OTHER
CULTURAL ORGANIZATIONS**

Alabama
Kentuck Association
500 McFarland Boulevard
Northport, AL 35476
ph: (205) 758-1257
fax: (205) 758-1258

Arizona
Arizona Historical Society
949 East Second Street
Tucson, AZ 85719
ph: (602) 623-8915

The Bead Museum
140 South Montezuma Street
Prescott, AZ 86303
ph: (520) 445-2431
fax: same

Casa Grande Valley
Historical Society
110 West Florence Boulevard
Casa Grande, AZ 85222
ph: (602) 836-2223

Desert Caballeros
Western Museum
La Senoras de Socorro Shop
P. O. Box 2252
Wickenburg, AZ 85358
ph: (602) 684-7075

Heard Museum Gift Shop
22 East Monte Vista
Phoenix, AZ 85004
ph: (602) 252-8840
fax: (602) 252-9757

Mesa Museum Guild Gift Shop
53 North MacDonald
Mesa, AZ 85201
ph: (602) 644-3283

Old Fort Museum
320 Rogers Avenue
Fort Smith, AZ 72901
ph: (602) 783-7841

Old Pueblo Museum
7401 North La Cholla Boulevard
Tucson, AZ 85741
ph: (602) 742-2355
fax: (602) 797-0936

Phippen Museum of Western Art
4701 Highway 89 North
Prescott, AZ 86301
ph: (602) 778-1385
fax: (602) 778-4524

Phoenix Art Museum
1625 North Central Avenue
Phoenix, AZ 85004
ph: (602) 257-1880
fax: (602) 253-8662

Scottsdale Cultural Society
7383 Scottsdale Mall
Scottsdale, AZ 85251
ph: (602) 994-2316
fax: (602) 994-7728

Sharlot Hall Museum
415 West Gurley Street
Prescott, AZ 86301
ph: (602) 445-3122

Sun Cities Art Museum
17425 North 115th Avenue
Sun City, AZ 85373
ph: (602) 972-0635

Tempe Historical Society
809 East Southern Avenue
Tempe, AZ 85282
ph: (602) 350-5141

Tucson Museum of Art
140 North Main Avenue
Tucson, AZ 85701
ph: (602) 624-2333

Arkansas
Discovery Depot Shop
Mid-America Museum
MacArthur Park
P. O. Box 2137
Little Rock, AR 72203
ph: (501) 372-4000
fax: (501) 375-8053

California
Anaheim Museum
P. O. Box 665
Anaheim, CA 92815
ph: (714) 778-3301

Bakersfield Museum of Art
P. O. Box 1911
Bakersfield, CA 93301
ph: (805) 323-7219
fax: (805) 323-7266

Bowers Museum Shop
2002 North Main Street
Santa Ana, CA 92706
ph: (714) 972-1900
fax: (714) 835-5937

California Craft Museum
Ghiradelli Square
900 North Point Street
San Francisco, CA 94109
ph: (415) 774-1919

Carnegie Art Museum
424 South C Street
Oxnard, CA 93030
ph: (805) 385-8157
fax: (805) 483-3654

Castle Air Museum Foundation
P. O. Box 488
Atwater, CA 95301
ph: (209) 723-2178

Catalina Island Museum
P. O. Box 366
Avalon, CA 90704
ph: (213) 510-2414

The Craft & Folk Art Museum
5800 Wilshire Boulevard
Los Angeles, CA 90036
ph: (213) 937-9099

Crocker Art Museum
216 O Street
Sacramento, CA 95814
ph: (916) 449-8256

De Young Museum
Golden Gate Park
San Francisco, CA 94118
ph: (415) 750-3642
fax: (415) 750-7680

Edward-Dean Museum
9401 Oak Glen Road
Cherry Valley, CA 92223
ph: (714) 845-2626

Fine Art Museum of San Francisco
California Palaces of the Legion
of Honor
Lincoln Park
San Francisco, CA 94121
ph: (415) 750-3600

Fresno Art Museum Shop
2233 North First Street
Fresno, CA 93703
ph: (209) 485-4810

Fullerton Museum Center
301 North Pomona Avenue
Fullerton, CA 92632
ph: (714) 738-6545

Grace Hudson Museum
431 South Main Street
Ukiah, CA 95482
ph: (707) 462-3370

Haggin Museum
1201 North Pershing Avenue
Stockton, CA 95203
ph: (209) 462-0830
fax: (209) 462-1404

The J. Paul Getty Museum
17985 Pacific Coast Highway
Malibu, CA 90265
ph: (310) 458-2003

Laguna Art Museum Store
307 Cliff Drive
Laguna Beach, CA 92651
ph: (714) 494-8971
fax: (714) 494-1530

La Tienda/The Mexican Museum
Grand Mark Building D
Fort Mason Center
San Francisco, CA 94123
ph: (415) 441-0445

Lindsay Museum Store
1901 First Avenue
Walnut Creek, CA 94596
ph: (510) 935-1978

Los Angeles County Museum of Art
5905 Wilshire Boulevard
Los Angeles, CA 90036
ph: (310) 857-6140
fax: (310) 935-0278

Los Angeles Crafts and Folk Art Museum
5800 Wilshire Boulevard
Los Angeles, CA 90036
ph: (205) 991-6600
fax: (205) 991-1479

Mingei International Museum and
Collector's Gallery
4405 La Jolla Village Drive
La Jolla, CA 92038
ph: (619) 755-5300
fax: (619) 453-0700

Mojave River Valley Museum
P. O. Box 1282
Barstow, CA 92311
ph: (619) 256-5452

Monterey Peninsula Museum of Art
559 Pacific Street
Monterey, CA 93940
ph: (408) 372-5477

Museum of African-American Art
4005 Crenshaw Boulevard, 3rd floor
Los Angeles, CA 90008
ph: (410) 294-7071

The Museum of Contemporary Art
250 South Grand Avenue
Los Angeles, CA 90012
ph: (213) 621-2766

Newport Harbor Art Museum
850 San Clemente Drive
Newport Beach, CA 92660
ph: (714) 759-1122

Norton Simon Museum
411 West Colorado Boulevard
Pasadena, CA 91101
ph: (818) 449-6840
fax: (818) 796-4978

Oakland Museum
1000 Oak Street
Oakland, CA 94607
ph: (510) 834-2129
fax: (510) 273-2258

Old Mission Museum Gift Shop
751 Palm Street
San Luis Obispo, CA 93401
ph: (805) 543-6850

Pacific Asia Museum
46 North Los Robles Avenue
Pasadena, CA 91101
ph: (818) 449-2742
fax: (818) 449-2754

Pacific Grove Museum
165 Forest Avenue
Pacific Grove, CA 93950
ph: (408) 372-4212

Redding Museum
P. O. Box 990427
Redding, CA 96099
ph: (916) 225-4155

Riverside Art Museum
3425 Seventh Street
Riverside, CA 92501
ph: (714) 787-4787
fax: (714) 787-4797

San Diego Museum of Art
P. O. Box 2107
San Diego, CA 92112
ph: (619) 232-7931
fax: (619) 232-9367

San Diego Museum of Man
1350 El Prado/Balboa Park
San Diego, CA 92101
ph: (619) 239-2001
fax: (619) 239-2749

San Francisco Craft and
Folk Art Museum
Landmark Building A
Fort Mason Center
San Francisco, CA 94123
ph: (415) 775-0990

San Jose Museum of Art
110 South Market Street
San Jose, CA 95113
ph: (408) 294-2789

Santa Barbara Museum of Art
1130 State Street
Santa Barbara, CA 93101
ph: (805) 963-4364
fax: (805) 966-6840

Santa Cruz Museum Association
1305 East Cliff Drive
Santa Cruz, CA 95062
ph: (408) 429-3773

Severin Wunderman Museum
3 Mason
Irvine, CA 92718
ph: (714) 472-1138
fax: (714) 472-2590

Southwest Museum Store
234 Museum Drive
Los Angeles, CA 90041
ph: (213) 221-2164
fax: (213) 224-8223

Triton Museum of Art
1505 Warburton Avenue
Santa Clara, CA 95050
ph: (408) 247-3754
fax: (408) 247-3796

Colorado
Adams County Museum
9601 Henderson Road
Brighton, CO 80601
ph: (303) 659-7103

City of Greeley Museum
919 Seventh Street
Greeley, CO 80631
ph: (303) 350-9223

Denver Art Museum
100 West 14th Avenue
Denver, CO 80204
ph: (303) 640-2295

Discovery Museum
4450 Park Avenue
Bridgeport, CO 06604
ph: (303) 372-3521

Loveland Museum and Gallery
Fifth and Lincoln
Loveland, CO 80537
ph: (303) 667-6130
fax: (303) 667-5773

Museum of Western Colorado
P. O. Box 20000-5020
Grand Junction, CO 81502
ph: (303) 242-0971

Southern Ute Indian Cultural Center
P. O. Box 737
Ignacio, CO 81137
ph: (970) 563-9583
fax: (970) 563-0396

Telluride Gallery Of Fine Art
General Delivery
P. O. Box 1900
Telluride, CO 81435
ph: (303) 728-3300

Connecticut
The Bruce Museum
Museum Drive
Greenwich, CT 06830
ph: (203) 869-0376
fax: (203) 869-0963

Connecticut River Museum
Main Street
P. O. Box 261
Essex, CT 06426
ph: (203) 767-8269

Florence Griswold Museum
96 Lyme Street
Old Lyme, CT 06371
ph: (203) 434-5542

Hill-Stead Museum
35 Mountain Road
Farmington, CT 06032
ph: (203) 677-4787

Lyman Allyn Museum
625 Williams Street
New London, CT 06320
ph: (203) 443-2545

Mattatuck Museum Store
144 West Main Street
Waterbury, CT 06702
ph: (203) 521-4583

New Britain Museum of
American Art
56 Lexington Street
New Britain, CT 06052
ph: (203) 229-0257

Noah Webster Museum
227 South Main Street
West Hartford, CT 06107
ph: (203) 521-5362

Stamford Museum and Nature Center
39 Scofieldtown Road
Stamford, CT 06903
ph: (203) 322-1646

Whitney Museum Of Art
Fairfield County
One Champion Plaza
Stanford, CT 06921
ph: (203) 358-7652

W. M. Benton Museum of Art
University of Connecticut
245 Glenbrook Road
Storrs, CT 06269
ph: (203) 486-4520
fax: (203) 486-0234

Delaware
Delaware Art Museum
2301 Kentmere Parkway
Wilmington, DE 19806
ph: (302) 571-9590
fax: (302) 571-0220

Hagley Museum
P. O. Box 3630
Barley Mill Road
Wilmington, DE 19807
ph: (302) 658-2400

Rockwood Museum
610 Shipley Road
Wilmington, DE 19809
ph: (302) 761-4340
fax: (302) 764-4570

District of Columbia

Anacostia Museum
Smithsonian Institute
1901 Fort Place S.E.
Washington, DC 20020
ph: (202) 287-3369
fax: (202) 287-3183

Arthur M. Sackler Gallery
Smithsonian Institution
1050 Independence Avenue S.W.
Washington, DC 20560
ph: (202) 357-4911
fax: same

Art Museum of the Americas
201 18th Street N.W.
Washington, DC 20006
ph: (202) 458-6016
fax: (202) 458-6121

Corcoran Gallery and School of Art
17th Street and New York
Avenue N.W.
Washington, DC 20006
ph: (202) 638-3211

Freer Gallery of Art
Smithsonian Institution
Jefferson Drive and 12th Street S.W.
Washington, DC 20560
ph: (202) 357-2700

National Building Museum
401 F Street Northwest
Washington, DC 20001
ph: (202) 272-2448

National Gallery of Art
Sixth and Constitution Avenue N.W.
Washington, DC 20565
ph: (202) 322-5900
fax: (202) 842-4043

National Geographic Society
1145 17th Street N.W.
Washington, DC 20036
ph: (202) 857-7000

National Museum of African Art
950 Independence Avenue S.W.
Washington, DC 20560
ph: (202) 357-4852

National Museum of American Art
Ninth and G Streets N.W.
Washington, DC 20560
ph: (202) 357-1300

National Museum of
American History
Constitution Avenue and
14th Street N.W.
Washington, DC 20560
ph: (202) 357-2700

National Museum of Natural History
Constitution Avenue and
10th Street N.W.
Washington, DC 20560
ph: (202) 357-2700

National Museum of
Women in Arts
1250 New York Avenue N.W.
Washington, DC 20005
ph: (202) 783-5000
fax: (202) 393-3235

National Portrait Gallery
Eighth and F Streets N.W.
Washington, DC 20560
ph: (202) 357-1915
fax: (202) 786-2565

The Phillips Collection
1600 21st Street N.W.
Washington, DC 20009
ph: (202) 387-2151
fax: (202) 472-3422

Renwick Gallery
Smithsonian Institution
17th Street and Pennsylvania
Avenue N.W.
MRC 510
Washington, DC 20560
ph: (202) 357-2531
fax: (202) 786-2810

Smithsonian Shops
600 Maryland Avenue S.W.,
Suite 295-B
Washington, DC 20024
ph: (202) 287-3563
fax: (202) 287-3080

Textile Museum
2320 S Street N.W.
Washington, DC 20008
ph: (202) 667-0441
fax: (202) 483-0994

Florida
The Bass Museum of Art
2121 Park Avenue
Miami, FL 33143
ph: (305) 673-7530

Brevard Art Center and Museum
1463 Highland Avenue
Melbourne, FL 32936
ph: (407) 242-0737
fax: (407) 242-0798

Center for the Arts
3001 Riverside Park Drive
Vero Beach, FL 32963
ph: (305) 231-0707
fax: (305) 231-0938

Center for the Fine Arts
101 West Flagler Street
Miami, FL 33130
ph: (305) 375-1729

The Deland Museum of Art
600 North Woodland Boulevard
Deland, FL 32720
ph: (904) 734-4371

Folk Museum of Art
800 East Palmetto Street
Lakeland, FL 33801
ph: (941) 688-7743

Harn Museum of Art
University of Florida
Building 309
Gainesville, FL 32611
ph: (904) 392-9826
fax: (904) 392-3892

The Henry B. Plant Museum
401 West Kennedy Boulevard
Tampa, FL 33606
ph: (813) 254-1891

Henry M. Flagler Museum
P. O. Box 969
Palm Beach, FL 33480
ph: (407) 655-2833
fax: (407) 655-2826

Indian Temple Mound Museum
P. O. Box 4009
Fort Walton Beach, FL 32549
ph: (904) 243-6521
fax: (904) 244-2045

Jacksonville Art Museum
4160 Boulevard Center Drive
Jacksonville, FL 32207
ph: (904) 398-8336
fax: (904) 348-3167

Lightner Museum
P. O. Box 334
St. Augustine, FL 32085
ph: (904) 824-2874

Lowe Art Museum
1301 Stanford Drive
Coral Gables, FL 33124
ph: (305) 284-3536
fax: (305) 284-2024

Museum of Art
1 East Las Olas Boulevard
Fort Lauderdale, FL 33301
ph: (305) 525-5500

Museum of Fine Arts
255 Beach Drive N.E.
St. Petersburg, FL 33701
ph: (813) 896-2667
fax: (813) 894-4638

Orlando Museum of Art
2416 North Mills Avenue
Orlando, FL 32803
ph: (407) 896-4231

Ringling Museum of Art
5401 Bay Shore Road
Sarasota, FL 34243
ph: (813) 355-5101

Tampa Museum of Art
601 Doyle Carlton Drive
Tampa, FL 33602
ph: (813) 223-8130

Tarpon Springs Cultural Center
101 South Pinellas Avenue
Tarpon Springs, FL 34689
ph: (913) 942-5605

Georgia
Albany Museum of Art
311 Meadowlark Drive
Albany, GA 31707
ph: (912) 439-8400

Columbus Museum
1251 Wynnton Road
Columbus, GA 31906
ph: (404) 322-0400

Georgia Museum of Art
University of Georgia
Athens, GA 30602
ph: (706) 542-3255
fax: (706) 542-1051

High Museum of Art
1280 Peachtree Street N.E.
Atlanta, GA 30309
ph: (404) 898-1155
fax: (404) 898-9578

Marietta/Cobb Museum of Art
30 Atlanta Street
Marietta, GA 30060
ph: (404) 424-8142

Morris Museum of Art
1 Tenth Street
Augusta, GA 30901
ph: (706) 724-7501
fax: (706) 724-7612

Hawaii
Alexander and Baldwin
Sugar Museum
P. O. Box 125
Puunene, HI 96784
ph: (808) 871-8058

Bernice P. Bishop Museum Shop
1525 Bernice Street
Honolulu, HI 96817
ph: (808) 848-4134

Mission Houses Museum
553 South King Street
Honolulu, HI 96813
ph: (808) 531-0481
fax: (808) 545-2280

Volcano Art Center
P. O. Box 104
Hawaii National Park, HI 96718
ph: (808) 967-8222
fax: (808) 967-8512

Idaho
Boise Art Museum
670 South Julia Davis Drive
Boise, ID 83702
ph: (208) 345-8330
fax: (208) 345-8333

Illinois
Anderson Fine Arts Center
226 West Eighth Street
Anderson, IL 46016
ph: (317) 649-1248

Columbia College Art Gallery
72 East 11th Street
Chicago, IL 60605
ph: (312) 663-1600

Krannert Art Museum
500 East Peabody Drive
Champaign, IL 61820
ph: (217) 333-1860

Mitchell Museum
Richview Road
P. O. Box 923
Mount Vernon, IL 62864
ph: (618) 242-1236
fax: (618) 242-9530

Museum of Contemporary Art
237 East Ontario
Chicago, IL 60611
ph: (312) 280-2679
fax: (312) 280-2687

Quincy Art Center
1515 Jersey Street
Quincy, IL 62301
ph: (217) 223-5900

The Smart Museum of Art
5550 South Greenwood Avenue
Chicago, IL 60637
ph: (312) 702-0528
fax: (312) 702-3121

Terra Museum of American Art
664 North Michigan Avenue
Chicago, IL 60611
ph: (312) 664-3939
fax: (312) 664-2052

World Heritage Museum
702 Wright Street
Urbana, IL 61801
ph: (217) 333-2360

Indiana

Columbus Museum
372 Commons Mall
Columbus, IN 47201
ph: (812) 376-2559
fax: (812) 375-2724

Eiteljorg Museum
500 West Washington Street
Indianapolis, IN 46204
ph: (317) 636-9378

Fort Wayne Museum of Art
311 East Main Street
Fort Wayne, IN 46802
ph: (219) 422-6467
fax: (219) 422-1374

Greater Lafayette Museum of Art
101 South Ninth Street
Lafayette, IN 47901
ph: (317) 742-1128

Indianapolis Museum of Art
1200 West 38th Street
Indianapolis, IN 46208
ph: (317) 923-1331

Matthers Museum
601 East Eighth Street
Bloomington, IN 47405
ph: (812) 855-7224

Monroe County Museum
202 East Sixth Street
Bloomington, IN 47408
ph: (812) 332-2517

South Bend Regional Museum of Art
120 South St. Joseph Street
South Bend, IN 46601
ph: (219) 235-9102

Iowa

Brunnier Art Museum Store
290 Scheman Building
Iowa State University
Ames, IA 50011
ph: (515) 294-4279
fax: (515) 294-7070

Davenport Museum of Art
1737 West 12th Street
Davenport, IA 52804
ph: (319) 326-7804
fax: (319) 326-7876

Des Moines Art Center
4700 Grand Avenue
Des Moines, IA 50312
ph: (515) 277-4405
fax: (515) 279-3834

Old Capitol Museum
The University of Iowa
Iowa City, IA 52242
ph: (319) 335-0548

Kansas

Reno County Museum
P. O. Box 664
Hutchinson, KS 67504
ph: (316) 662-4387

Smoky Hill Museum
211 West Iron Avenue
Salina, KS 67401
ph: (913) 826-7460
fax: (913) 826-7444

Spencer Museum of Art
University of Kansas
Lawrence, KS 66045
ph: (913) 864-4710
fax: (913) 864-3112

Wichita Art Museum
619 Stackman Drive
Wichita, KS 67203
ph: (316) 268-4975
fax: (316) 268-4980

Kentucky
Behringer Crawford Museum
P. O. Box 67
Covington, KY 41012
ph: (606) 491-4003

Headley-Whitney Museum
4435 Old Frankfort Pike
Lexington, KY 40510
ph: (606) 255-9112

J. B. Speed Art Museum
P. O. Box 2600
Louisville, KY 40201
ph: (502) 636-2893
fax: (502) 363-2899

Kentucky Center for the Arts
5 Riverfront Plaza
Louisville, KY 40202
ph: (502) 562-0164
fax: (502) 562-0150

Kentucky Highlands Museum
P. O. Box 1494
Ashland, KY 41105
ph: (606) 329-8888

Kentucky Museum Store
Western Kentucky University
Kentucky Building
Bowling Green, KY 42101
ph: (502) 745-6080

Louisiana
New Orleans Museum of Art
P. O. Box 19123
New Orleans, LA 70179
ph: (504) 488-2631
fax: (504) 484-6602

Stoner Arts Center
P. O. Box 44022
Shreveport, LA 71134

Maine
The Abbe Museum
P. O. Box 286
Bar Harbor, ME 04609
ph: (207) 288-3519

Museum of Art of Ogunquit
181 Shore Road
P. O. Box 815
Ogunquit, ME 03907
ph: (207) 646-4909

Museum Shop at the Brick Store
105 Main Street
Kennebunk, ME 04043
ph: (207) 985-3639

Portland Museum of Art
7 Congress Square
Portland, ME 04101
ph: (207) 775-6148
fax: (207) 773-7324

The Stanley Museum
School Street
P. O. Box 280
Kingfield, ME 04947
ph: (207) 265-2729

Maryland
Baltimore Museum of Art
Art Museum Drive
Baltimore, MD 21218
ph: (410) 396-6338

The Walters Art Gallery
600 North Charles Street
Baltimore, MD 21201
ph: (410) 547-9000

Massachusetts
Berkshire Museum
39 South Street
Pittsfield, MA 01201
ph: (413) 443-7171

Cahoon Museum of American Art
4676 Falmouth Avenue
P. O. Box 1853
Cotuit, MA 02635
ph: (508) 428-7581

Danforth Museum of Art
123 Union Avenue
Framingham, MA 01701
ph: (508) 620-0050
fax: (508) 872-5542

Fuller Museum of Art
455 Oak Street
Brockton, MA 02401
ph: (508) 588-6000

Museum of Fine Arts
295 Huntington Avenue
Boston, MA 02115
ph: (800) 342-7870
fax: (617) 267-5480

New Bedford Glass Museum
67 Allen Street
New Bedford, MA 02740
ph: (508) 990-0619

Old Sturbridge Village Museum
1 Old Sturbridge Village Road
Sturbridge, MA 01566
ph: (508) 347-3362

Peabody Museum Shop
East India Square
Salem, MA 01970
ph: (508) 744-3390

Springfield Museum of Fine Arts
49 Chestnut Street
Springfield, MA 01103
ph: (413) 732-6092
fax: (413) 732-1483

Thornton W. Burgess Museum
4 Water Street
P. O. Box 972
Sandwich, MA 02563
ph: (503) 888-4668

Wenham Museum
132 Main Street
Wenham, MA 01984
ph: (508) 468-2377

Worcester Art Museum
55 Salisbury Street
Worcester, MA 01609
ph: (508) 799-4406

Michigan
Cranbrook Art Museum
500 Lone Pine Road
P. O. Box 801
Bloomfield Hills, MI 48303
ph: (313) 645-3325

Ella Sharp Museum
3225 Fourth Street
Jackson, MI 49203
ph: (517) 784-3460

Fernwood
13988 Range Line Road
Niles, MI 49120
ph: (616) 695-6491

Grand Rapids Art Museum
155 Division North
Grand Rapids, MI 49503
ph: (616) 459-4677
fax: (616) 459-8491

Ojibwa Museum Gift Shop
500 North State Street
St. Ignace, MI 49781
ph: (906) 643-9161
fax: (906) 643-9393

Tri-Cities Museum
1 North Harbor
Grand Haven, MI 49417
ph: (616) 842-0700

Troy Museum Gift Shop
60 West Wattles Road
Troy, MI 48098
ph: (313) 524-3570

Minnesota
Glensheen Museum Shop
3300 London Road
Duluth, MN 55804
ph: (218) 724-1107

The Minneapolis Institute of Arts
2400 Third Avenue South
Minneapolis, MN 55404
ph: (612) 870-3200

Tweed Museum of Art
University of Minnesota
10 University Drive
Duluth, MN 55812
ph: (218) 726-8222

Mississippi
Choctaw Museum of the
Southern Indian
Route 7
P. O. Box 6010
Philadelphia, MS 39350
ph: (601) 656-5251

Lauren Rogers Museum
P. O. Box 1108
Laurel, MS 39441
ph: (601) 649-6374
fax: (601) 649-6379

Mississippi Museum of Art
201 East Pascagoula Street
Jackson, MS 39201
ph: (601) 960-1515
fax: (601) 960-1505

Walter Anderson Museum of Art
P. O. Box 328
Ocean Springs, MS 39564
ph: (601) 872-2370

Missouri
Albrecht-Kemper Museum of Art
2818 Frederick Boulevard
St. Joseph, MO 64506
ph: (816) 233-7003
fax: (816) 233-2413

Chatillon-DeMenil Mansion Museum
3352 DeMenil Place
St. Louis, MO 63122
ph: (314) 771-5828

The Kansas City Museum
3218 Gladstone
Kansas City, MO 64123
ph: (816) 483-8300

Powers Museum
P. O. Box 593
Carthage, MO 64836
ph: (417) 358-2667

Saint Louis Art Museum
1 Fine Arts Drive
St. Louis, MO 63110
ph: (314) 721-0067

Springfield Art Museum
1111 East Brookside Drive
Springfield, MO 65807
ph: (417) 866-2716

Montana

Missoula Museum of the Arts
335 North Pattee Street
Missoula, MT 59802
ph: (406) 728-0447

Nebraska

Sheldon Memorial Art Gallery
Sheldon Art and Gift Shop
12th and R Streets
Lincoln, NE 68588
ph: (402) 472-3637

Stuhr Museum
3133 West Highway 34
Grand Island, NE 68801
ph: (308) 381-5316
fax: (308) 391-5028

Western Heritage Museum
801 South 10th Street
Omaha, NE 68108
ph: (402) 444-5072

Nevada

Nevada Museum of Art
160 West Liberty Street
Reno, NV 89501
ph: (702) 329-3333
fax: (702) 329-1541

Stewart Indian Museum
Trading Post
5366 Snyder Avenue
Carson City, NV 89701
ph: (702) 882-1808

New Hampshire

Strawberry Banke Museum Shops
P. O. Box 300
Portsmouth, NH 03801
ph: (602) 433-1114

New Jersey

Monmouth Museum Store
Newman Springs Road
Lincroft, NJ 07738
ph: (201) 747-2266

Montclair Art Museum
3 South Mountain Avenue
Montclair, NJ 07042
ph: (201) 746-5555

The Morris Museum
Normandy Heights Road
Morristown, NJ 07960
ph: (201) 538-0454

Newark Museum
49 Washington Street
P. O. Box 540
Newark, NJ 07101

The Noyes Museum
Lily Lake Road
Oceanville, NJ 08231
ph: (609) 652-8848
fax: (609) 652-6166

Zimmerli Art Museum
Rutgers University
George and Hamilton Streets
New Brunswick, NJ 08903
ph: (908) 932-7237

New Mexico
Acoma Tourist Visitor Center
Museum and Gift Shop
P. O. Box 309
Acoma, NM 87034
ph: (505) 252-1139
fax: (800) 747-0181

Branigan Cultural Center Foundation
106 West Hadley
Las Cruces, NM 88001
ph: (505) 524-1422

Case Trading Post at the
Wheelwright Museum
P. O. Box 5153
Santa Fe, NM 87502
ph: (505) 982-4636
fax: (505) 989-7386

La Tienda del Museo
P. O. Box 7006
Albuquerque, NM 87194
ph: (505) 242-0434

Lincoln County Heritage Trust
P. O. Box 98
Lincoln, NM 88338
ph: (505) 653-4445

Millicent Rogers Museum
P. O. Box A
Taos, NM 87571
ph: (505) 758-4316
fax: (505) 758-5751

Museum of Indian Arts and Culture
P. O. Box 2087
Santa Fe, NM 87504
ph: (505) 827-6344

Museum of International Folk Art
P. O. Box 2087
706 Camino Lejo
Santa Fe, NM 87504
ph: (505) 827-6350

Regional Folk Art Gallery
141 Lincoln Avenue
Santa Fe, NM 87501
ph: (505) 983-1660

Roswell Museum and Art Center
100 West 11th Street
Roswell, NM 88201
ph: (505) 624-6744
fax: (505) 624-6765

University of New Mexico
Art Museum Shop
Fine Arts Center
Albuquerque, NM 87131
ph: (505) 277-4001

New York
Adirondack Center Museum
Court Street
Elizabeth, NY 12932
ph: (518) 873-6466

Adirondack Museum
P. O. Box 99
Blue Mountain Lake, NY 12812
ph: (518) 252-7650

American Craft Museum Shop
40 West 53rd Street
New York, NY 10019
ph: (212) 956-3535
fax: (212) 956-3699

Arnot Art Museum
235 Lake Street
Elmira, NY 14901
ph: (607) 734-3697
fax: (607) 734-5687

The Brooklyn Museum
200 Eastern Parkway
Brooklyn, NY 11238
ph: (718) 628-5000
fax: (718) 638-3731

Cooper-Hewitt Museum
2 East 91st Street
New York, NY 10128
ph: (212) 860-6939
fax: (212) 860-6909

Everson Museum of Art
401 Harrison Street
Syracuse, NY 13202
ph: (315) 474-6064

Friends of Clermont
87 Clermont Avenue, Suite 2
Germantown, NY 12526
ph: (518) 537-4240

Genesee Country Museum
Flint Hill Road
P. O. Box 310
Mumford, NY 14511
ph: (716) 538-6822

Hanford Mills Museum Store
P. O. Box 99
East Meredith, NY 13757
ph: (607) 278-5744

Heckscher Museum
2 Prime Avenue
Huntington, NY 11743
ph: (516) 351-3252
fax: (516) 423-2145

Herbert F. Johnson Museum of Art
Cornell University
Ithaca, NY 14853
ph: (607) 255-6464
fax: (607) 255-9940

Hudson River Museum
511 Warburton Avenue
Yonkers, NY 10701
ph: (914) 963-4550

Katonah Museum of Art
Route 22 at Jay Street
Katonah, NY 10536
ph: (914) 232-9555

Memorial Art Gallery
500 University Avenue
Rochester, NY 14607
ph: (716) 473-7720

Museum of American Folk Art
2 Lincoln Square
New York, NY 10023
ph: (212) 977-7170

Neuberger Museum Shop
State University of New York
at Purchase
Purchase, NY 10577
ph: (914) 251-6131
fax: (914) 251-6101

New York State Museum Shop
Culture Educational Center
Empire State Place
Albany, NY 12230
ph: (518) 449-1573
fax: (518) 486-5657

Parrish Art Museum Shop
25 Job's Lane
South Hampton, NY 11968
ph: (516) 283-2118

The Queens Museum
Flushing Meadows
New York City Building
Flushing, NY 11368
ph: (718) 592-9700
fax: (718) 592-5778

Sainte Marie Among the Iroquois
1 Onondaga Lake Parkway
P. O. Box 249
Liverpool, NY 13088
ph: (315) 453-6778

The Salt Museum
P. O. Box 249
Liverpool, NY 13088
ph: (315) 457-6715
fax: (315) 953-6762

Schenectady Museum
Nott Terrace Heights
Schenectady, NY 12308
ph: (518) 382-7890

Seneca-Iroquois National Museum
P. O. Box 442
Broad Street Extension
Salamanca, NY 14779
ph: (716) 945-1738
fax: (716) 945-1760

Storm King Art Center
Old Pleasant Hill Road
Mountainville, NY 10953
ph: (914) 534-3190

The Strong Museum
One Manhattan Square
Rochester, NY 14607
ph: (716) 263-2700

The Studio Museum in Harlem
144 West 125th Street
New York, NY 10027
ph: (212) 864-4500

Vanderbilt Museum
180 Little Neck Road
Centerport, NY 11721
ph: (516) 854-5555
fax: (516) 854-5527

North Carolina
Appalachian Heritage Museum
Route 1
P. O. Box 278
Blowing Rock, NC 28605
ph: (704) 264-2792

Discovery Place
301 North Tryon Street
Charlotte, NC 28202
ph: (704) 337-2651
fax: (704) 337-2670

Fayetteville Museum of Art
P. O. Box 35134
Fayetteville, NC 28303
ph: (919) 485-5121
fax: (919) 485-5223

Frisco Native American Museum and
Natural History Center
P. O. Box 399
Frisco, NC 27936
ph: (919) 995-4440

Furniture Discovery Center
101 West Green Drive
High Point, NC 27260
ph: (910) 887-3876
fax: (910) 884-4352

Hickory Museum of Art Shop
P. O. Box 2572
Hickory, NC 28603
ph: (704) 324-5864

High Point Museum
1805 East Lexington Avenue
High Point, NC 27262
ph: (919) 885-6859

Imagination Station
P. O. Box 2127
Wilson, NC 27893
ph: (919) 291-5113

North Carolina Museum of Art
2110 Blue Ridge Boulevard
Raleigh, NC 27607
ph: (919) 833-1935
fax: (919) 733-8034

Randolph Arts Guild Morings
Fine Crafts
P. O. Box 1033
123 Sunset Avenue
Asheboro, NC 27204
ph: (919) 629-4058

St. John's Museum of Art Shop
114 Orange Street
Wilmington, NC 28403
ph: (919) 763-0281

Tryon Palace Restoration Complex
P. O. Box 1007
New Bern, NC 28560
ph: (919) 638-1560

North Dakota
North Dakota Museum of Art
P. O. Box 7305
University Station
Grand Forks, ND 58202
ph: (701) 777-4195

Plains Art Museum
219 South Seventh Street
P. O. Box 2338
Fargo, ND 58108
ph: (701) 293-0903
fax: (701) 293-1082

Ohio
Cleveland Museum of Art
11150 East Boulevard
Cleveland, OH 44106
ph: (216) 421-7340
fax: (216) 421-0424

Columbus Museum of Art
480 East Broad Street
Columbus, OH 43215
ph: (614) 221-6801
fax: (614) 221-0226

Dayton Art Institute
P. O. Box 941
Dayton, OH 45401
ph: (513) 223-5277

McKinley Museum
800 McKinley Monument
Drive N.W.
Canton, OH 44708
ph: (216) 455-7043
fax: (216) 455-1137

Sharon Woods Village Shops
P. O. Box 62475
Cincinnati, OH 45262
ph: (513) 563-2503

The Taft Museum
316 Pike Street
Cincinnati, OH 45202
ph: (513) 241-0343
fax: (513) 241-7762

Toledo Museum of Art
P. O. Box 1013
Toledo, OH 43697
ph: (419) 255-8000
fax: (419) 255-5638

Oklahoma
Gilcrease Museum Shop
1400 North Gilcrease Museum Road
Tulsa, OK 74127
ph: (918) 596-2700

Oklahoma City Art Museum
3113 Pershing Boulevard
Oklahoma City, OK 73107
ph: (405) 946-4477
fax: (405) 946-7671

Philbrook Museum of Art
2727 South Rockford Road
Tulsa, OK 74114
ph: (918) 748-5357
fax: (918) 743-4230

Southern Plains Museum
P. O. Box 749
Anadarko, OK 73005
ph: (405) 247-6221

Oregon
The High Desert Museum
59800 South Highway 97
Bend, OR 97702
ph: (503) 382-4754
fax: (503) 382-5256

Horner Museum
Oregon State University
Corvallis, OR 97331
ph: (503) 737-2951

Museum of Art
University of Oregon
Eugene, OR 97403
ph: (503) 346-3027

Portland Art Museum
1219 Southwest Park
Portland, OR 97205
ph: (503) 226-2811

Pennsylvania
Abington Art Center Gallery Shop
515 Meetinghouse Road
Jenkintown, PA 19046
ph: (215) 887-4882

Afro-American Historical and
Cultural Museum
Seventh and Arch Streets
Philadelphia, PA 19106
ph: (215) 574-0380

Allentown Art Museum
P. O. Box 388
Allentown, PA 18105
ph: (215) 432-4333

Athenaeum of Philadelphia
219 South Sixth Street
Philadelphia, PA 19106
ph: (215) 925-2688

Brandywine River Museum
P. O. Box 141
Chadds Ford, PA 19317
ph: (215) 388-7601
fax: (215) 388-1197

Bucks County Historical Society
84 South Pine Street
Doylestown, PA 18901
ph: (215) 345-0210

Carnegie Museum Shops
4400 Forbes Avenue
Pittsburgh, PA 15213
ph: (412) 622-3320
fax: (412) 622-6258

Community Gallery of
Lancaster County
135 North Lime Street
Lancaster, PA 17602
ph: (717) 394-3497

Elfreth's Alley Museum
126 Elfreth's Alley
Philadelphia, PA 19106
ph: (215) 574-0560

Ephrata Cloister Museum Store
632 West Main Street
Ephrata, PA 17522
ph: (717) 733-2592
fax: (717) 733-4811

Erie Art Museum
411 State Street
Erie, PA 16501
ph: (814) 459-5477

Everhart Museum
Nay Aug Park
Scranton, PA 18510
ph: (717) 246-7186

Hope Lodge and Farmers Mill
553 Bethlehem Pike
Fort Washington, PA 19034
ph: (215) 646-1595

James A. Michener Art Museum
128 South Pine Street
Doylestown, PA 18901
ph: (215) 340-9800

Kemerer Museum of Decorative Arts
P. O. Box 1305
Bethlehem, PA 18016
ph: (610) 868-6868

Landis Valley Museum
Weather Vane Gift Shop
2451 Kissel Hill Road
Lancaster, PA 17601
ph: (717) 569-9312

Ligonier Valley Historical Society
Compass Inn Museum
P. O. Box 167
Laughlintown, PA 15655
ph: (412) 238-6818

Packwood House Museum
15 North Water Street
Lewisburg, PA 17837
ph: (717) 524-0323

Philadelphia Museum of Art
26th Street and Parkway
P. O. Box 7646
Philadelphia, PA 19101
ph: (215) 787-5472

Pittsburgh Center for the Arts
6300 Fifth Avenue
Pittsburgh, PA 15232
ph: (412) 361-0873

State Museum of Pennsylvania
Third and North Streets
P. O. Box 1026
Harrisburg, PA 17108
ph: (717) 787-5526

University of Pennsylvania
Museum Shop
33rd and Spruce Streets
Philadelphia, PA 19104
ph: (215) 898-4046
fax: (215) 898-0657

South Carolina
The Charleston Museum
360 Meeting Street
Charleston, SC 29403
ph: (803) 722-2996
fax: (803) 722-1784

Columbia Museum of Art
1112 Bull Street
Columbia, SC 29201
ph: (803) 343-2159
fax: (803) 343-2150

Gibbes Museum of Art
135 Meeting Street
Charleston, SC 29401
ph: (803) 722-2706
fax: (803) 720-1682

Greenville County Museum of Art
420 College Street
Greenville, SC 29601
ph: (803) 271-7570

McKissick Museum
University of South Carolina
Columbia, SC 29208
ph: (803) 777-7251
fax: (803) 777-3697

The Museum
P. O. Box 3131
Greenwood, SC 29648
ph: (803) 229-7093

The Museum of Hilton Head Island
P. O. Box 23497
Hilton Head Island, SC 29925
ph: (803) 689-6767
fax: (803) 689-6769

Museum of York County
4621 Mount Gallant Road
Rock Hill, SC 29732
ph: (803) 329-2121
fax: (803) 329-5249

South Dakota
Akta Lakota Museum
P. O. Box 89
Chamberlain, SD 57325
ph: (605) 734-3455

Dakota Prairie Museum
21 South Main
Aberdeen, SD 57401
ph: (605-622) 7117

Sioux Indian Museum
P. O. Box 1504
Rapid City, SD 57709
ph: (605)348-0557

Siouxland Heritage Museums
200 West Sixth Street
Sioux Falls, SD 57102
ph: (605) 335-4210

Tennessee
Cheekwood Museum Shop
Forrest Park Drive
Nashville, TN 37205
ph: (615) 353-2158

The Hermitage
4580 Rachel's Lane
Hermitage, TN 37076
ph: (615) 889-2941

Hunter Museum Shop
10 Bluff View
Chattanooga, TN 37403
ph: (615) 267-0968

McMinn Country Living
Heritage Museum
220 Lynwood Drive
Athens, TN 37303
ph: (615) 745-4783

National Ornamental
Metal Museum
374 West California Avenue
Memphis, TN 38106
ph: (901) 774-6380
fax: (901) 774-6382

Woodruff-Fontaine House and
Museum Shop
680 Adams Avenue
Memphis, TN 38105
ph: (901) 525-2695
fax: (901) 526-4531

Texas
Amon Carter Museum
P. O. Box 2365
Fort Worth, TX 76113
ph: (817) 738-1933

Art Museum of Southeast Texas
P. O. Box 3703
Beaumont, TX 77704
ph: (409) 832-3432
fax: (409) 832-8508

Art Museum of South Texas
1902 North Shoreline
Corpus Christi, TX 78401
ph: (512) 884-3844

Carson County Square
House Museum
P. O. Box 276
Panhandle, TX 79068
ph: (806) 537-3524
fax: (806) 537-3724

Center Gallery
300 Augusta Avenue
San Antonio, TX 78205
ph: (512) 224-1848

Dallas Museum of Art
1717 North Harwood
Dallas, TX 75201
ph: (214) 922-1270
fax: (214) 954-0174

El Paso Museum of Art
1211 Montana Avenue
El Paso, TX 79902
ph: (915) 541-4040
fax: (915) 533-5688

Fielder Museum Gift Shop
1616 Abram
Arlington, TX 76013
ph: (817) 460-4017

Heritage House Museum
905 West Division
Orange, TX 77630
ph: (409) 886-5385

International Museum of Cultures
7500 West Camp Wisdom
Dallas, TX 75236
ph: (214) 709-2406
fax: (214) 709-2433

Kimball Art Museum
3333 Camp Bowie Boulevard
Fort Worth, TX 76107
ph: (817) 332-8451
fax: (817) 877-1264

Laguna Gloria Art Museum
P. O. Box 5568
Austin, TX 78763
ph: (512) 477-0766

Mainland Museum
P. O. Box 1127
Texas City, TX 77592
ph: (713) 556-0444
fax: (713) 556-1860

Museum of Fine Arts Houston
P. O. Box 6826
Houston, TX 77265
ph: (713) 639-7554
fax: (713) 639-7597

San Angelo Museum of Fine Art
P. O. Box 3092
San Angelo, TX 76902
ph: (915) 658-4084

Strecker Museum
P. O. Box 97154
Waco, TX 76798
ph: (817) 755-1110
fax: (817) 744-2673

Texas Memorial Museum
2400 Trinity
Austin, TX 78705
ph: (512) 471-1604
fax: (512) 471-4794

Utah
Museum of Fine Arts
Brigham Young University
A-410 Harris
Fine Arts Center
Provo, UT 84602
ph: (801) 378-2819

Utah Museum of Fine Arts
University of Utah
101 Art and Architecture Center
Salt Lake City, UT 84112
ph: (801) 581-7049

Vermont
Bennington Museum
West Main Street
Bennington, VT 05201
ph: (802) 447-1571

Shelburne Museum
P. O. Box 10
Shelburne, VT 05482
ph: (802) 985-3346 ext. 382

Sheldon Museum
1 Park Street
Middlebury, VT 05753
ph: (802) 388-2117

Southern Vermont Arts Center
P. O. Box 617
Manchester, VT 05254
ph: (802) 362-1405

Virginia
Anderson Gallery Shop
P. O. Box 842514
Richmond, VA 23284
ph: (804) 828-1522

Art Museum of Western Virginia
Center in the Square, 2nd floor
One Market Square
Roanoke, VA 24011
ph: (540) 342-5760

The Chrysler Museum
245 West Olney Road
Norfolk, VA 23510
ph: (804) 664-6241
fax: (804) 664-6201

James Monroe Museum
908 Charles Street
Fredericksburg, VA 22401
ph: (540) 654-1043
fax: (540) 654-1106

Museum Store Consultants
5 Countryside Court
Richmond, VA 23229
ph: (804) 288-0528

Oatlands Gift Shop
Route 2
P. O. Box 352
Leesburg, VA 22075
ph: (703) 777-3174

The Petersburg Museum
15 West Bank Street
Petersburg, VA 23803
ph: (804) 733-2401

Southwest Virginia Museum
P. O. Box 742
10 West First Street
Big Stone, VA 24219
ph: (540) 523-1322
fax: (540) 523-6616

Washington
Bellevue Art Museum
301 Bellevue Square
Bellevue, WA 98004
ph: (206) 454-3322
fax: (206) 367-1799

Burke Museum
University of Washington
University of Washington Campus
Seattle, WA 98195
ph: (206) 685-0909
fax: (206) 685-3039

Cheney Cowles Museum
West 2316 First Avenue
Spokane, WA 99204
ph: (509) 456-3931

Museum and Arts Center
175 West Cedar
Sequim, WA 98382
ph: (206) 683-8110

Museum of History and Industry
2700 24th Avenue East
Seattle, WA 98112
ph: (206) 324-1126

Panaca Gallery
133 Bellevue Square
North Eighth Street
Bellevue, WA 98004
ph: (206) 454-0234

Seattle Art Museum
P. O. Box 22000
Seattle, WA 98122
ph: (206) 654-3164
fax: (206) 654-3135

Tacoma Art Museum
1123 Pacific Avenue
Tacoma, WA 98402
ph: (206) 272-4258
fax: (206) 627-1898

Whatcom Museum of
History and Art
121 Prospect Street
Bellingham, WA 98225
ph: (206) 676-6981

Wing Luke Memorial Museum
407 Seventh Avenue South
Seattle, WA 98104
ph: (206) 623-5124

Yakima Valley Museum Shop
2105 Tieton Drive
Yakima, WA 98902
ph: (509) 248-0747

West Virginia
Huntington Museum of Art
McCoy Road
Park Hills
Huntington, WV 25701
ph: (304) 529-2701
fax: (304) 529-7447

Sunrise Museums
746 Myrtle Road
Charleston, WV 25314
ph: (304) 344-8035

Wisconsin
Bergstrom-Mahler Museum
165 North Park Avenue
Neenah, WI 54956
ph: (414) 751-4658

Charles A. Wustum Museum
of Fine Arts
2519 Northwestern Avenue
Racine, WI 53404
ph: (414) 636-9177

Chippewa Valley Museum
P. O. Box 1204
Eau Claire, WI 54702
ph: (715) 834-7871

Elvehjem Museum of Art
800 University Avenue
Madison, WI 53706
ph: (608) 263-2240
fax: (608) 263-8188

Fox Cities Children's Museum
P. O. Box 9106
Appleton, WI 54911
ph: (414) 734-3226

Milton House Museum
18 South Janesville Street
Milton, WI 53563
ph: (608) 868-7772

Milwaukee Art Museum
750 North Lincoln Memorial Drive
Milwaukee, WI 53202
ph: (414) 271-9508
fax: (414) 271-7588

Milwaukee Public Museum
800 West Wells Street
Milwaukee, WI 53233
ph: (414) 278-2795
fax: (414) 278-6101

New Visions Gallery
1000 North Oak Avenue
Marshfield, WI 54449
ph: (715) 387-5562

Old World Wisconsin
South 103 West 37890
Highway 67
Eagle, WI 53119
ph: (414) 594-2116
fax: (414) 594-8958

Oneida Nation Museum
P. O. Box 365
Oneida, WI 54155
ph: (414) 869-2768

Paine Art Center
1410 Algoma Boulevard
Oshkosh, WI 54901
ph: (414) 235-6903
fax: (414) 235-6303

Wyoming
Buffalo Bill Historical Center
P. O. Box 2630
Cody, WY 82414
ph: (307) 587-3243
fax: (307) 587-5714

Nicolaysen Art Museum
400 East Collins
Casper, WY 82601
ph: (307) 235-5247
fax: (307) 235-0923

Old West Museum
P. O. Box 2824
Cheyenne, WY 82003
ph: (307) 778-7290

Wyoming State Museum
Barrett Building
Cheyenne, WY 82002
ph: (307) 777-7022

NATIONAL PARKS, GOVERNMENT PROGRAMS, AND COOPERATIVES

National parks and other government-sponsored artist-in-residence programs provide more exposure and creative market opportunity. National parks throughout the United States often feature crafts in their gift shops and sometimes offer artist residencies. They accept proposals from a variety of artists including photographers, writers, two-dimensional (2-D) and three-dimensional (3-D) artists, video- and filmmakers, composers, performers, and other art professionals. Each park has different requirements, including who can apply and in which mediums; application deadlines, requirement materials, and residency periods vary, so you need to contact each site separately.

The List of the 1995–96 Artist-in-Residence Programs in the National Parks, a pamphlet written by author and artist Bonnie Fournier, is a comprehensive list of the various programs and guidelines for each park. If these residencies interest you, this book is a valuable tool that is updated annually. Libraries can also provide useful information about many programs and locations. In addition, you can do more research by requesting free brochures from the national parks that interest you.

Many state associations and cooperatives also encourage and promote crafts and craftspeople from their own states. They create marketing opportunities for their member artisans and work to increase public awareness, knowledge, and appreciation of crafts. These organizations provide a forum to discuss craft issues, and they encourage professionalism and mutual support for their members. They also present a chance for craft designers to show their work with other craftspeople from their state. Not only do these cooperatives act as showcases for the best of the state's crafts, but they also serve as clearing houses for organizations that want to feature crafts from a particular state. It is one-stop shopping for busy buyers: various state cooperatives supply promotional material and represent their craftspeople as a group at wholesale trade shows. In addition, these groups often sponsor and jury additional crafts fairs throughout their own states.

As with the other lists in this book, these addresses are for organizations found in The Crafts Center database, but you could also try contacting other parks or government programs in your area.

NATIONAL PARKS

Alaska Natural History Association
Denali National Park Branch
P. O. Box 230
Denali National Park, AK 99755
ph: (907) 683-1258
fax: (907) 683-1408

ARA Bandelier Gift Shop
HCR 1
P. O. Box 1, Suite 17
Los Alamos, NM 87544
ph: (505) 672-9791

Badlands Natural History
Association
P. O. Box 6
Badlands National Park
Interior, SD 57750
ph: (605) 433-5361

Bryce Canyon Natural History
Association
Bryce Canyon National Park
Bryce Canyon, UT 84717
ph: (901) 834-5322

Canyonlands Natural History
Association
30 South 100 East
Moab, UT 84532
ph: (801) 259-6003
fax: (801) 259-8263

Colorado National Monument
Association
Colorado National Monument
Fruita, CO 81521
ph: (303) 858-3617
fax: (303) 858-0372

Death Valley Natural History
Association
P. O. Box 188
Death Valley, CA 92328
ph: (619) 786-3286
fax: (619) 786-2236

Denali Park Resorts
P. O. Box 109
Denali, AK 99755
ph: (907) 683-2220
fax: same

Denver Service Center
National Park Service
12795 West Alameda Parkway
P. O. Box 25287
Denver, CO 80225
ph: (303) 969-2100

Devils Tower Natural History
Association
P. O. Box 37
Devils Tower, WY 82714
ph: (307) 467-5283

Eastern National Park and Monument
446 North Lane
Conshohocken, PA 19428
ph: (215) 832-0555
fax: (215) 832-0242

Flagg Ranch Village
P. O. Box 187
Moran, WY 83013
ph: (307) 733-8761
fax: (307) 543-2536

Florida National Parks and Monument
P. O. Box 279
Homestead, FL 33030
ph: (305) 247-1216

Forever Resorts Padre Island Park
Company
Padre Island National Seashore
P. O. Box 18909
Corpus Christi, TX 78480
ph: (512) 949-9368

Fort Laramie Historical Association
Highway 160
P. O. Box 218
Fort Laramie, WY 82212
ph: (307) 837-2662

Glacier Natural History Association
P. O. Box 428
Glacier National Park
West Glacier, MT 59936
ph: (406) 888-5756

Golden Gate National Park Association
Fort Mason, Building 201
San Francisco, CA 94123
ph: (415) 776-0693
fax: (415) 776-2205

Grand Canyon National Park
P. O. Box 129
Grand Canyon, AZ 86023
ph: (602) 638-2401

Grand Canyon National Park Lodges
Fred Harvey
P. O. Box 699
Grand Canyon, AZ 86023
ph: (602) 638-2631

Grand Teton Natural History
Association
P. O. Box 170
Moose, WY 83012
ph: (307) 739-3404
fax: (307) 739-3438

Great Smoky Mountains Natural
History Association
115 Park Headquarters Road
Gatlinburg, TN 37738
ph: (615) 436-7318
fax: (615) 436-6884

Harpers Ferry Historical Association
P. O. Box 197
Harpers Ferry, WV 25425
ph: (304) 535-6881

Illinois State Museum Society
Spring and Edwards Street
Springfield, IL 62706
ph: (217) 782-7388

Jordan Pond House and the
Acadia Shops
85 Main Street
P. O. Box 24
Bar Harbor, ME 04609
ph: (207) 288-5592
fax: (207) 288-2420

Lake Mead National Recreation Area
601 Nevada Highway
Boulder City, NV 89005

La Quinta Sculpture Park
57325 Madison Street
P. O. Box 1566
La Quinta, CA 92253
ph: (619) 564-6464

Lincoln Home National Historical Site
406 South Eighth Street
Springfield, IL 61701
ph: (217) 524-1520

Los Compadres Gift Shop
6539 San Jose
San Antonio, TX 78214
ph: (512) 922-0360
fax: (512) 922-6800

Mesa Verde Museum Association
P. O. Box 38
Mesa Verde National Park, CO 81330
ph: (303) 529-4445

Mississippi Crafts Center
Natchez Trace Parkway
P. O. Box 69
Ridgeland, MS 39158
ph: (601) 856-7546

Mount Rainier National Park
Guest Services
55106 Kernahan Road East
P. O. Box 108
Ashford, WA 98304

National Park Service
U.S. Department of the Interior
P. O. Box 37127
Washington, DC 30013
ph: (202) 208-4621

National Park Service
143 South Third Street
Philadelphia, PA 19106
ph: (215) 597-7013

National Park Service
Guest Services
3055 Prosperity Avenue
Fairfax, VA 22031
ph: (703) 849-9300

National Zoological Park
3001 Connecticut Avenue N.W.
Washington, DC 20008
ph: (202) 673-4800

North Trading Post
P. O. Box 609
West Jefferson, NC 28694
ph: (919) 246-7172

Northwest Interpretive Association
909 First Avenue, Suite 630
Seattle, WA 98104

Parks and History Association
P. O. Box 40060
Washington, DC 20016
ph: (202) 472-3083
fax: (202) 472-3422

Petrified Forest Museum Association
P. O. Box 2277
Petrified Forest National Park, AZ 86028
ph: (602) 524-6228

Ramsey Canyon Preserve
27 Ramsey Canyon Road
Hereford, AZ 85615
ph: (602) 378-2785

Redwood Natural History Association
1111 Second Street
Crescent City, CA 95531
ph: (707) 464-9150
fax: (707) 464-1812

Regional Director of Alaska Region
National Park Service
2525 Gambell Street, Room 107
Anchorage, AK 99503
ph: (907) 257-2690

Regional Director of Midwest Region
National Park Service
1709 Jackson Street
Omaha, NE 68102
ph: (402) 221-3431

Regional Director of National
Capital Region
National Park Service
1100 Ohio Drive S.W.
Washington, DC 20242
ph: (202) 619-7005

Regional Director of North
Atlantic Region
National Park Service
15 State Street
Boston, MA 02109
ph: (617) 223-5001

Regional Director of Pacific Northwest
National Park Service
83 South King Street, Suite 212
Seattle, WA 98104
ph: (206) 442-5565

Regional Director of Rocky
Mountain Region
National Park Service
12795 West Alameda Parkway
Denver, CO 80225
ph: (303) 969-2500

Regional Director of Southeast Region
National Park Service
75 Spring Street
Atlanta, GA 30303
ph: (404) 331-5185

Regional Director of Southwest Region
National Park Service
P. O. Box 728
Santa Fe, NM 87504
ph: (505) 988-6004

Regional Director of Western Region
National Park Service
600 Harrison Street, Suite 600
San Francisco, CA 94107
ph: (415) 744-3876

Rocky Mountain National Park
Forever Resorts Rocky Mountain
Park Company
P. O. Box 2680
Estes Park, CO 80517
ph: (303) 586-9308
fax: (303) 586-8590

Sequoia and Kings Canyon
National Parks
Sequoia Guest Services
P. O. Box A-GF
Sequoia National Park, CA 93262
ph: (209) 565-3381
fax: (209) 565-3249

Sequoia Natural History Association
Ash Mountain
P. O. Box 10
Three Rivers, CA 93271
ph: (209) 565-3756
fax: (209) 565-3497

Shenandoah Natural History
Association
Route 4
P. O. Box 348
Luray, VA 22835
ph: (703) 999-3581

Southwest Natural and Cultural
Heritage Association
Drawer E
Albuquerque, NM 87103
ph: (505) 345-9498
fax: (505) 344-1543

Southwest Parks and Monuments
Association
221 North Court Avenue
Tucson, AZ 85701
ph: (602) 622-1999
fax: (602) 623-9519

Thunderbird Lodge
P. O. Box 548
Chinle, AZ 86503
ph: (602) 674-5841
fax: (602) 674-5844

Valley Forge Park Interpretive
Association
Valley Forge National Historical Park
Valley Forge, PA 19481
ph: (610) 783-1074

Virginia Peaks of Otter Company
P. O. Box 489
Bedford, VA 24523
ph: (703) 586-1081

Visitor Services Fort Laramie National
Historic Site
P. O. Box 218
Ft. Laramie, WY 82212
ph: (307) 837-2221
fax: (307) 837-2223

Wind Cave Concession
Wind Cave National Park
P. O. Box 310
Hot Springs, TN 57747
ph: (605) 745-3771

Yellowstone Association
P. O. Box 117
Yellowstone National Park, WY 82190
ph: (307) 344-2293

Yosemite Association
P. O. Box 230
El Portal, CA 95318
ph: (209) 379-2646

Yosemite National Park
Yosemite Concessions Services
Corporation
P. O. Box 455
Yosemite National Park, CA 95389
ph: (209) 372-1228
fax: (209) 372-1218

COOPERATIVES

Oklahoma Indian Arts and
Crafts Cooperative
P. O. Box 966
Anadarko, OK 73005
ph: (405) 247-3486

Village Artisans Cooperative
220 Xenia Avenue
Yellow Springs, OH 45387
ph: (513) 767-1209

RETAIL FAIRS AND STREET MARKETS

Burgers and barbecued chicken sizzle over the grill. Hints of hickory-smoked charcoal waft through the air, mingling with the enticing aroma of freshly popped corn. Guitar chords and harmonica sounds drift in and out of the subconscious, recalling familiar tunes. Adults weave in and out of stalls, lingering over the grooved lines of earthenware pots or running their fingers over smooth, lathe-turned wood bowls. "How much?" they ask. Sticky-fingered children scatter here and there looking for something other than pottery to amuse them. Originally conceived as outdoor venues, retail art fairs and festivals celebrate music and crafts and provide a relaxed atmosphere in which artists and customers can exchange ideas.

Retail fairs are ideally suited to both new craftspeople and veteran exhibitors alike. They put artisans in direct contact with their ultimate customers, and they provide the perfect place to test product marketability. Craftmakers get immediate consumer feedback and can test new designs and prices. Participation in these fairs allows for broad exposure to a variety of customers with relatively little cost and time commitment. Publicity is a key factor in enticing customers to these venues; fair organizers promote their fairs heavily and in doing so ensure a large audience turn out.

Not only do these fairs offer a showcase for crafts, but they also serve as a forum for networking with other artists. They afford a view of competing work and prices, and they provide craftspeople with professional opportunities to develop their marketing skills and expand their customer base. This may be the first time you receive important feedback about the marketability of your work. For example, wholesale buyers occasionally explore these shows looking for new products, giving you a chance at securing future orders, and sometimes even offering suggestions and direction.

Many of these fairs are exclusively craft oriented; others are general arts festivals. You can participate in juried and non-juried shows. Craft fairs often advertise in craft journals, or to learn more about specific shows, you can contact state arts agencies or state-wide craft organizations. To determine which retail fairs are right for you, consider these factors:

- Theme or mission of the craft fair.
- Fair sponsors.
- Booth fees and associated expenses (such as traveling).
- Booth space assignment.
- Fair location and logistics.
- Fair hours and duration.
- Other exhibitors.
- Publicity and promotional support from the organizers.
- On-site management support during the fair.
- Application deadlines and slide submissions.
- Inclement weather policy.

Bette Ann Libby, a ceramic artist and former organizer of the Mad River Valley Craft Fair in Waitsfield, Vermont, warns that these shows can be grueling. To conserve your energy she advises that you "get lots of sleep, eat well, focus on customers, and be organized."

As both a fair exhibitor and coordinator, she is sensitive to issues concerning both the buyers and the craftspeople. Her focus was that these shows maintain a balance between education (with appropriate craft demonstrations) and entertainment (amusing the children in a safe environment). She believes fairs should provide appreciation for how crafts are made, not just exist as exclusive venues for selling products.

"This is not high-pressured selling," Libby says. "I always thought of these fairs as giving a big party. You want people to be relaxed when they buy." She sees a benefit to exhibiting at the same fairs over and over. "Small shows can have longevity. They have developed a market, and repeat customers come to see what's new. People followed my work, invested in my history. Who you are as a person goes beyond the object and adds credibility. It makes it more interesting for [your customers].

"One of the great values of these shows is the networking. You make friendships that last. Everyone sets up their own booths, but craftspeople tend to help each other out and give advice to new people. It's not that competitive."

This selling experience is good for crafters. It's helpful to learn about market demands. In addition, Libby advises that you bring more lower-priced work, but also have a portfolio showing your expensive pieces. She suggests that you send advance notice about the fairs to your customers and also use these shows to develop your mailing lists. Once at the fair, talk to others working in your medium. And above all, enjoy the experience and get energized from it.

RETAIL FAIR ORGANIZERS

American Concern for Artistry
and Craftsmanship
P. O. Box 650
Montclair, NJ
ph: (201) 746-0091

American Craft Council
72 Spring Street
New York, NY 10012
ph: (212) 274-0630
fax: (212) 274-0650

American Craft Enterprises
P. O. Box 10
New Paltz, NY 12561
ph: (914) 255-0039

American Folk Arts Festival
601 North McDowell Boulevard
Petaluma, CA 94954
ph: (800) 321-1213

Artfolio
P. O. Box 136
Old Greenwich, CT 06870

Artrider Productions
4 Deming Street
Woodstock, NY 12498
ph: (914) 679-7277
fax: (914) 679-4185

California Artists
P. O. Box 1963
Burlingame, CA 94011
ph: (415) 348-7699

Carolina Craftsmen
1240 Oakland Avenue
Greensboro, NC 27403
ph: (910) 274-5550

Chautauqua Crafts Alliance
P. O. Box 389
Fredonia, NY 14063
ph: (716) 679-3413

Connie Hines and Fine Company
P. O. Box 1020
Monroe, LA 71210

Country Folk Art Shows
8393 East Holly Road
Holly, MI 48442
ph: (810) 634-4151
fax: (810) 634-3718

Crafter's Corner
Route 1
P. O. Box 307-R
Croghn, NY 13327
ph: (315) 346-6944

Craft Producers
P. O. Box 490
Charlotte, VT 05445
ph: (802) 425-3399
fax: (802) 425-3711

Crafts America
P. O. Box 603
Greens Farms, CT 06436
ph: (203) 254-0486

Craftsmen's Guild of Mississippi
Mississippi Crafts Center
P. O. Box 69
Ridgeland, MS 39158
ph: (601) 856-7546
fax: (601) 981-0019

Eckerstrom Productions
5151 Cold Springs Drive
Foresthill, CA 95631
ph: (916) 367-4557

Fieldstone Shows
6 Deerfield Drive
Medfield, MA 02052
ph: (508) 359-6546

G and C Crafters
P. O. Box 4798
Sonora, CA 95370
ph: (209) 533-2400

Guilford Handcraft Center
P. O. Box 589
411 Church Street
Guilford, CT 06437
ph: (203) 453-5947
fax: (203) 453-6237

International Artists
P. O. Box 3039
San Bernadino, CA
ph: (909) 883-2061

Kentuck Association
500 McFarland Boulevard
Northport, AL 35476
ph: (205) 758-1257
fax: (205) 758-1258

Laumeier Sculpture Park
12580 Rott Road
St. Louis, MO 63127
ph: (314) 821-1209
fax: (314) 821-1248

Marketechs
3425 Woodbridge Court, Suite 4
York, PA 17402
ph: (717) 764-2588

Mid-America Festivals
3525 145th Street West
Shakopee, MN 55379
ph: (612) 445-7361

Minnesota Art Fairs
2400 Third Avenue South
Minneapolis, MN 55404
ph: (612) 870-3200

National Black Arts Festival
236 Forsyth Street
Atlanta, GA 30303
ph: (404) 730-7315

North East Promotions
274 Silas Deane Highway
Wethersfield, CT 06109
ph: (203) 529-2123
fax: (203) 529-2317

Pennsylvania National Arts
and Crafts Show
P. O. Box 449
New Cumberland, PA 17070
ph: (717) 763-1254

The Philadelphia Craft Show
P. O. Box 7646
Philadelphia, PA 19101

Portland Craft Show
6 Dow Road
P. O. Box 228
Deer Isle, ME 04627
ph: (207) 348-9943

Quilts Incorporated
7660 Woodway Drive, Suite 550
Houston, TX 77063
ph: (713) 496-0033

Rockwood Museum
610 Shipley Road
Wilmington, DE 19809
ph: (302) 761-4340
fax: (302) 764-4570

Southwest Arts and Crafts Festival
525 San Pedro N.E., Suite 107
Albuquerque, NM 87108
ph: (505) 262-2448

Summerfair
P. O. Box 8287
Cincinnati, OH 45208
ph: (513) 531-0050

United Craft Enterprises
P. O. Box 326
Masonville, NY 13804
ph: (607) 265-3230

Washington Crafts Show
Women's Committee of Smithsonian
Associates
Arts and Industries Building
Smithsonian Institute
Washington, DC 20560
ph: (202) 357-2700

Waterfront Festivals
4 Greenleaf Woods Drive, Suite 302
Portsmouth, NH 03801
ph: (207) 439-2021
fax: (207) 439-1433

Wyoming State Museum
Barrett Building
Cheyenne, WY 82002
ph: (307) 777-7022

SOCIALLY RESPONSIBLE BUSINESSES
AND ALTERNATIVE TRADE ORGANIZATIONS

Companies that address today's environmental and social issues belong to a network of businesses that are described as "socially responsible." Often referred to as *green* businesses, they care about their communities and the environment, invest in businesses that create jobs, and support fair trade. These organizations promote crafts that make use of recycled material or environmentally sound packaging and thereby contribute to a sustainable future for their surrounding communities.

Often these companies work in conjunction with alternative- or fair-trade organizations (ATOs). For instance, The Body Shop, founded by Anita Roddick, is an example of a socially conscious business that works with fair-trade groups to improve economic conditions and foster healthy communities around the world. Its "Values and Visions" division encourages job opportunities and sustainable development both locally and internationally. For example, it buys from Urban Alternatives in Baltimore, a group that works with at-risk youths to collect abandoned pallets, recycle them, and turn them into soap dishes for The Body Shop. This dedication fosters long-term commitment to preserving the balance of ecosystems and improving both the workplace and social problems. As Paul Hawken, founder of *Smith & Hawken,* is quoted as saying in a fact sheet on green businesses, "Business is the only mechanism on the planet today powerful enough to reverse global environmental and social degradation."

If you are part of this "green" effort, you might consider joining Co-op America, a national nonprofit group that deals with these concerns. Its annual directory, *National Green Pages,* lists environmentally and socially responsible businesses in America (call 202-872-5307 to order). If you create crafts using renewable or recycled material, networking with similarly minded groups might introduce new marketing options to you.

A product that is not recyclable, reusable, or sustainable must at least be ecologically sound in order for Stan Dobert to consider offering it in Ecoworks, his store in Austin, Texas. "Our mission," he says, "is to try to present recycling and environmental awareness to mainstream America in an economical way." Dobert believes that only a small segment of the population has this awareness. By offering three major categories of attractive, in-demand merchandise—gifts, clothes, and shoes—he creates an easy involvement for customers who want to contribute to this effort but don't know how.

Ecoworks' products, Dobert says, are "cool, funky, and real attractive." He wants to make it convenient for consumers to participate in the ecological movement, and also to improve the lives of people around the world. "I hear customers saying, 'Look at this, isn't it cool? And it helps the environment.'

"We built the whole store from recycled material—the entire infrastructure. We took a hardwood floor from an old mansion south of Dallas, disassembled and remilled it for our floor. We added recycled glass tiles to lead people on a path through the store, and we used corrugated tin (similar to iron) for the infrastructure and compact florescent lighting throughout the store. The 2 × 4s and the 4 × 4s, which usually go to a landfill when a building is gutted, we bought from Habitat for Humanity, which puts disabled people to work."

Ecoworks sells gifts, jewelry, and clothes that reuse old items—things like recycled computer chips, old license plates, inner tubes, and even silver nitrate that Eastman Kodak discards from its film production. Dobert is willing to try almost any craft that incorporates something recycled; however, he is a businessman as well as a socially responsible business, and he will stop carrying an item that doesn't sell well. He feels that artisans don't think often enough about their final retail prices, and he offers this advice: "Sometimes a product is too expensive. First you must see if there is consumer acceptance. Build a few samples, find the right price, see if they sell. Then adjust your prices. People come in with weird items they haven't tried in the market. Before you invest in the machinery and materials, find out if the product is salable. And, be price conscious." In other words, do market surveys, research, and analysis first.

Also socially responsible, culturally sensitive, and protective of the environment, alternative trade organizations share the goals of businesses such as Ecoworks. These international trade groups view the promotion and selling of crafts as a positive effort to increase and sustain economic development in low-income communities around the world. ATOs provide technical assistance to artisans, help them obtain fair prices and find viable markets for their products, assist them in becoming self-sufficient, and encourage them to conserve resources and protect the environment.

ATOs, usually nonprofit organizations, purchase crafts from producers in developing countries. They strive to create fair trade relationships, working on a lower profit margin than for-profit importers by returning a higher monetary percentage back to the artisan. They also attempt to educate customers about indigenous crafts and the people who create them.

Wholesalers, retailers, and producers who work in fair trade venues or support the mission through product-development assistance, market links, education, or technical services can become members of the Fair Trade Federation (FTF). The FTF can be a valuable resource; consider getting resources from an FTF member if you incorporate imported, indigenous handwork into your own craft pieces. For example, you might buy fabric from one of these groups to use in a handmade garment.

SOCIALLY RESPONSIBLE BUSINESSES

Art-Y-Facts
2002 W Olmos Drive
San Antonio, TX 78201

The Beaded Lizard
732 North New Street
West Chester, PA 19380
ph: (610) 429-9366

Cadeaux du Monde
140 Bellevue Avenue
Newport, RI 02840
ph: (401) 848-0550
fax: (401) 624-8224

Colleen's Gardens and Native Arts
P. O. Box 68
Marvin, SD 57251
ph: (605) 398-6923

Cottonwoods
155 East Wilson Street
Madison, WI 53703
ph: (608) 251-7507

Coxberry Bookshop
1102 North Rolling Road
Catonsville, MD 21228
ph: (410) 788-1900

Crafty Lady and Book Trader
1194 Scenic Way
Rimforest, CA 92378
ph: (909) 355-5355

Cross Cultural Crafts
499-C Pennsylvania Avenue
Glen Ellyn, IL 60137
ph: (708) 790-1166

Crowded Closet
1121 Gilbert Court
Iowa City, IA 52240
ph: (319) 337-5924

Down to Earth
P. O. Box 865
Madison, VA 22727
ph: (540) 948-6257

Dove of Peace
3445 North 980 West
Shipshewana, IN 46565
ph: (219) 768-4221

Earthcare Paper
P. O. Box 8507
Uriah, WI 95482
ph: (608) 277-2900

Earth Savers
5501 Magazine Street
New Orleans, LA 70115
ph: (504) 899-8555

Ecosentials
69 Elliot Street
Brattleboro, VT 05301
ph: (802) 257-9377

Ecoworks
2901 Capital of Texas Highway
Austin, TX 78746
ph: (512) 328-6422
fax: (512) 328-6456

Environmental Realists
Trading Company
Route 179
P. O. Box 1970
Sedona, AZ 86336
ph: (602) 282-4945

Everything Under the Sun
211 Main Street
P. O. Box 493
Punta Arena, CA 95468
ph: (707) 882-2161

Family Bookshelf and Global Crafts
1511 North Abbe Road
Fairview, MI 48621
ph: (517) 848-5400

Ginger Blossom
3016 Route 173
Richmond, IL 60071
ph: (815) 678-4015
fax: same

Global Gallery
682 North High Street
Columbus, OH 43215
ph: (614) 621-1744

The Global Trader
30 Main Street
Amherst, MA 01002
ph: (413) 256-0769
fax: (413) 549-1135

Good Green Fun
P. O. Box 27
Miami, FL 33257
ph: (800) 684-8882
fax: (305) 663-0605
http://www.gate.net/good-green-fun/

Grass Roots Goods
Denver Urban Ministries
216 South Grant Street
Denver, CO 80209
ph: (303) 777-4896

Grassroots Handcrafts
46 East Main Street
Newark, DE 19711
ph: (302) 453-9751
fax: (302) 369-3406

Green Star Cooperative
P. O. Box 753
Ithaca, NY 14850
ph: (607) 273-9392

Hands Across the Water
24761 77th Crescent
Bellerose, NY 11426
ph: (718) 347-8904

Hands of the World
1501 Pike Place, Suite 428
Seattle, WA 98101
ph: (206) 622-1696

Heartbeats
2052 West 101st Street
Cleveland, OH 44102
ph: (216) 281-7875

Heritage Store
314 Laskin Road
Virginia Beach, VA 23451
ph: (804) 428-0400

Humboldt Express
3301 Interstate B-5 North
Charlotte, NC 28269
ph: (704) 598-8866

International Arts and Gifts
16102 South Park Avenue
South Holland, IL 60473
ph: (708) 596-7281

Just Us
P. O. Box 526
Ouray, CO 81427
ph: (970) 325-4091
fax: (970) 325-0505

Leslie Grace Associates
2068 East 23rd Avenue
Seattle, WA 98112
ph: (206) 323-6668
fax: (206) 323-7656

Los Pastores
Main Street
P. O. Box 118
Los Ojos, NM 87551
ph: (505) 588-7821
fax: (505) 588-9514

Loving Hands Gifts
710 South Rancho Santa Fe
San Marcos, CA 92069
ph: (619) 727-5607

Lydia's Place
1509 River Terrace Drive
East Lansing, MI 48823
ph: (517) 351-9059

Magic Mill
2862 University Avenue
Madison, WI 53705
ph: (608) 238-2630

Many Nations Crafts Shop
2101 West 41st Street
Sioux Falls, SD 57105
ph: (605) 335-6209

Meridian Arts
Rural Route 2
Belgrade Road
P. O. Box 1900
Mount Vernon, ME 04352
ph: (207) 293-2239

Mixik
162 Ripley Street
San Francisco, CA 94110
ph: (415) 285-8596
fax: (415) 285-8597

Moon Dog Traders
29 Katonah Avenue
Katonah, NY 10536
ph: (914) 232-4547

Moravian Tibetan Rug Shop
5045 Reynolda Road
Winston-Salem, NC 27106
ph: (919) 924-9725

Mountainside Market
Gay Street
Little Washington, VA 22747
ph: (540) 987-9100

Multiweave
1300 South Layton Boulevard
Milwaukee, WI 53215
ph: (414) 645-2511

Native Arts and Crafts
109 West 27th Street, 8th floor
New York, NY 10001

Native Material
605 Whitehead Street
Key West, FL 33040
ph: (305) 296-0466

Nobody's Business
P. O. Box 415
Laytonville, CA 95454
ph: (707) 984-6311
fax: (707) 984-8855

Nomads
815 Dempster Street
Evanston, IL 60201
ph: (708) 328-4009
fax: (708) 328-2858

North Country Cooperative
2129 Riverside Avenue South
Minneapolis, MN 55454
ph: (612) 338-3110

Olive Branch
119 Southwest Sixth Street
Topeka, KS 66603
ph: (913) 233-4811

One World Goods
118 Fairport Village Landing
Fairport, NY 14450
ph: (716) 223-6370

One World Handcrafts
226 East Main Street
North Manchester, IN 46962
ph: (219) 982-8540
fax: (219) 982-6868

One World Market
2041 Englewood Avenue
Durham, NC 27705
ph: (919) 286-4036

One World Shoppe
19321 Detroit Avenue
Rocky River, OH 44116
ph: (216) 333-7709
fax: (216) 961-0004

Peacecraft
325-A Chestnut Street
Berea, KY 40403
ph: (606) 986-8666

Penn Alps Craft Store
P. O. Box 5
Grantsville, MD 21536
ph: (301) 895-5986

Planetweavers Treasure Store
1573 Haight Street
San Francisco, CA 94117
ph: (415) 864-4415
fax: (415) 864-7103

Plowshare Gifts
301 West Main Street
Waukesha, WI 53186
ph: (414) 547-5188

Plowsharing Crafts
6271 Delmar Boulevard
St. Louis, MO 63130
ph: (314) 863-3723

River Rats
233 South Second Street
Stillwater, MN 55082
ph: (612) 439-3308

Rowe Pottery Works
404 England Street
Cambridge, WI 53523
ph: (608) 764-5435
fax: (608) 423-4273

Salt of the Earth
509 Market Street
Cheraw, SC 29520

Spiritual Renewal Center Gift Shop
1118 Court Street
Syracuse, NY 13208
ph: (315) 472-6546

Trade Winds
304 Washington Street Mall
Cape May, NJ 08204
ph: (609) 884-6720

United Nations Gift Center
United Nations Plaza
New York, NY 10017
ph: (212) 963-7700

Unique World Gifts
2609 North Center Street N.W.
Hickory, NC 28601
ph: (704) 328-5595

Window to the World
1056 St. Charles Avenue N.E.
Atlanta, GA 30306
ph: (404) 892-5307

Window to the World
835 East First Street North
Wichita, KS 67202
ph: (316) 267-6013

World Marketplace
10 College Street
Asheville, NC 28801
ph: (704) 254-8374

World's Attic
109 East Main Street
Somerset, PA 15501
ph: (814) 445-4886

The World's Window
4120 Pennsylvania, Suite 10
Kansas City, MO 64111
ph: (816) 756-1514
fax: same

World Treasures
P. O. Box 1397
Fort Dodge, IA 50501
ph: (515) 955-6734

Worldwide Gifts
105 North Walnut Street
Champaign, IL 61820
ph: (217) 352-8200

SPECIALIZED ART GALLERIES

Up-scale art galleries that specialize in a specific field can provide an alternate way to show your work. If you produce high-end crafts, or get your business through commissions, you may want to seek out this exclusive representation.

Michael Monroe, former director of the Smithsonian Institution's Renwick Gallery, expert in the field of American crafts, and current curator-in-charge of the Peter Joseph Gallery in New York City, explains the emergence of these galleries. "In 1972, when Lloyd Herman (founding director of the Renwick) organized the landmark exhibition, Wooden Works, there was only a handful of craft artists making museum-quality, one-of-a-kind pieces in wood. Back in the 1940s, '50s, and '60s, as a result of the GI Bill, hundreds of artisans went back to school to the craft field. With secure teaching jobs at universities, artists were free to take risks while they earned a living. From a handful of artists to hundreds of students, there was now mass participation in the craft movement. With the emergence of craft fairs, the market started to recognize different layers of creativity, financial stratification, and definitions of the state of the craft field."

Now, there is a greater variety of defined markets that specialize in representing all these levels of creativity. For example, the Peter Joseph Gallery show artists working in one particular field. Formed in 1990 by Peter Joseph as a Manhattan venue for wood-craft designers, this gallery represents 19 furniture makers. Its focus is museum-quality, contemporary furniture design.

"Each gallery has a different look, different aesthetic interests," says Monroe. He believes that an artist should visit a gallery several times over the course of a year to understand what it is about. When new artists try to show him their work, he always asks, "Have you been to the gallery before?" If the answer is "no," he wonders, "How serious are you? Would you want to marry someone you've never seen?"

Prices at the Peter Joseph Gallery range from about $1,500 to $100,000. The gallery promotes the careers of its artists, placing their work in museums and with collectors; it has a commitment to its artists. Not only does the gallery give them space and care, but it is also responsible for being "attuned to what is going on in the field" and generating interest among, and educating, the public, thereby creating a popular understanding and appreciation of its artists.

If you're approaching a gallery, Monroe stresses the importance of understanding its role. "No one has time to fiddle around with anyone who doesn't," he says. "It tells you this person is not professional. Someone wanted to show me pewter wall reliefs, but we are known for wood furniture. Visit the gallery; you might have the most wonderful work in the world, but it should be appropriate to the gallery—the same vision, materials, style."

Monroe also wants to see a portfolio that is pulled together professionally with slides, biography, and résumé, and he offers these other suggestions if you want to break into the art-gallery world:

- Enter juried competitions. Look at who's doing the jurying—it should be a museum or recognized gallery because you want to get your work in front of the power brokers who might jot your name down.
- Know your long-term goals. Don't be wishy-washy about what you want to achieve; articulate what you want and work toward it.
- Study your role models.
- Seek out advice as you go up the ladder to the top—and work on the *appropriate* ladder. You have to know which one you want to climb, so pick out one or two. There is no one path, but you must know what you want and who to use in a world so tightly wound. You may flounder if you try too many different areas, and this venue isn't as kind to floaters. It's no different from other fields—it's competitive.
- Prepare and do your homework. Learn everything you can.

The following listing of galleries in The Crafts Center database is fairly extensive but you can check your local directory for additional galleries.

SPECIALIZED ART GALLERIES

Alabama
Jefferson Street Gallery
13 East Jefferson Street
Montgomery, AL 36104
ph: (205) 263-5703

Maralyn Wilson Gallery
10 Cahaba Road
Birmingham, AL 35223
ph: (205) 879-0582

Olland Smith Gallery
1 Jefferson Street North
Huntsville, AL 35801
ph: (205) 534-1982

Alaska
Tonington Gallery
515 F Street
Anchorage, AK 99501
ph: (907) 272-1489

Arizona
Artamerica Gallery of Art
9301 East Shea Boulevard
Scottsdale, AZ 85260
ph: (602) 661-8772

Artistic Galleries
7077 East Main Street
Scottsdale, AZ 85251
ph: (602) 945-6766

Ausi Gallery
38 Camino Otero
Tubac, AZ 85646
ph: (602) 398-3193

Bentley Tomlinson Gallery
4161 North Marshall Way
Scottsdale, AZ 85251
ph: (602) 941-0078

Berta Wright Gallery
260 East Congress Street
Tucson, AZ 85701
ph: (602) 742-4134

Berta Wright Gallery Shops
260 East Congress Street
Tucson, AZ 85701
ph: (602) 882-7043

El Prado Galleries
P. O. Box 1849
Sedona, AZ 86339
ph: (602) 282-7390

Es Posible Gallery
34505 North Scottsdale Road
Scottsdale, AZ 85262
ph: (602) 488-3770

Gallery Ten
7045 East Third Avenue
Scottsdale, AZ 85251
ph: (602) 994-0405

Gallery Three
3819 North Third Street
Phoenix, AZ 85012
ph: (602) 277-9540

Hand and the Spirit
Joanne Rapp Gallery
4222 North Marshall Way
Scottsdale, AZ 85251
ph: (602) 949-1262

Hatathli Gallery
Navajo Community College
Development Foundation
Tsaile, AZ 86556
ph: (602) 724-3311

Honani Crafts Gallery
P. O. Box 221
Second Mesa, AZ 86043
ph: (602) 737-2238

Imagine Gallery
Conrad Leather Boutique
34505 North Scottsdale Road E-8
Scottsdale, AZ 85262
ph: (602) 488-2190

La Fuente Gallery
B123 Tlaquepaue
P. O. Box 2169
Sedona, AZ 86339
ph: (602) 282-5276

The Mind's Eye Craft Gallery
4200 North Marshall Way
Scottsdale, AZ 85251
ph: (602) 941-2494

Obsidian Gallery
4340 North Campbell Avenue,
Suite 90
Tucson, AZ 85718
ph: (602) 577-3598
fax: (602) 577-9018

Pink Adobe Gallery
222 East Congress Street
Tucson, AZ 85701
ph: (602) 623-2828

Raku Gallery
General Delivery
P. O. Box 965
Jerome, AZ 86331
ph: (602) 639-0239

Sun West Gallery
152 South Montezuma Street
Prescott, AZ 86303
ph: (602) 778-1204

Suzanne Brown Galleries
7160 East Main Street
Scottsdale, AZ 85251
ph: (602) 945-8475

Totally Southwestern Gallery
5575 River Road, Suite 181
Tucson, AZ 85715
ph: (602) 577-2295

Arkansas
Contemporanea Gallery
516 Central Avenue
Hot Springs, AR 71901
ph: (501) 624-0516

California
Affinity Gallery
1592 Union Street, Suite 103
San Francisco, CA 94123
ph: (415) 567-5508

Allen Fine Art Gallery
37656 Bankside Drive
Cathedral City, CA 92234
ph: (619) 341-8655

Allrich Gallery
251 Post Street
San Francisco, CA 94108
ph: (415) 398-8896

Ambiance Gallery
405 Second Street
Eureka, CA 95501
ph: (707) 445-8950
fax: (707) 443-3654

The Art Collector's Gallery
4151 Taylor Street
San Diego, CA 92110
ph: (619) 299-3232
fax: (619) 299-8709

Artifax Int'l Gallery & Gifts
450 First Street East, Suite C
Sonoma, CA 95476
ph: (707) 996-9494

Artists' Collaborative Gallery
1007 Second Street
Old Town
Sacramento, CA 95814
ph: (916) 444-3764

Banaker Gallery
251 Post Street, Suite 310
San Francisco, CA 94108
ph: (415) 397-1397

Bayside Gallery
P. O. Box 182208
Coronado, CA 92178

Bendice Gallery
380 First Street, Suite W
Sonoma, CA 95476
ph: (707) 938-2775

Beth Christensen Fine Art
538 Silverado Drive
Tiburon, CA 94920
ph: (415) 435-2314

The Braunstein Quay Gallery
250 Sutter Street
San Francisco, CA 94108
ph: (415) 392-5532

Brendan Walter Gallery
1001 Colorado Avenue
Santa Monica, CA 90401
ph: (310) 395-1155

CA Contemporary Crafts
Association Gallery
109 Corte Madera Town Center
Corte Madera, CA 94925
ph: (415) 331-8520

California Art Gallery
305 North Coast Highway, Suite A
Laguna Beach, CA 94966
ph: (415) 927-3158

Caskey Lees Gallery
P. O. Box 1409
Topanga, CA 90290
ph: (310) 455-2886

Cavanaugh Gallery
415 Main Street
Half Moon Bay, CA 94019
ph: (415) 726-7771

Cecile Moochnek Gallery
1809-D Fourth Street
Berkeley, CA 94710
ph: (510) 549-1018

Cedanna Gallery
400 Main Street
Half Moon Bay, CA 94019
ph: (415) 726-6776

Claudia Chapline Gallery
3445 Shoreline Highway
P. O. Box 946
Stinson Beach, CA 94970
ph: (415) 868-2308

Clyde Street Gallery
34 Clyde Street
San Francisco, CA 94107
ph: (415) 546-5185

Coast Galleries
P. O. Box 223519
Carmel, CA 93922
ph: (408) 625-4145
fax: (408) 625-3575

Coast Gallery
Highway One
Big Sur, CA 93920
ph: (408) 667-2301

CODA Gallery
73151 El Paseo
Palm Desert, CA 92260
ph: (619) 346-4661

Collage Studio Gallery
1345 18th Street
San Francisco, CA 94107
ph: (415) 282-4401

Compositions Gallery
317 Sutter Street
San Francisco, CA 94108
ph: (415) 693-9111

The Courtyard Gallery
1349 Park Street
Alameda, CA 94501
ph: (415) 521-1521

Couturier Gallery
166 North La Brea Avenue
Los Angeles, CA 90036
ph: (213) 933-5557

David Austin Contemporary Art
355 West El Portal
Palm Springs
San Francisco, CA 92264
ph: (619) 322-7709

Del Mano Gallery
11981 San Vicente Boulevard
Los Angeles, CA 90049
ph: (310) 476-8508

Del Mano Gallery
33 East Colorado Boulevard
Pasadena, CA 91105
ph: (818) 793-6648

DEVERA Gallery
334 Hayes Street
San Francisco, CA 94102
ph: (415) 861-8480

The Devorzon Gallery
8687 Melrose Avenue, Suite BL-88
Los Angeles, CA 90069
ph: (310) 659-0555

Dorothy Weiss Gallery
256 Sutter Street
San Francisco, CA 94108
ph: (415) 397-3611

Editions Limited/The Joanne
Chappel Gallery
625 Second Street, Suite 400
San Francisco, CA 94107
ph: (415) 777-1390
fax: same

Eileen Kremen Gallery
619 North Harbor Boulevard
Fullerton, CA 92632
ph: (714) 879-1391

Elegant Earth Gallery
13101 Highway 9
Boulder Creek, CA 95006
ph: (408) 338-3646

Elizabeth Fortner Gallery
100 West Micheltorena Street
Santa Barbara, CA 93101
ph: (805) 969-9984

Feingarten Galleries
P. O. Box 5383
Beverly Hills, CA 90209
ph: (310) 274-7042

Fine Gallery
P. O. Box 1494
Sutter Creek, CA 95685
ph: (209) 267-0571

Fine Woodworking Gallery
1201-C Bridgeway
Sausalito, CA 94965
ph: (415) 332-5770

Freehand Gallery
8413 West Third Street
Los Angeles, CA 90048
ph: (213) 655-2607

The Gallery
329 Promrose Road
Burlingame, CA 94010
ph: (415) 347-9392

Gallery Alexander
7850 Girard Avenue
La Jolla, CA 92037
ph: (619) 459-9433
fax: (619) 459-0080

Gallery Eight
7464 Girard Avenue
La Jolla, CA 92037
ph: (619) 454-9781

Gallery Fair
P. O. Box 263
Mendocino, CA 95460
ph: (707) 937-5121
fax: (707) 937-2405

Gallery Fourteen
300 Napa Street, Slip 21
Sausalito, CA 94965
ph: (510) 547-7608

Gallery K
314 Meadowbrook Drive
Santa Barbara, CA 93108
ph: (818) 907-5560

A Gallery of Fine Art
73580 El Paseo
Palm Desert, CA 92260
ph: (619) 346-8885

Gallery of Functional Art
2429 Main Street
Santa Monica, CA 90405
ph: (310) 450-2827

Gallery One
32 Liberty Street
Petaluma, CA 94952
ph: (707) 778-8277

Garrett White Gallery
664 South Coast Highway
Laguna Beach, CA 92652
ph: (909) 982-3349

Garth Clark Gallery
170 South La Brea
Los Angeles, CA 90036
ph: (213) 939-2189

Gregory Gallery
3406 Via Lido
Newport Beach, CA 92663
ph: (714) 723-0887
fax: (714) 723-0889

Gump's Gallery
250 Post Street
San Francisco, CA 94108
ph: (415) 982-1616

Hank Baum Gallery
2842 Pierce Street
San Francisco, CA 94123
ph: (415) 752-4336

Henley's Gallery
1000 Annapolis Road
Sea Ranch, CA 95497
ph: (707) 785-2951

Highlands Sculpture Gallery
Dolores between Fifth and Sixth Streets
Carmel, CA 93921
ph: (408) 624-0535

Highlight Gallery
P. O. Box 1515
45052 Main Street
Mendocino, CA 95460
ph: (707) 937-3132

ICAAN Galleries
223 Manhattan Beach Boulevard,
Suite 107
Manhattan Beach, CA 90266
ph: (310) 376-6171

International Gallery
643 G Street
San Diego, CA 92101
ph: (619) 235-8255

Ira Wolk Gallery
1235 Main Street
St. Helena, CA 94574
ph: (707) 963-8801

Joanne Chappel Gallery
625 Second Street, Suite 302
San Francisco, CA 94107
ph: (415) 777-5711

Joan Robey Gallery
2912 Fourth Street
Santa Monica, CA 90405
ph: (310) 394-5181

John Natsoulas Gallery
140 F Street
Davis, CA 95616
ph: (916) 756-3938

Joslyn Studio & Art Gallery
General Delivery
P. O. Box 596
Coloma, CA 95613
ph: (916) 621-2049

Kurland/Summers Gallery
13428 Maxella Avenue, Suite 388
Marina Del Rey, CA 90292
ph: (213) 659-7098

La Vae Gallery
4703 Spring Street
La Mesa, CA 91941
ph: (619) 463-3886

Legends Gallery
483 First Street West
Sonoma, CA 95476
ph: (707) 939-8100

Lori's Art Gallery
20929 Ventura Boulevard
Woodlands Hills, CA 91364
ph: (818) 884-1110

Martin Lawrence Galleries
2855 Stevens Creek Boulevard
Santa Clara, CA 95050
ph: (408) 985-8885

Master's Mark Gallery
3228 Sacramento Street
San Francisco, CA 94115
ph: (415) 885-6700

Matrix Gallery
1725 F
Sacramento, CA 95814
ph: (916) 441-4818

The Meadowlark Gallery
317 Corte Madera Avenue
Town Center
Corte Madera, CA 94925
ph: (415) 924-2210

Michael Himovitz Gallery
1020 Tenth Street
Sacramento, CA 95814
ph: (916) 448-8723

A New Leaf Gallery
1286 Gilman Street
Berkeley, CA 94706
ph: (510) 525-7621

The Outside-In Gallery
6909 Melrose Avenue
Los Angeles, CA 90038
ph: (213) 933-4096

The Pacific Gallery
P. O. Box 844
Dana Point, CA 92629
ph: (714) 494-8732

Painted Lady Gallery
1407 Jackson Gate Road
Jackson, CA 95642
ph: (209) 223-1754

The Palumbo Gallery
Dolores Street (at Sixth)
P. O. Box 5727
Carmel, CA 93921
ph: (408) 625-5727

Pazar Gallery
23561 Malibu Colony Road
Malibu, CA 90265
ph: (310) 456-1142

The Plaza Gallery
746 Higuera Street, Suite 8
San Luis Obispo, CA 93401
ph: (805) 543-5681

Plums Contemporary Art
5096 North Palm Avenue
Fresno, CA 93704
ph: (209) 227-5389

Posner Gallery
1119 Montana Avenue
Santa Monica, CA 90403
ph: (310) 260-8858
fax: (310) 260-8860

Potpourri Gallery
4100 Redwood Road
Oakland, CA 94619
ph: (510) 531-1503

Primavera Gallery
214 East Ojai Avenue
Ojai, CA 93023
ph: (805) 646-7133

Red Rose Gallery
2251 Chestnut Street
San Francisco, CA 94123
ph: (415) 776-6871

Roberge Gallery
73520 El Paseo
Palm Desert, CA 92260
ph: (619) 340-5045

Rookie-To Gallery
14300 Highway 128
P. O. Box 606
Boonville, CA 95415
ph: (707) 895-2204

Ruth Bachofner Gallery
2046 Broadway
Santa Monica, CA 90404
ph: (310) 458-8007

Santa Fe Gallery
2797 Union Street
San Francisco, CA 94123
ph: (415) 346-0181

Schwartz Cierlak Gallery
26106 Paolino Place
Valencia, CA 91355
ph: (213) 396-3814

Seekers Collection & Gallery
2450 Main Street
Cambria, CA 93428
ph: (805) 927-8626

Sharon Park Gallery
325 Sharon Park Drive
Menlo Park, CA 94025
ph: (415) 854-6878

Sherwood Gallery
460 South Coast Highway
Laguna Beach, CA 92651
ph: (714) 497-3185

Signature Gallery
3693 Fifth Avenue
San Diego, CA 92103
ph: (619) 297-0430

Simpson Heller Gallery
2289 Main Street
Cambria, CA 93428
ph: (805) 927-1800

Soft Touch Artists Collective Gallery
1580 Haight Street
San Francisco, CA 93428
ph: (805) 927-1800

Stary Sheets Fine Art Gallery
14988 Sand Canyon Avenue
Irvine, CA 92718
ph: (714) 733-0445

Steve Stein Gallery
13934 Ventura Boulevard
Sherman Oaks, CA 91423
ph: (818) 990-0777

Summer House Gallery
14 Miller Avenue
Mill Valley, CA 94941
ph: (415) 383-6695

Susan Cummins Gallery
12 Miller Avenue
Mill Valley, CA 94941
ph: (415) 383-1512

TAFOYA Gallery
2105 South Bascom Street
Lincoln Court Building 110
Campbell, CA 95008
ph: (408) 559-6161

TAKADA Fine Arts Gallery
251 Post, 6th floor
San Francisco, CA 94108
ph: (415) 956-5288

Tarbox Gallery
1202 Kettner Boulevard
San Diego, CA 92101
ph: (619) 234-5020

Taylor Gratzer Gallery
8667 West Sunset Boulevard
West Hollywood, CA 90069
ph: (213) 659-6422

Ten Directions Gallery
723 Santa Ysabel Avenue
Los Osos, CA 93402
ph: (805) 528-4574

Tercera Gallery
24 North Santa Cruz Avenue
Los Gatos, CA 95030
ph: (408) 354-9482

Tesori Gallery
319 South Robertson Boulevard
Los Angeles, CA 90048
ph: (213) 273-9890

Tesori Gallery
30 East Third Avenue
San Mateo, CA 94401
ph: (415) 344-4731

Third World Art Exchange
2016 North Hillhurst Avenue
Los Angeles, CA 90027
ph: (213) 666-9357

Tops Gallery
23410 Civic Center Way
Malibu, CA 90265
ph: (310) 456-8677

The Trove Gallery
73700 El Paseo
Palm Desert, CA 92260
ph: (619) 346-1999

Valerie Miller Fine Art
611 South Muirfield Road
Los Angeles, CA 92260
ph: (213) 467-1511

Valerie Miller Fine Art
73100 El Paseo
Palm Desert, CA 92260
ph: (619) 773-4483

Victor Fischer Galleries
1525 Santanella Terrace
Corona Del Mar, CA 92625
ph: (714) 644-9655

Victor Fischer Galleries
1300 Clay Street, Suite 510
Oakland, CA 94612
ph: (510) 464-8044

The Viewpoint Gallery
224 The Crossroads
Carmel, CA 93923
ph: (408) 624-3369

Viewpoints Gallery
11315 Highway
P. O. Box 670
Point Reyes Station, CA 94956
ph: (415) 663-8861

Virginia Breier Gallery
3091 Sacramento Street
San Francisco, CA 94115
ph: (415) 929-7173

Walter White Fine Arts
107 Capitol Avenue
Capitola, CA 95010
ph: (408) 476-7001

Wellspring Gallery
3330 South Robertson Boulevard
Los Angeles, CA 90034
ph: (310) 441-4204

Wellspring Gallery
120 Broadway, Suite 105
Santa Monica, CA 90401
ph: (310) 451-1924

The Wild Blue Gallery
7220 Melrose Place
Los Angeles, CA 90046
ph: (213) 939-8434

Wing Gallery
13529 Ventura Boulevard
Sherman Oaks, CA 91423
ph: (818) 981-9464
fax: (818) 981-2787

Z Gallery
5500 West 83 Street
Los Angeles, CA 90045
ph: (310) 410-6655

Colorado
Aspen Mountain Gallery
555 East Durant
Aspen, CO 80206
ph: (303) 925-5083

Canyon Road Gallery
257 Fillmore Street
Denver, CO 80206
ph: (303) 321-4139

David Floria Gallery
6 Wood Creek Place
Wood Creek, CO 81656
ph: (303) 923-5705

Four Directions Gallery
117 Eighth Street
Steamboat Springs, CO 80487
ph: (303) 870-9188

Gingerbread Square Gallery
649 Quince Circle
Boulder, CO 80304
ph: (303) 443-3180

Gothelf's Gallery
122 East Meadow Drive
Vail, CO 81657
ph: (303) 476-1777

Heather Gallery
555 East Durant Avenue
Aspen, CO 81611
ph: (303) 925-6641

Hibberd McGrath Gallery
General Delivery
P. O. Box 7638
Breckenridge, CO 80424
ph: (303) 453-6391

Howell Gallery
1420 Larimer Street
Denver, CO 80202
ph: (303) 820-3925

J. Cotter Gallery
234 Wall Street
P. O. Box 385
Vail, CO 81657
ph: (303) 476-3131

Maxims Art Gallery
818 Ninth Street
Greeley, CO 80631
ph: (970) 352-9341

Mill Street Gallery
112 South Mill Street
Aspen, CO 81611
ph: (303) 925-4988

The Panache Craft Gallery
315 Columbine Street
Denver, CO 80206
ph: (303) 321-8069

Reiss Gallery
429 Acoma Street
Denver, CO 80204
ph: (303) 778-6924
fax: (303) 776-6633

Robischon Gallery
1740 Wazee Street
Denver, CO 80202
ph: (303) 298-7788

A Show of Hands Gallery
2440 East Third Avenue
Denver, CO 80206
ph: (303) 920-3071

Susan Duval Gallery
525 East Cooper Street
Aspen, CO 81611
ph: (303) 925-9044

Tavelli Gallery
555 North Mill Street
Aspen, CO 80206
ph: (303) 920-3071

21st Century Gallery
235 Fillmore Street
Denver, CO 80206
ph: (303) 320-0926

The Unique Gallery
11 East Bijou Street
Colorado Springs, CO 80903
ph: (719) 473-9406

The Upperedge Gallery
Snowmass Village, Upper Level
P. O. Box 5294
Snowmass Village, CO 81615
ph: (303) 923-5373

The White Hart Gallery
843 Lincoln Avenue
Steamboats Springs, CO 80487
ph: (303) 879-1015

Connecticut
Atelier Studio Gallery
27 East Street
New Milford, CT 06776
ph: (203) 354-7792

Brown-Grotta Gallery
39 Grumman Hill Road
Wilton, CT 06897
ph: (203) 834-0623

Endleman Gallery
1014 Chapel Street
New Haven, CT 06510
ph: (203) 776-2517

Evergreen Gallery
21 Boston Street
Guilford, CT 06437
ph: (203) 453-4324

Fisher Gallery Shop
Farmington Valley Arts Center
25 Arts Center Lane
Avon Park North
Avon, CT 06001
ph: (203) 678-1867

Gallery Shop at Wesleyan Potters
350 South Main Street
Middletown, CT 06457
ph: (203) 344-0039

The Gifted Hand Gallery
966-B Farmington Avenue
West Hartford, CT 06107
ph: (860) 236-9978
fax: (860) 236-9979

Heron American Craft Gallery
P. O. Box 535
Main Street
Kent, CT 06757
ph: (203) 927-4804

Mendelson Gallery
Titus Square
Washington Depot, CT 06794
ph: (203) 868-0307

The Red Pepper Gallery
41 Main Street
Chester, CT 06412
ph: (203) 526-4460

The Silo Gallery
44 Upland Road
New Milford, CT 06776
ph: (203) 335-0300

Starshire Gallery
319 Horse Hill Road
Westbrook, CT 06498
ph: (203) 399-5149

Variations Gallery
P. O. Box 246
Route 20
Riverton, CT 06065
ph: (203) 379-2964

Delaware
Blue Streak Gallery
1723 Delaware Avenue
Wilmington, DE 19806
ph: (302) 429-0506

The Station Gallery
3922 Kennett Pike
Greenville, DE 19807
ph: (302) 654-8638

District of Columbia
Aaron Gallery
1717 Connecticut Avenue N.W.
Washington, DC 20009
ph: (202) 234-3311

Addison/Ripley Gallery
9 Hillyer Court N.W.
Washington, DC 20008
ph: (202) 328-2332

Anne O'Brien Gallery
4829 Bending Lane Northwest
Washington, DC 20007
ph: (202) 265-9697

The Collector Art Gallery
1500 New Hampshire Avenue N.W.
Dupont Plaza Hotel
Washington, DC 20036
ph: (202) 797-0160

Jackey Chalkley Gallery
Chevy Chase Plaza
5301 Wisconsin Avenue N.W.
Washington, DC 20015
ph: (202) 686-8882

Jackey Chalkley Gallery
1455 Pennsylvania Avenue N.W.
Washington, DC 20004
ph: (202) 683-3060

Jackey Chalkley Gallery
5301 Wisconsin Avenue N.W.
Washington, DC 20015
ph: (202) 537-6100

Jackey Chalkley Gallery
3301 New Mexico Avenue N.W.
Washington, DC 20016
ph: (202) 686-8882

Jewelers Werk Galerie
2000 Pennsylvania Avenue N.W.
Washington, DC 20006
ph: (202) 293-0249

Maureen Littleton Gallery
1667 Wisconsin Avenue N.W.
Washington, DC 20007
ph: (202) 333-9307

Miya Gallery
410 Eighth Street N.W.
Washington, DC 20004
ph: (202) 347-6330

Sun Gallery Goldsmiths
2322 18th Street N.W.
Washington, DC 20009
ph: (202) 265-9341

The Touchstone Gallery
2009 R Street N.W.
Washington, DC 20009
ph: (202) 797-7278

Florida
Albertson Peterson Gallery
329 South Park Avenue
Winter Park, FL 32789
ph: (407) 628-1258

Alexander's Fine Arts Gallery
1517 East Seventh Avenue, Suite A
Tampa, FL 33605
ph: (813) 247-6363

Bayfront Gallery
713 South Palafox Street
Pensacola, FL 32501
ph: (904) 438-7556

Belvetro Glass Gallery
934 Lincoln Road
Miami Beach, FL 33139
ph: (305) 673-6677

Center Street Gallery
136 South Park Avenue
Winter Park, FL 32389
ph: (407) 644-1545

Christy/Taylor Galleries
410 Plaza Real
Mizner Park
Boca Raton, FL 33432
ph: (407) 750-7302

Clay Space Gallery
924 Lincoln Road
Miami Beach, FL 39139
ph: (305) 534-3339

Clayton Galleries
4105 South Macdill Avenue
Tampa, FL 33611
ph: (813) 831-3753

Collectors Gallery
213 West Venice Avenue
Venice, FL 34285
ph: (813) 488-3029

EG Cody Gallery
80 Northeast
40th Street
Miami, FL 33137
ph: (305) 374-4777

Florida Global Gallery
3020 Penmar Drive
Clearwater, FL 34619
ph: (813) 276-3957

Galeria of Sculpture
11 Via Parigi Worth Avenue
Palm Beach, FL 33480
ph: (407) 659-7557

Gallery Camino Real
Gallery Center
608 Banyan Trail
Boca Raton, FL 33428
ph: (407) 241-1606

Gallery Contemporanea
526 Lancaster Street
Jacksonville, FL 32204
ph: (904) 359-0016

Gallery Five
363 Tequesta Drive
Tequesta, FL 33469
ph: (407) 747-5555

Gallery One
1301 Third Street South
Naples, FL 33940
ph: (813) 263-0835

Grand Central Gallery
442 West Central Avenue, Suite 100
Tampa, FL 33606
ph: (813) 254-4977

Green Gallery
1541 Brickell Avenue, Suite 1503
Miami, FL 33129
ph: (305) 858-7868

Habitat Galleries
608 Banyan Trail
Boca Raton, FL 33431
ph: (407) 241-4544

HB Brickell Gallery
905 South Bayshore Drive
Miami, FL 33131
ph: (305) 358-2088

Heller Gallery Palm Beach
203 Worth Avenue
Palm Beach, FL 33480
ph: (407) 833-4457

Hodgell Gallery
46 South Palm Avenue
Sarasota, FL 34236
ph: (813) 366-1146

Hoffman Gallery
4070 Northeast 15th Terrace
Fort Lauderdale, FL 33334
ph: (305) 561-7300

Images Art Gallery
7400 Tamiami Trail North, Suite 101
Naples, FL 33963
ph: (813) 598-3455

J. Lawrence Gallery
535 West Eau Gallie Boulevard
Melbourne, FL 32935
ph: (407) 728-7051

Lewis Charles Gallery
1627 West Snow Circle
Tampa, FL 33606
ph: (813) 254-8700

Lucky Street Gallery
919 Duval Street
Key West, FL 33040
ph: (305) 294-3976

Marie Ferrer Gallery
309 North Park Avenue
Winter Park, FL 32789
ph: (407) 647-7680

Masterpiece Gallery
449 Plaza Real
Boca Raton, FL 33432
ph: (407) 394-0070

Nancy Kaye Gallery
201 East Palmetto Park Road
Boca Raton, FL 33432
ph: (407) 392-8220
fax: (407) 347-1782

Oehlschlaeger Gallery II
253 Bird Key Drive
Sarasota, FL 34236
ph: (813) 366-0652

The Park Shore Galleries
501 Goodlette Road, Suite B-204
Naples, FL 33940
ph: (813) 434-0833

Passage West Fine Art Gallery
3020 North Federal Highway
Fort Lauderdale, FL 33306
ph: (305) 565-8009

Presidio Gallery
36 Spanish Street
St. Augustine, FL 32084
ph: (904) 826-1758

Prodigy Gallery
4320 Gulf Shore Boulevard,
Suite 206
Naples, FL 33940
ph: (813) 263-5881

The Rain Forest Gallery
5535 Tamiami Trail, Suite 8
Naples, FL 33963

Raleigh Gallery
1855 Griffin Road
Dania, FL 33004
ph: (305) 922-3330

Rick Sanders Galleries
310 Bay Road
Sarasota, FL 34239
ph: (813) 364-9911

Robert Windsor Gallery
1855 Griffin Road, Suite A-108
Dania, FL 33004
ph: (305) 923-9100

Seldom Seen Gallery
820 East Las Olas Boulevard
Fort Lauderdale, FL 33316
ph: (305) 764-5590
fax: (305) 764-0004

Sokolsky Gallery For Fine Arts
942 Lincoln Avenue
South Florida Art Center
Miami Beach, FL 33139
ph: (305) 674-8278

State Street Gallery
1517 State Street
Sarasota, FL 34236
ph: (813) 362-3767

A Step Above Gallery
500 North Tamiami Trail
Sarasota, FL 34236
ph: (813) 955-4477

Tequesta Galleries
361 Tequesta Drive
Tequesta, FL 33469
ph: (407) 744-2534

Timothy's Gallery
212 Park Avenue North
Winter Park, FL 32789
ph: (407) 629-0707

The Turnberry Art Gallery
1907 Turnberry Way
Miami, FL 33180
ph: (305) 931-5272

Zoo Gallery
209 Airport Road, Suite 8
Destin, FL 32541
ph: (904) 650-2611

Georgia
Aliya, Gallery at Morningside
1402 North Highland Avenue
Northeast, Suite 6
Atlanta, GA 30306
ph: (404) 892-2835

Avery Gallery
390 Roswell Street
Marietta, GA 30060
ph: (404) 427-2459

Connell Gallery
333 Buckhead Avenue N.E.
Atlanta, GA 30305
ph: (404) 261-1712

Eve Mannes Gallery
116 Bennett Street Northwest, Suite A
Atlanta, GA 30309
ph: (404) 351-6651

Fay Gold Gallery
247 Buckhead Avenue N.E.
Atlanta, GA 30305
ph: (404) 233-3843

Goldsmith Gallery
200 Worth Drive N.W.
Atlanta, GA 30327
ph: (404) 841-9264

Heath Gallery
416 East Paces Ferry Road N.E.
Atlanta, GA 30305
ph: (404) 262-6407

Lagerquist Gallery
3235 Paces Ferry Place Northwest
Atlanta, GA 30305
ph: (404) 261-8273

The Lowe Gallery
75 Bennett Street N.W., Suite A-7
Atlanta, GA 30309
ph: (404) 352-8114

The Main Street Gallery
North Main Street
Clayton, GA 30525
ph: (706) 782-2440

The McIntosh Gallery
One Virginia Hill
587 Virginia Avenue
Atlanta, GA 30306
ph: (404) 892-4023

Rainblue Gallery
1205 Johnson Ferry Road, Suite 117
Marietta, GA 30068
ph: (404) 973-1091

The Signature Shop & Gallery
3267 Roswell Road N.E.
Atlanta, GA 30330
ph: (404) 237-4426

Trinity Gallery
940 Myrtle Street N.E., Apt. 8
Atlanta, GA 30309
ph: (404) 525-7546

The Tula Galleries
75 Bennett Street Northwest,
Suite D1
Atlanta, GA 30309
ph: (404) 351-6724

Up The Creek Gallery
Highways 115 & 105
Demorest, GA 30535
ph: (404) 754-4130

Vespermann Glass Gallery
2140 Peachtree Street N.W.
Atlanta, GA 30309
ph: (404) 350-9698

Weinberg's Gallery
375 Pharr Road N.E., Suite 204
Atlanta, GA 30305

Winn/Regency Gallery
2344 Lawrenceville Highway
Atlanta, GA 30033
ph: (404) 633-1789

Hawaii
Coast Gallery
P. O. Box 565
Hana, HI 96713
ph: (808) 248-8636

Madaline Michaels Gallery
108 Lopaka Place
Kula, HI 96790
ph: (800) 635-9369

The Village Gallery
120 Dickenson Street
Lahaina, HI 96761
ph: (808) 669-0585

Idaho
Anne Reed Gallery
P. O. Box 597
Ketchum, ID 83340
ph: (208) 726-3036
fax: (208) 726-9630

Gail Severn Gallery
620 Sun Valley Road
P. O. Box 1679
Ketchum, ID 83340
ph: (208) 726-5079

Richard Kavesh Gallery
P. O. Box 6080
Ketchum, ID 83340
ph: (208) 726-2523

Roland Gallery
601 Sun Valley Road
P. O. Box 221
Ketchum, ID 83340
ph: (208) 726-2333
fax: (208) 726-6266

Illinois
Ann Nathan Gallery
134 Merchandise Mart
Chicago, IL 60654
ph: (312) 664-6622

Ann Nathan Gallery
210 West Superior Street
Chicago, IL 60610
ph: (312) 664-6622

Artisan Shop and Gallery
1515 Sheridan Road
Plaza Del Lago
Wilmette, IL 60091
ph: (708) 251-3775

Atlas Galleries
549 North Michigan Avenue
Chicago, IL 60611
ph: (800) 423-8702

Betsy Rosenfield Gallery
212 West Superior Street
Chicago, IL 60610
ph: (312) 787-8020

Billy Hork Gallery
272 East Golf Road
Arlington Heights, IL 60005
ph: (708) 640-7272

Carey Gallery
1062 West Chicago Avenue
Chicago, IL 60622
ph: (312) 942-1884

Center For Contemporary Art
325 West Huron Street
Chicago, IL 60610
ph: (312) 944-0094

Chicago Street Gallery
204 South Chicago Street
Chicago, IL 62656
ph: (217) 732-5937

Douglas Dawson Gallery
222 West Huron Street
Chicago, IL 60610
ph: (312) 751-1961

Dream Fast Gallery
2035 West Wabansia Avenue
Chicago, IL 60647
ph: (312) 235-4779

Eva Cohon Gallery
301 West Superior, 2nd floor
Chicago, IL 60610
ph: (312) 664-3669

Fabrile Gallery
2945 North Broadway
Chicago, IL 60657
ph: (312) 929-7471

Fabrile Gallery
224 South Michigan Avenue
Chicago, IL 60604
ph: (312) 427-1510

Fumie Gallery
126 South Franklin Street
Chicago, IL 60606
ph: (312) 726-0080

Gallery Moya
835 North Michigan Avenue
Chicago, IL 60611
ph: (312) 337-2900

Graphic Source Art Gallery
200 Applebee Street
Barrington, IL 60010
ph: (708) 381-2476

Gwenda Jay Gallery
301 West Superior Street, 2nd floor
Chicago, IL 60610
ph: (312) 664-3406

Hokin Kaufman Gallery
P. O. Box 14761
Chicago, IL 60614
ph: (312) 266-1212

Jayson Gallery
1915 North Clybourn Avenue
Chicago, IL 60614
ph: (312) 525-3100

Joy Horwich Gallery
226 East Ontario Street
Chicago, IL 60611
ph: (312) 787-0171

Kaleidoscope Gallery
205 South Cook Street
Barrington, IL 60010
ph: (708) 381-4840

Lill Street Gallery
1021 West Lill Avenue
Chicago, IL 60614
ph: (312) 477-6185

Lindsey Gallery
146 North Oak Park Avenue
Oak Park, IL 60301
ph: (708) 386-5272

Lovely Fine Arts
18 West 100 22nd Street
Oakbrook Terrace, IL 60181
ph: (708) 369-2999

Martha Schneider Gallery
230 West Superior Street
Chicago, IL 60610
ph: (312) 988-4033

Marx Gallery
1090 Johnson Drive
Buffalo Grove, IL 60610
ph: (312) 573-1400

Marx Gallery
230 West Superior Street
Chicago, IL 60610
ph: (312) 573-1400

Perimeter Gallery
750 New Orleans Street
Chicago, IL 60610
ph: (312) 266-9473

The Plum Line Gallery
1515 Chicago Avenue
Evanston, IL 60201
ph: (708) 328-7586

Portia Gallery
1702 North Dames
Chicago, IL 60647
ph: (312) 862-1700

Prestige Art Galleries
3909 Howard Street
Skokie, IL 60076
ph: (708) 679-2555

Princeton Art Gallery
1844 First Street
Highland Park, IL 60035
ph: (708) 432-1930

R. C. Danon Gallery
1224 West Lunt Avenue, Suite 1
Chicago, IL 60610
ph: (312) 988-4033

Schneider-Bluhm-Loeb Gallery
230 West Superior Street
Chicago, IL 60610
ph: (312) 988-4033

Studio of Long Grove Gallery
360 North Old McHenry Road
Long Grove, IL 60047
ph: (708) 634-4244

Vale Craft Gallery
207 West Superior Street
Chicago, IL 60610
ph: (312) 337-3525
fax: (312) 337-3530

Wentworth Gallery
835 North Michigan Avenue, fifth level
Chicago, IL 60611
ph: (312) 944-0079

Wood Street Gallery
1239 North Wood Street
Chicago, IL 60622
ph: (312) 227-3306

Indiana
By Hand Gallery
104 East Kirkwood Avenue
Bloomington, IN 47408
ph: (812) 334-3255

Centre Art Gallery
3018 East Carmel Drive
Carmel, IN 46032
ph: (317) 844-6421

Chesterton Art Gallery
115 South Fourth Street
Chesterton, IN 46304
ph: (219) 926-4711

Cornerstone Gallery
176 West Main Street
Greenwood, IN 46142
ph: (317) 887-2778

Fables Gallery
317 Lincoln Way East
Mishawaka, IN 46544
ph: (219) 255-9191

JM Mallon Galleries
Editions Limited
4040 East 82nd Street
Indianapolis, IN 46250
ph: (317) 253-7800

Jubilee Gallery
121 West Court
Jeffersonville, IN 47130
ph: (812) 282-9997

Katherine Todd Fine Arts
5356 Hillside Avenue
Indianapolis, IN 46220
ph: (317) 253-0250

Lake Street Gallery
615 South Lake Street
Gary, IN 46403
ph: (219) 938-4566

Sigman's Gallery
930 Broad Ripple Avenue
Indianapolis, IN 46220
ph: (317) 253-9953

Sycamore Gallery
6116 Breamore Road
Indianapolis, IN 46220
ph: (317) 255-9794

Trilogy Gallery
120 East Main Street
P. O. Box 200
Nashville, IN 47448
ph: (812) 988-4030

Iowa
Cornerhouse Gallery & Frame
2753 First Avenue Southeast
Cedar Rapids, IA 52402
ph: (319) 365-4348
fax: (319) 365-1707

Iowa Artisans Gallery
117 East College
Iowa City, IA 52240
ph: (319) 351-8686

Jean Sample Studio Gallery
3111 Ingersoll Avenue
Des Moines, IA 50312

Kansas
Gallery At Hawthorne
4833 West 119th Street
Overland Park, KS 66209
ph: (913) 469-8001

Kentucky
Art Biz Gallery
414 Baxter Avenue
Louisville, KY 40204
ph: (502) 585-2809

Artique Gallery
410 West Vine Street, First Level
Lexington, KY 40507
ph: (606) 233-1774

Benchmark Gallery
1-75 Interchange
Berea, KY 40403
ph: (606) 986-9413

Chestnut Street Gallery
3409 Nicholasville Road
Lexington, KY 40503
ph: (606) 273-7351

Commonwealth Gallery
Hyatt Regency
313 Fourth Avenue
Louisville, KY 40202
ph: (502) 589-4747

Edenside Gallery
1422 Bardstown Road
Louisville, KY 40204
ph: (502) 459-2787

Liberty Gallery
416 West Jefferson
Louisville, KY 40202
ph: (502) 566-2081

Payton Glass Studio/Gallery
1825 Eastern Parkway
Louisville, KY 40204
ph: (502) 456-9253

Promenade Gallery
204 Center Street
Berea, KY 40403
ph: (606) 986-1609

The Zephyr Gallery
812 West Main Street
Louisville, KY 40202
ph: (502) 585-5646

Louisiana
Baton Rouge Gallery
1442 City Park Avenue
Baton Rouge, LA 70808
ph: (504) 383-1470

Carol Robinson Gallery
4537 Magazine Street
New Orleans, LA 70115
ph: (504) 895-6130

Gallery Insightful Objects
1812 Magazine Street
New Orleans, LA 70130
ph: (504) 581-2113
fax: (504) 581-2114

Hilderbrand Galleries
4524 Magazine Street
New Orleans, LA 70115
ph: (504) 895-3312

Maggio Gallery
941 Rue Royal
New Orleans, LA
ph: (504) 523-4093

Morehead Fine Arts Gallery
603 Jula Street
New Orleans, LA 70130
ph: (504) 568-9754

Maine
Abacus Handcrafters Gallery
8 McKown Street
Booth Bay Harbor, ME 04538
ph: (207) 633-2166

The Blue Heron Gallery
Church Street
Deer Isle, ME 04627
ph: (207) 348-6051

Compliments Gallery
P. O. Box 567-A
Kennebunkport, ME 04046
ph: (207) 967-2269

Elements Gallery
190 Danforth Street
Portland, ME 04102
ph: (207) 729-1108

Frick Gallery
139 High Street
Belfast, ME 04915
ph: (207) 338-3671

Hand in Hand Crafts Gallery
8 School Street
Freeport, ME 04032
ph: (207) 865-1705

Nancy Margolis Gallery
367 Fore Street
Portland, ME 04101
ph: (207) 775-3822

The Shore Road Gallery
12 Shore Road
Ogunquit, ME 03907
ph: (207) 646-5046

Stein Gallery Contemporary Glass
20 Milk Street
Portland, ME 04101
ph: (207) 772-9072

Turtle Gallery
39 Morning Street
Portland, ME 04101
ph: (207) 774-0621

Victorian Stable Gallery
9 Water Street
P. O. Box 728
Damariscotta, ME 04543
ph: (207) 563-1991

Maryland
The Art Gallery
Art-Sociology Building
The University of Maryland
College Park, MD 20742
ph: (301) 405-2763
fax: (301) 314-9148

Art Institute & Gallery
Route 50 and Lemmon Hill Lane
Salisbury, MD 21801
ph: (301) 546-4748

Aurora Gallery
67 Maryland Avenue
Annapolis, MD 21401
ph: (301) 263-9150

Barbara Fendrick Gallery
4104 Leland Street
Bethesda, MD 20815

Gallery 44
103 Belhany Road
Ellicott City, MD 21043
ph: (410) 465-5200

The Glass Gallery
44720 Hampden Lane
Bethesda, MD 20814
ph: (301) 657-3478

Joyce Michaud Gallery
9043 Allington Manor Circle West
Frederick, MD 21701
ph: (301) 698-0929
fax: (301) 846-0035

Margaret Smith Gallery
8090 Main Street
Ellicott City, MD 21043
ph: (410) 461-0870

Meredith Gallery
805 North Charles Street
Baltimore, MD 21201
ph: (410) 837-3575

Ruby Blakeney Gallery
Savage Mill
8600 Foundry Street
Savage, MD 20763
ph: (410) 880-4935

Massachusetts
Andrea Marquit Fine Arts
38 Newbury Street
Boston, MA 63210
ph: (617) 859-0190

Artful Hand Galleries
P. O. Box 131
Orleans, MA 02653
ph: (508) 255-2969

The Artful Hand Gallery
36 Copley Place
100 Huntington Avenue
Boston, MA 06651
ph: (617) 262-960

Artique Gallery
400 Cochituate Road
Farmingham Mall
Farmingham, MA 01701
ph: (508) 872-3373

The Artisan Gallery
150 Main Street
Northampton, MA 01060
ph: (413) 586-1942

Artisans Gallery
10 Oak Street
Quincy, MA 02169
ph: (617) 847-1612

Artists & Craftsmen Gallery
72 Main Street
West Harwich, MA 02671
ph: (508) 432) 7604

Artwork Gallery
261 Park Avenue
Worcester, MA 01609
ph: (508) 755-7808

Baracca Gallery
P. O. Box 85
North Hatfield, MA 01266
ph: (413) 247-5262

Bhadon Gift Gallery
1075 Pleasant Street
Worcester, MA 01602
ph: (508) 978-0432
fax: same

Bramhall & Dunn Gallery
16 Federal Street
Nantucket, MA 02554
ph: (508) 228-4688

Clark Gallery
Lincoln Station
P. O. Box 339
Lincoln, MA 01773
ph: (617) 259-8303

Croma Gallery
94 Central Street
Wellesley, MA 02181
ph: (617) 235-6230

Designers Gallery
1 Design Center Place, Suite 329
Boston, MA 02210
ph: (617) 426-5511

Ferrin Gallery at Pinch Pottery
179 Main Street
Northampton, MA 01060
ph: (413) 586-4509

Gallerie Oceana
18 North Summer Street
Edgartown, MA 02539
ph: (508) 627-3121

Gallery at Chatham
595 Main Street
Chatham, MA 02633
ph: (508) 945-5449

Gallery Naga
67 Newbury Street
Boston, MA 02116
ph: (617) 267-9060

Gifted Hand Gallery
32 Church Street
Wellesley, MA 02181
ph: (617) 235-7171
fax: (203) 236-9979

G/M Galleries
Main Street
West Stockbridge, MA 97225

Hand of Man Craft Gallery
The Curtis Shops
Walker Street
Lenox, MA 01201
ph: (413) 637-0632

Hand of Man Craft Gallery
29 Wendell Avenue
Pittsfield, MA 01201
ph: (413) 637-0632

Holsten Galleries
General Delivery
Stockbridge, MA 01262
ph: (413) 298-3044

Hoorn Ashby Gallery
10 Federal Street
Nantucket, MA 02554
ph: (508) 228-9314

Northside Craft Gallery
933 Main Street
Yarmouth Port, MA 02675
ph: (508) 362-5291

Rice Polak Gallery
432 Commercial Street
Provincetown, MA 02657
ph: (508) 487-1052

Signature Gallery
Dock Square
24 North Street
Boston, MA 02109
ph: (617) 227-4885

Signature Gallery
10 Steeple Street
Mashpee, MA 02649
ph: (508) 539-0029

Skera Gallery
221 Main Street
Northampton, MA 01060
ph: (413) 586-4563

Towne Gallery
88 Main Street
Lenox, MA 01240
ph: (413) 637-0053

Michigan
Ackerman Gallery
327 Abbott Road
East Lansing, MI 48823
ph: (517) 332-6818

Alice Simsar Gallery
P. O. Box 7089
Ann Arbor, MI 48107
ph: (313) 665-4883

Animalia Gallery
403 Water Street
P. O. Box 613
Saugatuck, MI 49453
ph: (616) 857-3227

Ariana Gallery
119 South Main Street
Royal Oak, MI 48067
ph: (810) 546-8810

Artisans Gallery
2666 Charlevoix Avenue
Petoskey, MI 49770
ph: (616) 347-6466

Art Leaders Gallery
26111 Novi Road
Novi, MI 48375
ph: (810) 348-5540

The Bell Gallery
257 East Main Street
Harbor Springs, MI 49740
ph: (616) 526-9855

Belstone Gallery
321 East Front
Traverse City, MI 49684
ph: (616) 946-0610

Carol Hooberman Gallery
124 South Woodward Avenue,
Suite 12
Birmingham, MI 48009
ph: (313) 647-3666

Carol James Gallery
301 South Main Street
Royal Oak, MI 48067
ph: (313) 541-6216

C. Corcoran Gallery
608 Lake Drive
Muskegon, MI 49445
ph: (616) 722-2370

The Courtyard Gallery
813 East Buffalo Street
New Buffalo, MI 49117
ph: (616) 469-4110

Donna Jacobs Gallery
574 North Woodward Avenue,
2nd floor
Birmingham, MI 48009
ph: (313) 540-1600

Gallerie 454
15105 Kercheval Street
Grosse Pointe, MI 48230
ph: (313) 822-4454

Gallery Four Fourteen
414 Detroit Street
Ann Arbor, MI 48104
ph: (313) 747-7004

Gallery On The Alley
611 Broad Street
St. Joseph, MI 49085
ph: (616) 983-6161

Habitat Galleries
32255 Northwestern Highway
Triatria Building, Suite 45
Farmington Hills, MI 48334
ph: (313) 851-9090

Joyce Petter Gallery
134 Butler Street
Douglas, MI 49453
ph: (616) 857-7861

Judith Racht Gallery
General Delivery
Harbert, MI 49115
ph: (517) 469-1080

Koucky Gallery
319 Bridge Street
Charlevoix, MI 49720
ph: (616) 547-2228

Linda Hayman Gallery
5 Pine Gate Court
Bloomfield Hills, MI 48304

Mesa Arts Gallery
32800 Franklin Road
Franklin, MI 48025
ph: (313) 851-9949

Nicol Studio & Gallery
2531 Charlevoix Avenue
Petoskey, MI 49770
ph: (616) 347-0227

Northwood Gallery
144 East Main Street
Midland, MI 48640
ph: (517) 631-0390

The Pine Tree Gallery
824 East Cloverland Drive
US Highway 2
Ironwood, MI 49938
ph: (906) 932-5120

The Posner Gallery
32407 North Western Highway
Farmington Hills, MI 48332
ph: (313) 626-6450

Preston Burke Gallery
37622 West 12 Mile Road
Farmington Hills, MI 48331
ph: (313) 963-2350

Private Collection Gallery
6736A Orchard Lake Road
West Bloomfield, MI 48322
ph: (313) 737-4050

Robert Kidd Gallery
107 Townsend Street
Birmingham, MI 48009
ph: (313) 642-3909

Russell Klatt Gallery
1467 South Woodward Avenue
Birmingham, MI 48009
ph: (313) 647-6655

The Sajon May Gallery
6251 Island Lake Drive
East Lansing, MI 48823

Saper Gallery
433 Albert Avenue
East Lansing, MI 48823
ph: (517) 351-0815

Selo Shevel Gallery
335 South Main Street
Ann Arbor, MI 48104
ph: (313) 761-6263

Spitler Gallery
2007 Pauline Court
Ann Arbor, MI 48103
ph: (313) 662-8914

Suzie Vigland Gallery
1047 Michigan Avenue
Benzonia, MI 49616
ph: (616) 882-7203

The Sybaris Gallery
202 East Third Street
Royal Oak, MI 48067
ph: (313) 544-3388

Tewlews Gallery
54 East Eighth Street
Holland, MI 49423
ph: (616) 396-2653

T'Marra Gallery
111 North First Street
Ann Arbor, MI 48104
ph: (313) 769-3223

Touch of Light Gallery
23426 Woodward Avenue
Ferndale, MI 48220
ph: (313) 543-1868

Troy Art Gallery
515 South Lafayette Avenue
Royal Oak, MI 48067
ph: (313) 548-7919

The Yaw Gallery
550 North Woodward Avenue
Birmingham, MI 48009
ph: (313) 747-5470

Minnesota
Anderson & Anderson Gallery
414 First Avenue North
Minneapolis, MN 55401
ph: (612) 332-4889

Art Lending Gallery
25 Groveland Terrace
Minneapolis, MN 55403
ph: (612) 377-7800

Art Resources Gallery
494 Jackson Street
St. Paul, MN 55101
ph: (612) 222-4431

ATAZ Gallery
3480 West 70th Street
Edina, MN 55435
ph: (612) 925-4883

Bois Fort Gallery
130 East Sheridan Street
Ely, MN 55731
ph: (218) 365-5066

Forum Gallery
1235 Yale Place, Apt. 1308
Minneapolis, MN 55403
ph: (612) 333-1825

Goldstein Gallery
250 McNeal Hall
1985 Buford Avenue
St. Paul, MN 55108
ph: (612) 624-7434

Grand Avenue Frame & Gallery
964 Grand Avenue
St. Paul, MN 55105
ph: (612) 224-9716

Kess Gallery
130 East Sheridan Street
Ely, MN 55731
ph: (218) 365-5066

Made in the Shade Gallery
600 East Superior Street
Duluth, MN 55802
ph: (218) 722-1929

Peter M. David Gallery
3351 St. Louis Avenue
Minneapolis, MN 55416
ph: (612) 339-1825

Raymond Avenue Gallery
761 Raymond Avenue
St. Paul, MN 55114
ph: (612) 644-9200

Rourkes's Gallery
523 Fourth Street South
Moorhead, MN 56560
ph: (218) 236-8861

The Rumors Gallery
5632 Sanibel Drive
Minnetonka, MN 55343
ph: (612) 822-9490

Sayer Strand Gallery
275 Market Street, Suite 222
Minneapolis, MN 55405
ph: (612) 375-0838

Signature Gallery
2132 Ford Parkway
St. Paul, MN 55116
ph: (612) 698-5348

Sonia's Gallery
400 First Avenue North, Suite 318
Minneapolis, MN 55401
ph: (612) 338-0350

Suzanne Kohn Gallery
1690 Grand Avenue
St. Paul, MN 55105
ph: (612) 699-0417

Technic Gallery
1055 Grand Avenue
St. Paul, MN 55105
ph: (612) 222-0188

Thomas Barry Fine Arts
400 First Avenue North, Suite 304
Minneapolis, MN 55401
ph: (612) 338-3656

The White Oak Gallery
3939 West 50th Street
Edina, MN 55424

Mississippi
The Attic Gallery
1406 Washington Street
Vicksburg, MS 39180
ph: (601) 638-9221

Bryant Galleries
2845 Lakeland Drive
Jackson, MS 39208
ph: (601) 932-1993

The Old Trace Gallery
120 East Jefferson Street
P. O. Box 307
Kosciusko, MS 39090
ph: (601) 289-9170

Serenity Gallery
126 1/2 Main Street
Bay St. Louis, MS 39520
ph: (601) 467-3061

The Third Dimension Gallery
201 Banner Hall
4465 1-55 North
Jackson, MS 39206
ph: (601) 366-3371

Missouri
Art Attack Gallery
420 West Seventh Street
Kansas City, MO 64105
ph: (816) 474-7482

Austral Gallery
2115 Park Avenue
St. Louis, MO 63104
ph: (314) 776-0300

Barucci Gallery
8101 Maryland Avenue
Clayton, MO 63105
ph: (314) 727-2020

Barucci Gallery
8121 Maryland Avenue
St. Louis, MO 63105
ph: (314) 727-2020

Boody Fine Arts
10706 Trenton Avenue
St. Louis, MO 63132
ph: (314) 423-2255

Central Park Gallery
1644 Wyandotte Street
Kansas City, MO 64108
ph: (816) 417-7711

Gallery 525
770 Forsyth Boulevard
St. Louis, MO 63105
ph: (314) 991-0770

Glynn Brown Design Gallery
420 West Seventh Street
Kansas City, MO 64105
ph: (816) 842-2115

Griffin Gallery
9712 Clayton Road
St. Louis, MO 63124
ph: (314) 993-5200

Leedy Voulkos Gallery
2012 Baltimore Avenue
Kansas City, MO 64108
ph: (816) 474-1919
fax: same

The Morgan Gallery
412 Delaware Street, Suite A
Kansas City, MO 64105
ph: (816) 842-8755

Nancy Sachs Gallery
7700 Forsyth Boulevard
St. Louis, MO 63105
ph: (314) 727-7770
fax: (314) 991-8727

Portfolio Gallery
3514 Delmar Boulevard
St. Louis, MO 63103
ph: (314) 533-3323

Private Stock Gallery
4550 Warwick Boulevard
Kansas City, MO 64111
ph: (816) 561-1191

Pro Art Gallery
625 South Skinker Boulevard,
Suite 503
St. Louis, MO 63105
ph: (314) 231-5848

Union Hill Arts Gallery
3013 Main Street
Kansas City, MO 64108
ph: (816) 561-3020

Montana
Chandler Gallery
Front Street
Missoula, MT 59802
ph: (406) 721-5555

Nebraska
Adam Whitney Gallery
8725 Shamrock Road
Omaha, NE 68114
ph: (402) 393-1051

Anderson O'Brien Gallery
8724 Pacific Street
Omaha, NE 68114
ph: (402) 390-0717

Haymarket Gallery
119 South Ninth Street
Lincoln, NE 68508
ph: (402) 475-1061

Nevada
Mark Masuoka Gallery
1149 South Maryland Street
Las Vegas, NV 89104
ph: (702) 366-0377

Moira James Gallery
P. O. Box 50049
Henderson, NV 89016
ph: (702) 454-4800

Moonstruck Gallery
6368 West Sahara Avenue
Las Vegas, NV 89102
ph: (702) 634-0531

River Gallery
15 North Virginia Street
Reno, NV 89501
ph: (702) 329-3698

Ryan Galleries
2972 South Rainbow Boulevard
Las Vegas, NV 89102
ph: (702) 368-0545

Shutler/Ziv Art Group
3119 West Post Road
Las Vegas, NV 89118
ph: (702) 896-2218
fax: (702) 896-3488

Stremmel Gallery
1400 South Virginia Street
Reno, NV 89502
ph: (702) 786-0558

New Hampshire
Art 3 Gallery
44 West Brook Street
Manchester, NH 03101
ph: (603) 668-6650

Ava Gallery
4 Bank Street
Lebanon, NH 03766
ph: (603) 448-3117

Gallery Thirty Three
111 Market Street
Portsmouth, NH 03801
ph: (603) 431-7403

Woodworkers Gallery
469 Nashua Street
Milford, NH 03055
ph: (603) 673-7977

New Jersey
Alice White Gallery
105 Pulis Avenue
Franklin Lakes, NJ 07417
ph: (201) 848-1855

CBL Fine Art
459 Pleasant Valley Way
West Orange, NJ 07052
ph: (201) 736-7776

Clayphernalia Gallery
P. O. Box 276
Rocky Hill, NJ 08555
ph: (609) 924-6394

The Elvid Gallery
P. O. Box 5267
Englewood, NJ 07631
ph: (201) 871-8747

Galerie Atelier
347 Kings Highway West
Haddonfield, NJ 08033
ph: (215) 627-3624

Gallery At Bristol-Meyers
P. O. Box 4000
Princeton, NJ 08543
ph: (609) 921-5896

Kornbluth Gallery
7-21 Fair Lawn Avenue
Fair Lawn, NJ 07410
ph: (201) 791-3374

Melme Gallery
Bridgewater Commons
400 Commons Way, Suite 256
Bridgewater, NJ 08807
ph: (908) 722-0933

Nathans Gallery
205 McBride Avenue
West Paterson, NJ 07424
ph: (201) 785-9119

Scherer Gallery
93 School Road West
Marlsboro, NJ 07746
ph: (201) 536-9465

Sheila Nussbaum Gallery
341 Millburn Avenue
Millburn, NJ 07041
ph: (201) 467-1720

Strand Gallery
9209 Ventnor Avenue
Margate City, NJ 08402
ph: (609) 822-8800

Thaine Gallery
150 Kings Highway East
Haddonfield, NJ 08033
ph: (609) 428-6961

Vitti Gallery
590 Valley Road
Upper Montclair, NJ 07043
ph: (201) 746-1715

Walker-Kornbluth Art Gallery
7-21 Fair Lawn Avenue
Fair Lawn, NJ 07410
ph: (201) 791-3374

Williams Gallery
8 Chambers Street
Princeton, NJ 08542
ph: (609) 921-1142

New Mexico
Andrews Pueblo Gallery
400 San Felipe Street Northwest
Albuquerque, NM 87104
ph: (505) 243-0414

Bareiss Contemporary Art
P. O. Box 2739
Taos, NM 87571
ph: (505) 776-2284

Clay & Fiber Gallery
126 West Plaza
Taos, NM 87571
ph: (505) 758-8093

Contemporary Southwest Gallery
123 West Palace Avenue
Santa Fe, NM 87501
ph: (800) 283-0440

El Prado Gallery
112 West San Francisco Street
Santa Fe, NM 87501
ph: (505) 988-2906

Garland Gallery
125 Lincoln Avenue, Suite 113
Santa Fe, NM 87501
ph: (505) 984-1555

Gerald Peters Gallery
P. O. Box 908
Santa Fe, NM 87504
ph: (505) 988-8961

Handsel Gallery
306 Camino Del Monte Sol
Santa Fe, NM 87501
ph: (505) 988-4030

Joan Cawley Gallery
133 West San Francisco Street
Santa Fe, NM 87501
ph: (505) 984-1464

Kent Galleries
130 Lincoln Avenue
Santa Fe, NM 87501
ph: (505) 988-1001

Lew Allen Gallery
225 Galisteo Street
Santa Fe, NM 87501
ph: (505) 988-5387

The Lightside Gallery
225 Canyon Road
Santa Fe, NM 87501
ph: (505) 982-5501

Lilly's Gallery
P. O. Box 342
Acoma Pueblo, NM 87034
ph: (505) 552-9501

Made In the USA Gallery
110 West San Francisco Street
Santa Fe, NM 87501
ph: (505) 982-3232

Mariposa Gallery
113 Romero Street N.W.
Albuquerque, NM 87104
ph: (505) 842-9097

Mariposa Gallery
225 Canyon Road
Santa Fe, NM 87501
ph: (505) 982-3032

Michael Wigley Galleries
1111 Paseo De Peralta
Santa Fe, NM 87501
ph: (505) 984-8986

Misi Lakia-Bi Kisi Gallery
312 Read Street
Santa Fe, NM 87501
ph: (505) 984-0119

New Trend Gallery
225 Canyon Road
Santa Fe, NM 87501
ph: (505) 988-1199

Off The Wall Gallery
616 Canyon Road
Santa Fe, NM 87501
ph: (505) 983-8337

Okun Gallery
301 North Guadalupe Street
Santa Fe, NM 87501
ph: (505) 989-4300

The Running Ridge Gallery
640 Canyon Road
Santa Fe, NM 87501
ph: (800) 584-6830

Santa Fe Weaving Gallery
124 1/2 Galileo Street
Santa Fe, NM 87501
ph: (505) 982-1737

Shidoni
Contemporary Gallery
General Delivery
P. O. Box 250
Tesuque, NM 87574
ph: (505) 988-8001

Weaving Southwest Gallery
216B Paseo Del Pueblo Sur
Taos, NM 87571
ph: (505) 758-0433

Weems Gallery
2801 M Eubank Boulevard N.E.
Albuquerque, NM 87112
ph: (505) 293-6133

Weyrich Gallery
2935-D Louisiana Boulevard N.E.
Albuquerque, NM 87110
ph: (505) 883-7410

Worth Gallery
112-A Camino de la Placita
Taos, NM 87571
ph: (505) 750-0816
fax: (505) 751-0817

New York
Aaron Faber Gallery
666 Fifth Avenue
New York, NY 10103
ph: (212) 586-8411
fax: (212) 582-0205

Accessory Resource Gallery
7 West 36th Street, Suite 11-A
New York, NY 10018
ph: (212) 971-7300

America House Gallery
466 Piermont Avenue
Piermont, NY 10968
ph: (914) 359-0106

Austin Harvard Gallery at
Northfield Common
50 State Street
Pittsford, NY 14534
ph: (716) 383-1472

Babcock Galleries
724 Fifth Avenue
New York, NY 10019
ph: (212) 767-1852

Balaman Craft Gallery
1031 Lexington Avenue
New York, NY 10021
ph: (212) 472-8366

Barry Palum Gallery
21 Prince Street
Rochester, NY 14607
ph: (716) 244-9407

Bernice Steinbaum Gallery
132 Greene Street
New York, NY 10012
ph: (212) 431-4224

Charles Cowles Gallery
420 West Broadway
New York, NY 10012
ph: (212) 925-3500

Clay Hand Gallery
212 West 105th Street
New York, NY 10025
ph: (212) 865-9190

Contemporary Porcelain Gallery
105 Sullivan Street
New York, NY 10012
ph: (212) 219-2172

The Craftman's Gallery
648 Central Park Avenue, Suite 125
Scarsdale, NY 10583

Distant Origin Gallery
150 Mercer Street
New York, NY 10012
ph: (212) 941-0024

Elaine Benson Gallery
P. O. Box 3034
2317 Montauk Highway
Bridgehampton, NY 11932
ph: (516) 537-3233

Engel Gallery
51 Main Street
East Hampton, NY 11937
ph: (516) 324-6462

Eric Zetterquist Gallery
24 East 81st Street, Apt. Suite 5-C
New York, NY 10028
ph: (212) 988-3399

Fast Forward Gallery
580 Fifth Avenue, Penthouse
New York, NY 10036
ph: (212) 302-5518

Franklin Parrasch Gallery
584 Broadway
New York, NY 10012
ph: (212) 925-7090

Gallery at the Courtyard
223 Katonah Avenue
Katonah, NY 10536
ph: (914) 232-9511

Gallery Authentique
1499 Old Northern Boulevard
Roslyn, NY 11576
ph: (516) 484-7238

Gallery 514
98 Wheatley Road
Old Westbury, NY 11568
ph: (516) 626-0387

Gallery Muhr
P. O. Box 572
Port Washington, NY 11050
ph: (816) 883-1057

Gallery Ninety One
91 Grand Street
New York, NY 10013
ph: (212) 966-3072

Gallery North
90 North Country Road
Setauket, NY 11733
ph: (516) 751-2676

Gallery 10
7 Greenwich Avenue
New York, NY 10014
ph: (212) 206-1058

Garth Clark Gallery
24 West 57th Street
New York, NY 10019
ph: (212) 246-2205

Gayle Willson Gallery
16 Jobs Lane
Southampton, NY 11968
ph: (516) 283-7430

Gift Gallery
6584 Nash Road
North Tonawanda, NY 14120

Gimpel Weitzenhoffer Gallery
P. O. Box 20006
New York, NY 10011
ph: (212) 925-9060

Gloria Plevin Gallery
P. O. Box 188
Chautauqua, NY 14722
ph: (716) 753-3277

Graham Gallery
1014 Madison Avenue
New York, NY 10021
ph: (212) 535-5767

Hammer Gallery
33 West 57th Street
New York, NY 10019
ph: (212) 644-4400

Heller Gallery
71 Greene Street
New York, NY 10012
ph: (212) 966-5948

Henoch Gallery
90 Wooster Street
New York, NY 10012
ph: (212) 966-0303

Holthaus Fiber Art Gallery
Eleven Wildwood Gons
Port Washington, NY 11050
ph: (516) 883-8620

Hudson River Gallery
217 Main Street
Ossining, NY 10562
ph: (914) 762-5300

Images Art Gallery
1157 Pleasantville Road
Briarcliff Manor, NY 10510
ph: (914) 762-3000

Impressive Interior Gallery
14 Old Indian Trail
Milton, NY 12547
ph: (914) 795-5101

Jaro Art Galleries
955 Madison Avenue
New York, NY 10021
ph: (212) 734-5475

Joel Schwalb Gallery
12 South Broadway
Nyack, NY 10960
ph: (914) 358-1701

John Christopher Gallery
43 Main Street
Cold Spring Harbor, NY 11724
ph: (516) 367-3978

Julie Artisan's Gallery
687 Madison Avenue
New York, NY 10021
ph: (212) 688-2345

Lee Gallery
83 Main Street
Southampton, NY 11968
ph: (516) 287-2361

Lewis Dolin Gallery
P. O. Box 239
Katonah, NY 05361
ph: (212) 941-8130

Limestone Gallery
205 Thompson Street
Fayetteville, NY 13066
ph: (315) 637-0460

Mark Milliken Gallery
1200 Madison Avenue
New York, NY 10128
ph: (212) 534-8802

Max Protech Gallery
560 Broadway
New York, NY 10012
ph: (212) 966-5454

Melissa D. Gallery
24 Woodbine Avenue
Northport, NY 11768
ph: (516) 757-5503

Michael Ingbar Gallery Of Art
568 Broadway
New York, NY 10012
ph: (212) 334-1100

Miller Gallery
560 Broadway (at Prince Street),
4th floor
New York, NY 10012
ph: (212) 226-0702

Nancy Margolis Gallery
251 West 21st Street
New York, NY 10011
ph: (212) 255-0386

Nan Miller Gallery
3450 Winton Place
Rochester, NY 14623
ph: (716) 292-1430

Neil Isman Gallery
1100 Madison Avenue
New York, NY 10028
ph: (212) 628-3688

New Glass Gallery
345 West Broadway
New York, NY 10013
ph: (212) 431-0050

Noho Gallery
168 Mercer Street
New York, NY 10012
ph: (212) 219-2210

Northport Crafters Gallery
106 Main Street
Northport, NY 11768
ph: (516) 757-1603

Peter Joseph Gallery
745 Fifth Avenue
New York, NY 10151
ph: (212) 751-5500

Pritam & Eames Gallery
29 Race Lane
East Hampton, NY 11937
ph: (516) 324-7111

Raku Gallery
171 Spring Street
New York, NY 10012
ph: (212) 226-6636

The Rice Gallery
135 Washington Avenue
Albany, NY 12210
ph: (518) 463-4478

Roberta Wood Gallery
6907 East Genesee Street
Lyndon Plaza
Fayetteville, NY 13066
ph: (315) 445-0423

Rochester Memorial Gallery
500 University Avenue
Rochester, NY 14607
ph: (716) 473-7720

Ruth Raible Gallery
41 Forest Avenue
Hastings-on-Hudson, NY 10706
ph: (914) 478-0585

Sculpture Fields Gallery
P. O. Box 94
Kenoza Lake, NY 12750
ph: (914) 482-3669

Sedoni Gallery
304-A New York Avenue
Huntington, NY 11743
ph: (516) 547-4811

Silver Fox Gift Gallery
7935 Boston State Road
Hamburg, NY 14075
ph: (716) 649-0300

Steinhardt Gallery
370 New York Avenue
Huntington, NY 11743
ph: (516) 549-4430

Studio 5 Gallery
Pelham Engine Shop
450 Highbrook Avenue
Pelham Manor, NY 10803
ph: (914) 738-5707

Studio Gallery
369 Hillside Avenue
Williston Park, NY 11596
ph: (516) 742-6226

Sweetheart Gallery
34-C Tinker Street
Woodstock, NY 12498
ph: (914) 679-4900

Terracotta Gallery
259 West 4th Street
New York, NY 10014
ph: (212) 243-1952

The Unique Gallery
5701 Transit Road
East Amherst, NY 14051
ph: (716) 689-2160

Ward Masse Gallery
178 Prince Street
New York, NY 10012
ph: (212) 925-6951

The West End Gallery
87 West Market Street
Corning, NY 14830
ph: (607) 962-8692

West Harbour Gallery
237 Centre Island Road
Oyster Bay, NY 11771
ph: (516) 922-7070

The White Buffalo Gallery
13 Mill Road
Woodstock, NY 12498
ph: (800) 724-2113

The White Tree Gallery
140 King Street
Chappaqua, NY 10514
ph: (914) 238-4601

Winter Tree Gallery
147 Spring Street
New York, NY 10012
ph: (212) 343-2220

Works Gallery
1250 Madison Avenue
New York, NY 10128
ph: (212) 996-0300

North Carolina
Broadhurst Gallery
800 Midland Road
Pinehurst, NC 28374
ph: (910) 295-2296

Cedar Creek Gallery
1150 Fleming Road
Creedmoor, NC 27522
ph: (919) 528-1041

Compton Art Gallery
409 West Fisher Avenue
Greensboro, NC 27401
ph: (919) 370-9147

Creative Heart Gallery
207 West Sixth Street
Winston-Salem, NC 27101
ph: (910) 722-2345
fax: (910) 722-9596

First Light Gallery
8508 Park Road, Suite 123
Charlotte, NC 28210
ph: (704) 543-9939

Hayden Gallery
7 South Main Street
Burnsville, NC 28714
ph: (704) 682-7998

Heartwood Gallery
P. O. Box 546
Saluda, NC 28773

Hodges Taylor Gallery
227 North Tryon Street
Charlotte, NC 28202
ph: (704) 334-3799

Horizon Gallery
905 West Main Street
Durham, NC 27701
ph: (919) 688-0313

Greenleaf Gallery
6917 South Croatan
P. O. Box 755
Nags Head, NC 27959
ph: (919) 480-3555

Grovewood Gallery
111 Grovewood Road
Asheville, NC 28804
ph: (704) 253-7651

Island Art Gallery
P. O. Box 265
Highway 64
Manteo, NC 27954
ph: (919) 473-2838

Julia Rush Gallery
Southern National Center
Charlotte, NC 28202
ph: (704) 324-0409

Little Art Gallery
North Hills Mall
Raleigh, NC 27609
ph: (919) 787-6317

Makado Gallery
307 North Front Street
The Cotton Exchange
Wilmington, NC 28401
ph: (919) 762-8922

Master Works Gallery
Wright Square
Main Street
Highlands, NC 28741
ph: (704) 526-2633

Moondance Gallery
141 South Square Mall
Durham, NC 27707
ph: (919) 493-3132

Morning Star Gallery
Route 1
P. O. Box 292-10
Banner Elk, NC 28604
ph: (704) 898-6047

New Elements Gallery
216 North Front Street
Wilmington, NC 28401
ph: (919) 343-8997

New Morning Gallery
7 Boston Way
Biltmore Village
Asheville, NC 28803
ph: (704) 274-2831

Peden Gallery II
132 East Hargett Street
Raleigh, NC 27601
ph: (919) 834-9800

Raleigh Contemporary Gallery
134 Hargett Street
Raleigh, NC 27601
ph: (919) 828-6500

Skillbeck Gallery
238 South Sharon Amity Road
Charlotte, NC 28211
ph: (704) 366-8613

The Sommerhill Gallery
3 East Gate Shopping Center
East Franklin Street
Chapel Hill, NC 27514
ph: (919) 868-8868

Southern Expressions Gallery
2157 New Hendersonville Avenue
Pisgah Forest, NC 28768
ph: (704) 884-6242

Touchstone Gallery
318 North Main Street
Hendersonville, NC 28792
ph: (704) 692-2191

Weatherspoon Art Gallery
Spring Garden and Tate Streets
Greensboro, NC 27412
ph: (919) 334-95770

Whitewoven Gallery
201 1/2 North Main Street
Waynesville, NC 28786
ph: (704) 452-4864

Ohio

American Crafts Gallery
13010 Larchmere Avenue
Cleveland, OH 44120
ph: (216) 231-2008

The Art Bank Gallery
317 West Fourth Street
Cincinnati, OH 45202
ph: (513) 621-7779

Arternative Gallery
2034 Madison Road
Cincinnati, OH 45208
ph: (513) 871-2218

Artspace Center For Contemporary Art
8501 Carnegie Avenue
Cleveland, OH 44106
ph: (216) 421-8671

Avante Gallery
2094 Murray Hill Road
Cleveland, OH 44106
ph: (216) 791-1622

Brenda Kroos Gallery
1360 West Ninth Street
Cleveland, OH 44113
ph: (216) 621-1164

Chelsea Galleries
23225 Mercantile Road
Beachwood, OH 44122
ph: (216) 591-1066
fax: (216) 591-1068

Drumm Studios & Gallery
437 Crouse Street
Akron, OH 44311
ph: (216) 253-6268

Fiori-Omni Gallery
2072 Murray Hill Road
Cleveland, OH 44106
ph: (216) 721-5319

The Gallery
24 South Gamble Street, Suite 10
Shelby, OH 44875
ph: (419) 347-4206

Gallery at Studio B
140 West Main Street
Lancaster, OH 43130
ph: (614) 653-8424

Gallery 400
4659 Dressler Road Northwest
Canton, OH 44718
ph: (216) 492-2600

Heliotrope Art Gallery
3001 Caltapa Drive
Dayton, OH 45405
ph: (513) 275-1071

Images Art Gallery
3154 Markway Road
Toledo, OH 43606
ph: (419) 537-1400

Kaufman Gallery
P. O. Box 185
Berlin, OH 44610
ph: (216) 893-2842

Kussmaul Gallery
103 North Prospect Street
Granville, OH 43023
ph: (614) 587-4640

The Malton Gallery
2709 Observatory Avenue
Cincinnati, OH 45208
ph: (513) 321-8014

Miller Gallery
2715 Erie Avenue
Cincinnati, OH 45208
ph: (513) 871-4420
fax: (513) 871-4429

Ohio Designer Craftsmen Gallery
1665 West Fifth Avenue
Columbus, OH 43212
ph: (614) 486-7119

Osher Osher Gallery
5662 Mayfield Road
Lyndhurst, OH 44124
ph: (216) 646-9191

The Pump House Art Gallery
Enderlin Circle
P. O. Box 1613
Chillicothe, OH 45601
ph: (614) 772-5783

Riley Hawk Glass Gallery
2026 Murray Hill Road, Suite 103
Cleveland, OH 44106
ph: (216) 421-1445

Riley Hawk Glass Gallery
642 North High Street
Columbus, OH 43215
ph: (614) 228-6554

Santa Clara Gallery
1942 North Main Street
Dayton, OH 45405
ph: (513) 279-9100

William Busta Gallery
2021 Murray Hill Road
Cleveland, OH 44106
ph: (216) 231-7363

Woodbourne Gallery
9885 Montgomery Road
Cincinnati, OH 45242
ph: (513) 793-1888

Woodbourne Gallery
175 East Alex Bell Road, Suite 208
Dayton, OH 45459
ph: (513) 434-3565

Oklahoma
Doran Gallery
3509 South Peoria Avenue
Tulsa, OK 74105
ph: (918) 748-8700

Oregon
Alder Gallery & Art Service
160 East Broadway
Eugene, OR 97401
ph: (503) 342-6411

Art Decor Gallery
136 High Street Southeast
Salem, OR 97301
ph: (503) 378-0876

Contemporary Crafts Gallery
3934 Southwest
Corbett Avenue
Portland, OR 97201
ph: (503) 223-2654

Earthworks Gallery
2222 Highway 101 North
Yachats, OR 97498
ph: (503) 547-4300

Gango Gallery
205 Southwest First Avenue
Portland, OR 97204
ph: (503) 222-3850

Graystone Gallery
3279 Southeast
Hawthorne Boulevard
Portland, OR 97214
ph: (503) 238-0651

Hoffman Gallery
8245 Southwest Barnes Road
Portland, OR 97225
ph: (503) 297-5544

The Indigo Gallery
311 Avenue B, Suite 8
Lake Oswego, OR 97034
ph: (503) 636-3454

Laura Russo Gallery
805 Northwest 21st Avenue
Portland, OR 97209
ph: (503) 635-7419

Lawrence Gallery
P. O. Box 187
Sheridan, OR 97378
ph: (503) 843-3633

Maveety Gallery
P. O. Box 148
Gleneden Beach, OR 97388
ph: (503) 764-2318

Montage Gallery
5875 Southwest Elm Avenue
Beaverton, OR 97005
ph: (503) 643-7513

Quintana's Gallery of Indian and
Western Art
139 Northwest Second Avenue
Portland, OR 97209
ph: (503) 223-1729
fax: (503) 223-0339

The Real Mother Goose Gallery
927 Southwest Yamhill Street
Portland, OR 97205
ph: (503) 223-3737

Skylark Gallery
130 Spaulding Avenue
Brownsville, OR 97327
ph: (503) 466-5221

Sunbird Gallery
916 Northwest Wall Street
Bend, OR 97701
ph: (503) 389-9196

The White Bird Gallery
North Hemlock Road
P. O. Box 502
Cannon Beach, OR 97145
ph: (503) 436-2681

The Wood Gallery
818 Southwest Bay Boulevard
Newport, OR 97365

Pennsylvania
Art Effects Gallery
277 Montgomery Avenue
Bala Cynwyd, PA 19004
ph: (610) 668-0992
fax: same

Artisans Gallery
Peddlers Village
P. O. Box 133
Lahaska, PA 18931
ph: (215) 794-3112

Art Vark Gallery
The Warwick
17th at Locust
Philadelphia, PA 19103
ph: (215) 735-5600

Artworks Fine Arts and Crafts Gallery
121 East State Street
Kennett Square, PA 19348
ph: (215) 444-6544

Calico Cat Gallery
16 West King Street
Lancaster, PA 17603
ph: (717) 397-6372

Catherine Starr Gallery
4235 Main Street
Philadelphia, PA 19127
ph: (215) 482-7755

Chadds Ford Gallery
US Highway 1 and 100
P. O. Box 179
Chadds Ford, PA 19317
ph: (610) 459-5510

Clay Place Gallery
Mineo Building
5416 Walnut Street
Pittsburgh, PA 15232
ph: (412) 682-3737

Craftsmen's Gallery
1377 Hemlock Farms
Hawley, PA 18428
ph: (717) 226-4111

Design Arts Gallery
Nesbitt College of Design Arts
33rd and Market Streets
Philadelphia, PA 19104
ph: (215) 895-2386

Dina Porter Gallery
1655 Hausman Road
Allentown, PA 18104
ph: (215) 434-7363

Doris Fordham Gallery
Rural Route 2
P. O. Box 2502
Factoryville, PA 18419
ph: (717) 945-7434

Downingtown Art Gallery
305 Manor Avenue
Downingtown, PA 19335
ph: (610) 269-5414

Earthworks Gallery
227 Haverford Avenue
Narberth, PA 19072
ph: (215) 667-1143

Eyes Gallery
402 South Street
Philadelphia, PA 19147
ph: (215) 925-0193
fax: (215) 574-0967

479 Gallery
55 North Second Street
Philadelphia, PA 19106
ph: (215) 922-1444

Galleria Tricia
2 Harrison Drive
New Cumberland, PA 70701
ph: (717) 691-0263

Gallerie Nadeau
118 North Third Street
Philadelphia, PA 70701
ph: (717) 691-0263

The Gallery at Cedar Hollow
2447 Yellow Springs Road
Malvern, PA 19355
ph: (610) 640-2787

The Gallery At The Clay Lady
General Delivery
Uwchland, PA 19480
ph: (610) 458-8262

Gallery 500
Church and Old York Road
Elkins Park, PA 19117
ph: (215) 572-1203

Gallery G
211 Ninth Street
Pittsburgh, PA 52221
ph: (412) 562-0912

Gallery of First Impressions
4 East Lancaster Avenue
Paoli, PA 19301
ph: (610) 647-4433

Gallery Riggione Fine Crafts
130 Almshouse Road
Richboro, PA 18954
ph: (215) 322-5035

Glass Growers Gallery
701 Holland Street
Erie, PA 16501
ph: (814) 453-3758

Greene & Greene Gallery
88 South Main Street
New Hope, PA 89381
ph: (215) 862-9620

Hahn Gallery
8439 Germantown Avenue
Philadelphia, PA 19188
ph: (215) 247-8439

Helen Drutt Gallery
1721 Walnut Street
Philadelphia, PA 19103
ph: (215) 735-1625
fax: (215) 557-9417

Indigo Gallery
1102 Pine Street
Philadelphia, PA 19103
ph: (215) 440-0202

Jab Gallery
225 Race Street
Philadelphia, PA 19106
ph: (215) 923-8122

James Gallery
2892 West Liberty Avenue
Pittsburgh, PA 15216
ph: (412) 343-1366

Jessica Berwind Gallery
301 Cherry Street
Philadelphia, PA 19106
ph: (215) 574-1645

Jun Gallery
114 Market Street
Philadelphia, PA 19106
ph: (215) 627-5020

Kaiser Newman Gallery
134 North Third Street
Philadelphia, PA 19106
ph: (215) 923-7438

Langman Gallery
Willow Grove Park
2500 Moreland Road
Willow Road, PA 19090
ph: (215) 657-8333

Latitudes Gallery
4325 Main Street
Philadelphia, PA 19127
ph: (215) 482-0417

Locks Gallery
600 South Washington Square
Philadelphia, PA 19106
ph: (215) 629-1000

Made By Hand Gallery
303 South Craig Street
Pittsburgh, PA 15213
ph: (412) 684-8346

Moser Showroom & Gallery
210 West Washington Square
Philadelphia, PA 19106
ph: (215) 922-6440

Nexus Gallery
137 North Second Street
Philadelphia, PA 19106
ph: (215) 629-1103

OLC Gallery
152 North Third Street, Suite 154
Philadelphia, PA 19106
ph: (215) 923-6085

Owen Patrick Gallery
4345 Main Street
Philadelphia, PA 19127
ph: (215) 482-9395

The Painted Bride Gallery
230 Vine Street
Philadelphia, PA 19106
ph: (215) 925-9914

Raintree Gallery
122 West High Street
Elizabethtown, PA 17022
ph: (717) 367-2990
fax: (717) 367-8998

Reisboro Gallery
4313 Main Street, Suite 17
Philadelphia, PA 19127
ph: (215) 483-3232

Rosenfeld Gallery
113 Arch Street
Philadelphia, PA 19106
ph: (215) 922-1376

Ruth Zafir Gallery
13 South Second Street
Philadelphia, PA 19106
ph: (215) 627-7098

Sande Webster Gallery
2018 Locust Street
Philadelphia, PA 19103
ph: (215) 732-8850

Simcoe Gallery
1925 Main Street
Northampton, PA 18067
ph: (215) 262-8154

Snyderman Gallery
303 Cherry Street
Philadelphia, PA 19106
ph: (215) 238-9576

The Works Gallery
319 South Street
Philadelphia, PA 19147
ph: (215) 922-7775

Zephyr Gallery
28 South Main Street
New Hope, PA 18938
ph: (610) 862-9765

Rhode Island
Sun Up Gallery
95 Watch Hill Road
Westerly, RI 02891
ph: (401) 596-0800

Virginia Lynch Gallery
4 Cornell Road
3883 Main Road
Tiverton, RI 02878
ph: (401) 624-3392

South Carolina
The Blue Heron Gallery
D2 Lagoon Road Coligny Plaza
Hilton Head, SC 29928
ph: (803) 785-3788

Carol Saunders Gallery
922 Gervais Street
Columbia, SC 29201
ph: (803) 256-3046

Checkered Moon Gallery
208 West Street
Beaufort, SC 29902
ph: (803) 522-3466

Craftseller Gallery
818 Bay Street
P. O. Box 1968
Beaufort, SC 29902
ph: (803) 525-6104

Duke Street Gallery
109 Duke Street
Pendleton, SC 29670
ph: (803) 646-3469

Llyn Strong Gallery
119 North Main Street
Greenville, SC 29601
ph: (864) 233-5900

Smith Galleries of Fine Crafts
The Village At Wexford, Suite J-11
Hilton Head Island, SC 29928
ph: (803) 842-2280

Southern Galleries
402 Southeast Main Street
Simpsonville, SC 29681
ph: (803) 963-4893

Tennessee
Artifacts Gallery
1007 Oakhaven Road
Memphis, TN 38119
ph: (901) 767-5236

Boones Creek Potter's Gallery
4903 Kingsport Highway 36
Johnson City, TN 37615
ph: (615) 282-2801

Cumberland Gallery
4107 Hillsboro Circle
Nashville, TN 37215
ph: (615) 297-0296

Hovanec Gallery
1010 Laurel Avenue
Knoxville, TN 37916
ph: (615) 524-5312

Kurts Bingham Gallery
766 South White Station Road
Memphis, TN 38117
ph: (901) 683-6200

The River Gallery
400 East Second Street
Bluff View
Chattanooga, TN 37403
ph: (615) 267-7353

Robert Tino Gallery
812 Old Douglas Dam Road
Sevierville, TN 37876
ph: (615) 428-6519

Texas
Adelle M Gallery
3317 McKinney Avenue, Suite 203
Dallas, TX 75204
ph: (214) 220-0300

Artables Gallery
2625 Colquitt
Houston, TX 77098
ph: (713) 528-0405

Artisans Fine Crafts Gallery
10000 Research Boulevard
Austin, TX 78759
ph: (512) 345-3001

Banks Fine Art
3316 Royal Lane
Dallas, TX 75229
ph: (214) 352-1811

Blaire Carnahan Fine Art
418 La Villita Street
San Antonio, TX 78205
ph: (210) 227-6313

Boardwalk Gallery Goldsmiths
5175 Westheimer, Suite 2350
Houston, TX 77056
ph: (713) 961-3552
fax: (713) 626-9608

Bowden Gallery
6981 Blanco Road
San Antonio, TX 78216
ph: (512) 341-4367

Circa Now Gallery
2162 Portsmouth Street
Houston, TX 77098
ph: (713) 529-8234

Creative Arts Gallery
836 North Star Mall
San Antonio, TX 78216
ph: (210) 342-8659

Debusk Galleries
3813 North Commerce Street
Fort Worth, TX 76106
ph: (817) 625-8476

Eclectic Ethnographic Gallery
916 West 12th Street
Austin, TX 78703
ph: (512) 477-1816
fax: (512) 477-1876

Free Flight Gallery
603 Munger Avenue, Suite 309
Dallas, TX 75202
ph: (214) 720-9147

Freelight Gallery
13350 Dallas Parkway, Suite G-137
Dallas, TX 75240
ph: (214) 239-5990

The Gallery At Los Patios
2015 Northeast Loop, Suite 410
San Antonio, TX 78217
ph: (210) 655-0538

Golden Eye Gallery
20035 Katy Freeway
Katy, TX 77450
ph: (713) 678-2820

Hanson Galleries
800 West Sam Houston Parkway,
Suite E-118
Houston, TX 77024
ph: (713) 984-1242

Heartland Gallery
Brodie Oaks Center
4006 South Lamar
Austin, TX 78704
ph: (512) 447-1171

Jack Meier Gallery
2310 Bissonnet Street
Houston, TX 77005
ph: (713) 526-2983

Judy Youens Gallery
3115 Damico Street
Houston, TX 77019
ph: (713) 527-0303

Keene Gallery
242 Losoya Street
San Antonio, TX 78205
ph: (210) 299-1999

Lyons Matrix Gallery
1712 Lavaca Street
Austin, TX 78701
ph: (512) 479-0068

The New Gallery
2639 Colquitt Street
Houston, TX 77098
ph: (713) 520-1753

The Rock House Gallery
1311 West Abram Street
Arlington, TX 76013
ph: (817) 265-5874

Sable V Fine Art Gallery
P. O. Box 1792
Wimberley, TX 78676
ph: (512) 847-8975

The Spicewood Gallery
1206 West 38th Street
Austin, TX 78705
ph: (512) 458-6575

Spirit Echoes Gallery
701 Brazos, Suite 720
Austin, TX 78701
ph: (512) 320-1492

Sol Del Rio Gallery
1020 Townsend Avenue
San Antonio, TX 78209
ph: (210) 828-5555

The Two Friends Gallery
2301 Strand
Galveston, TX 77550
ph: (409) 765-7477

The Ursuline Gallery
Southwest Craft Center
300 Augusta Avenue
San Antonio, TX 78205
ph: (512) 224-1848

West Bank Gallery
4201 Bee Caves Road, Suite A100
Austin, TX 78746
ph: (512) 329-8514

William Campbell Contemporary Art
4935 Byers Avenue
Fort Worth, TX 76107
ph: (817) 737-9566

Utah
Phillips Gallery
444 East 200 South
Salt Lake City, UT 84111
ph: (801) 364-8284

Utah Designer Crafts Gallery
38 West 200 South
Salt Lake City, UT 84101
ph: (801) 359-2770

Vermont
Emotional Outlet Gallery
170 Billings Hill Road
Stowe, VT 05672
ph: (802) 253-7407

North Wind Artisan Gallery
81 Central Street
Woodstock, VT 05091
ph: (802) 457-4587

The Spiral Gallery
P. O. Box 29
Marlboro, VT 05344
ph: (802) 257-5696

Woodstock Gallery of Art
Gallery Place
Route 4 East
Woodstock, VT 05091
ph: (802) 457-1900

Virginia
Andreas Galleries
8545 Leesburg Pike
Vienna, VA 22182
ph: (703) 448-2222

Blue Skies Gallery
120 West Queens Way, Suite 201
Hampton, VA 23669
ph: (804) 727-0028

Broadway Gallery
11213 J Lee Highway
Fairfax, VA 22030
ph: (703) 273-2388

Buffalo Gallery
127 South Fairfax Street
Alexandria, VA 22314
ph: (703) 549-3338

Crafters Gallery
Rural Route 12
P. O. Box 97
Charlottesville, VA 22901
ph: (804) 295-7006

Electric Glass Gallery
1 East Mellen Street
Hampton, VA 23663
ph: (804) 722-6300

Enamelists Gallery
Torpedo Factory Art Center
105 North Union Street
Alexandria, VA 22314
ph: (703) 836-1561

House Unique Gallery
112 Market Street S.E.
Roanoke, VA 24011
ph: (703) 345-0697

Potomac Craftsmen Gallery
Torpedo Factory Art Center
105 North Union Street
Alexandria, VA 22314
ph: (703) 548-0935

Signet Gallery
P. O. Box 753
Charlottesville, VA 22902
ph: (804) 296-6463

Washington
Anderson Glover Gallery
303 Kirkland Avenue
Kirkland, WA 98033
ph: (206) 739-0303

fax: (206) 739-0308

Artworks Gallery
155 South Main Street
Seattle, WA 98104
ph: (206) 625-0932

Fireworks Gallery
210 First Avenue South
Seattle, WA 98104
ph: (206) 682-8707

Foster White Gallery
311 1/2 Occidental Avenue South
Seattle, WA 98104
ph: (206) 622-2833
fax: (206) 622-7606

Gallery One
408 1/2 North Pearl Street
Ellensburg, WA 98926
ph: (309) 925-2670

Glass Eye Gallery
1902 Post Alley
Seattle, WA 98101
ph: (206) 441-3221

Grover/Thurston Gallery
532 First Avenue South
Seattle, WA 98104
ph: (206) 223-0816

Janet Huston Gallery
P. O. Box 845
La Conner, WA 98257
ph: (206) 466-5001

Lynn McAllister Gallery
1028 Lakeview Boulevard East, Apt. 5
Seattle, WA 98102
ph: (206) 624-6864

Northwest Gallery
202 First Avenue South
Seattle, WA 98104
ph: (206) 625-0542

Northwest Gallery of Fine
Woodworking
317 Northwest Gilman Boulevard
Issaquah, WA 98027
ph: (206) 391-4221

Northwest Gallery of Fine
Woodworking
202 First Avenue West
Seattle, WA 98104
ph: (206) 625-0542

Peterson Art Furniture Gallery
122 Central Way
Kirkland, WA 98033
ph: (206) 827-8053

Phoenix Rising Gallery
2030 Western Avenue
Seattle, WA 98121
ph: (206) 728-2332

Ron Segal Gallery
1420 Fifth Avenue, Suite 208
Seattle, WA 98101
800) 688-2788

Stonington Gallery
2030 First Avenue
Seattle, WA 98121
ph: (206) 443-1108

West Virginia
High Country Gallery
124 West Washington Street
Lewisburg, WV 24901
ph: (304) 647-3453

Sanguine Gryphon Gallery
P. O. Box 3120
Shepherdstown, WV 25443
ph: (304) 876-6569

Wisconsin
Art Elements Gallery
10050 North Port Washington Road
Mequon, WI 53092
ph: (414) 241-7040
fax: (414) 963-2126

Artisan Gallery
6858 Paoli Road
Belleville, WI 53508
ph: (608) 845-6600

Blue Dolphin House Gallery
10320 North Water Street
Ephraim, WI 54211
ph: (414) 854-4113

Edgewood Orchard Gallery
4140 Peninsula Players Road
Fish Creek, WI 54212
ph: (414) 868-3579

Fanny Garver Gallery
7432 Mineral Point Road
Madison, WI 53717
ph: (608) 833-8000

Katie Gingrass Gallery
241 North Broadway
Milwaukee, WI 53202
ph: (414) 289-0855
fax: (414) 289-9255

M. V. Knowles Gallery
117 North Broadway
De Pere, WI 54115
ph: (414) 339-7800

TV AND ON-LINE SHOPPING SITES

The television shopping industry is a $3 billion electronic-retailing business that is dominated by a few networks, such as QVC and Home Shopping Network. These are merchandise-oriented vending channels on cable television, and their program formats vary. They might feature crafts along with a wide range of other consumer products. Live, on-camera demonstrations by program hosts answer questions about materials, techniques, product history, and care. This item information is a key selling factor; viewer-shoppers can discuss the merchandise on-air with customer service representatives, or they can order directly through an automated voice-response unit. This venue offers broad exposure to middle-class consumers, who have the option to pay for their purchases in monthly installments.

This is a single-product business (carrying only one craft item from an artisan, much like a catalog house) in which production capability, quantity back-up, and quality control are vital. If you craft only one-of-a-kind items, this market isn't for you; the shopping networks depend on large quantities. It is a tough, unforgiving business, which is item driven. Buyers basically look for goods that fit in where they have programming needs (for example, they might have a segment on teddy bears as collectibles and want to feature handmade bears), and they test the products in time slots. If merchandise doesn't test well, it doesn't get a second chance. In fact, the opportunity for a similar item is then equally slim. Buyers in this market expect to sell at least $2,000-worth of product per minute of television time.

No doubt you've read news accounts of famous personalities selling millions of dollars of merchandise on cable channels, and you may even have heard about lesser-known people who have made fortunes in this market. Still, there are many reasons to approach this market with caution. For example, if you don't have an introduction, getting to the buyer is a daunting effort in and of itself.

Once your product passes the selection process, the buyer then sends it to quality control for rigorous testing. The quality assurance department at QVC test-drops your samples several times. Your packaging must hold up for shipping via UPS. According to Stephanie Schus, a marketing consultant who places products on shopping networks, even if your packing withstands testing "you're likely to get knocked out if quality assurance perceives any return problems. One glass craftsman tried repackaging a vase several times so it would pass the test, spending a lot of money in that effort. Then the vase didn't sell well."

Another hurdle is quantity. The first question you will probably be asked is, "Can you supply quantity?" Buyers usually test an item with a large opening order of $10,000 to $15,000. When they place the order, they expect you to ship on consignment, and if your craft doesn't sell, you'll get it back. You must consider whether you can afford to take back that inventory. On the other hand, if your piece sells well, the buyer might want a reorder four to six weeks later, and you'll have to be able to supply it. If your fulfillment takes longer, you might be able to persuade the buyer to postpone a rerun of your craft until you can handle delivery.

Clearly, this is risky business. If you want to pursue this selling opportunity, Schus advises that you go into this in a way that won't make or break your operation. "In the worst-case scenario, you sell only 10 percent, and you get the rest back. What would that do to you? You have to assess the impact on your business." She suggests that you look at the endeavor as a promotional opportunity. "Think of it as seven minutes of national television-ad time." Viewed in this way, even with limited sales, the experience of national exposure could ultimately bring profitable business in the future.

Other relatively recent developments in marketing venues are on-line shopping sites. On-line shopping generated approximately $700 to $800 million dollars in 1995 and is expected to expand to the $5 billion range by 1998. That is an anticipated annual growth rate of 200 percent. While no one has precise figures, newspaper and magazine polls indicate a growing attraction to on-line purchasing. Approximately 17.6 million people use the World Wide Web, and insiders anticipate that by 1998 there will be 130 million users, 10 percent of whom may become shoppers.

To date, successful Internet marketing offers services and products, such as information, advertising, computer products and software, electronics, books, compact discs, travel services, and flowers. Although this is a business in its infancy, other companies are preparing for the future by establishing a presence on the Internet with home pages and web sites. Crafts sites, such as "The CraftWEB Project" and "The Arts and Crafts Society," provide on-line communities for both craft professionals and consumers interested in crafts. These services create an opportunity to exchange information and promote crafts worldwide.

"The CraftWEB Project" invites artisans and others to discuss issues; allows them access to chat rooms, a bookstore, resources, and a help desk; and offers a calendar and newsletter. Similarly, "The Arts and Crafts Society" hosts an on-line "home," a home page in the spirit of the societies inspired by the Arts and Crafts movement, and they provide the following:

- *An events calendar* listing national conferences, exhibits, tours, auctions, lectures and related happenings.
- *A forum* for interactive discussions with a variety of people in the field, including researchers, experts, and collectors, and a classified ad section.
- *Archives* containing a compendium of resources pertaining to the Arts and Crafts movement, plus annotations, and images.
- *A marketplace* featuring products and services from current artisans, studios, and merchants.

"The Internet," says Lauren Freedman, president of e-tailing Group, an on-line retail consulting company based in Chicago, "is a good place to get industry information, communicate with peers, and learn about tips, outside events, and special projects in an open forum." If you want to establish your own site, however, she cautions, "Be realistic and establish goals. Set a budget—even if it's a small one."

You can establish a quick classified ad for $1,500 (with the relatively inexpensive help of a high school or university student) or go to a full-service company to build a site. Freedman advises users to have a design concept. "Shop around, then apply the vision. Figure out where you want to be, where you're going to reside. Research and select your designer wisely."

Once you establish a site, you should change your look and content frequently to ensure continued consumer interest; alter pictures and revise descriptions. Be innovative. Note that monthly maintenance fees vary depending on the amount of camera-ready images used and other services, such as linkage to additional sites.

To help you get started on-line, Freedman offers 10 rules for designing a retail Internet site:

1. "Don't package—redefine." —Barry Diller (This means don't just present exactly what you already have; tailor your crafts to better suit this venue.)
2. Time is of the essence—Internet users are impatient.
3. No one reads—keep your text and paragraphs to a minimum.
4. Be visual—maximize your use of graphics, taking modem speed into account.
5. Be interactive—allow your users to talk back.
6. Tell your users how to order early and often.
7. Tell your users where to find you.
8. Keep any additional pages as interesting as your main menus.
9. Don't over-merchandise—be more information-oriented.
10. Exploit the dynamism of the medium—be creative.

Freedman warns that in designing a site, as in other things, there is the "pay nothing, get nothing theory." She also emphasizes the importance of linking and promoting in the right places by connecting your site to other, related web sites. Other factors to consider involve graphics. For example, graphic quality is important—computer screen and browser software (which allows you to view graphics) can create color alterations, resulting in an inaccurate representation of your crafts; after establishing the initial contact and interest, sending actual photographs may better help your potential customers. You should also take computer speed in downloading graphics into account—too many images on a page will substantially increase the downloading time; fewer images can reduce this time.

Initiating actual consumer purchasing may take some time and confidence. Customers might be concerned about secure transactions. Freedman sees this as a nonissue, however, because the major players have developed secure encryption codes, off-line pin numbers, and protected passwords. "There will always be hackers, but there is the $50 [credit card] liability limit. The reality is that it is difficult to pick up 15 numbers flying through cyberspace." As customers get used to this form of business, credit security won't inhibit sales, but Freedman still suggests keeping revenue goals realistic. Initially, you should view on-line shopping as product-information advertising.

The advantages of the Internet are multifaceted. The global reach and speed provide access to your peers and customers through efficient communication. This direct customer contact lowers marketing costs. While the quality of graphics is limited, the potential with added video and audio is tremendous. Value selling (as opposed to hard selling) provides information and answers consumer questions, allowing for networking opportunities and product knowledge.

TV SHOPPING SITES

QVC
Goshen Corporate Park
West Chester, PA 19380
ph: (215) 430-8979

ON-LINE SHOPPING SITES

AAA Craft Link
http://www.primenet.com/~higley/

Add Your Own Ceramics Link
http://apple.sdsu.edu/ceramicsweb/
Userlink/userlinks.html

Allan's Country Craft Cupboard
http://www.inquo.net/~crafts/

All-Internet Shopping Directory:
Arts & Crafts
http://www.webcom.com/~tbrown/
artcraft.html

The American Smorgasboard's
Calendar of Arts/Crafts Events
http://www.nic.com/~circa/calendar.htm

Arts and Crafts Search Page
http://www.ro.com/av/search/

Biggest Little Craft Mall
http://www.craftmall.com/

CKSINFO
http://www.cyberus.ca/~cksinfo

Craft Mall
http://www.craft.com//shops.html

CraftNet
http://mkn.co.uk/help/extra/craftnet/
craft

CraftWeb
http://www.craftweb.com/

Cyberspace Hand Craft Market
http://www.craft.com/craft/market

Design Studio Internet Catalog
http://www.spectracom.com/
designstudio/

For Sale For Sale
http://tc.frontiercomm.net/~tcross/
OCG.htm

New England Crafts Fair
http://www.tiac.net/users/penink/
necf.html

R Crafts Gift Catalog
http://www.kemero.com/catalog.shtml

Top Notch
http://www.vitinc.com/topnotch/

Welcome to Madcrafts
http://www.madcrafts.com/

WHOLESALERS, SALES REPRESENTATIVES, AND EXPORT AGENTS

Wholesalers (either individuals or businesses) gather numerous products from various sources and act as collective sales representatives. They may just take orders and collect a commission for representing your work, or they may assume the burden of order fulfillment and marketing. They select products that they can sell successfully to their established client base. Price, quantity, producer reliability, and quality are important considerations in their craft choices. They evaluate costs and buy products with enough profit margin to allow them to wholesale to their customers. Wholesalers usually need several samples to show at trade shows or to distribute to their sales representatives for use when they call on buyers.

Sales representatives (also called sales "reps") are commissioned agents who usually cover a particular geographic area, selling crafts to retail accounts. Working independently or for wholesalers, they service clients in regions that you may not be able to cover, thereby giving your work broader exposure. Though negotiable, their commission is commonly based on 15 percent of the total wholesale order. They usually carry the work of several craftspeople or other gift lines, all of which they show by scheduling buyer appointments or exhibiting at their own trade-show booths; they then pass any orders on to the artisans, who handle fulfillment. Sales reps can help reach a broad client base and maintain customer relations for you by following up on problems and reorders, and showing new designs. To find a good sales rep, ask for recommendations from your favorite buyers, or walk through a trade show and talk to reps whose product lines and sales manners impress you.

Similar to sales reps, export agents can also be independent or work for companies. They represent your line overseas, and they work on commission or purchase crafts from you at wholesale prices and hold the inventory for export to global markets. If they are individual sales reps, they show your work (and that of others) at trade shows or make specific buyer appointments; then, they take orders and pass them on to you for fulfillment. If, however, they are import or wholesale businesses in their country, then the company assumes the burden of order fulfillment, transportation, and warehousing of crafts.

Export agents select items that they think they can sell successfully to their retail accounts in other countries. Price, quantity, producer reliability, and consistency of quality are important considerations in their choice of craft. They evaluate costs and buy products with enough margin to cover customs and overseas freight and still make a profit. They require samples, which they show or test-market at wholesale trade shows in various countries. If they get sufficient orders, they will warehouse inventory for their clients.

Leta Stathacos, former buyer for the Albright-Knox Art Gallery Shop, represents contemporary craft artists at wholesale trade shows. As an independent sales rep, who covers domestic and foreign markets, she believes this is a natural extension of the museum experience. "I bring to the marketplace—nationally and internationally—people I admire, craft artists, designers, and creative people who are producing a product that stems from a unique talent and self-mission. That unusual aspect becomes an educational tool."

As a sales rep, Stathacos assumes responsibility for educating customers. "I like people to think about what they're holding," she says. "Is it useful, a cultural adaptation, funky, or minimal?" She explains that the process of making an object, and the story of who makes it, sets it apart. "I am terrified by the increasing lack of thought [about a product] that the consumer is developing because of the discount mentality. A person who is representing a craft artist must explain the object to a wholesale buyer."

Educating the customer is just one of the many responsibilities of a good sales rep. To select a rep, Stathacos says, "Talk to the sales rep first, send photos, then talk and ask questions. I choose parts of lines. To make a selection, I need visual literature—color photos on a plain background. Products do not need a setting. I need to just see the product. I don't know what they're selling if the background conflicts [with the craft]." In addition, Stathacos sees the whole world as her sales territory, rather than just one geographical area.

After selecting your sales rep, information is critical. Find out what your rep needs to represent you in the most advantageous way. Each rep will have slightly different requirements. "If price sheets are not clear, it increases the possibility of mistakes," says Stathacos. "I don't like sheets and sheets of paper. Use the back of sheets; use three sheets instead of six."

Stathacos believes that good communication between the rep and the craftsperson is the key to a successful relationship. Establishing trust, as well as good communication, is important in your sales relationship. Stathacos says, "I don't like begging for commission checks. We need to function in a businesslike setting. Send a monthly statement and include the check." Craftspeople should honor their commitments to their sales reps. If you aren't sending a check, communicate with your rep and explain why. Stathacos expects ethical behavior on both sides. "I work hard to establish someone and get a big order," she says. "Then the artist gets greedy and says 'I'll handle the business.' People need to be ethical. You have a relationship." To cement that relationship Stathacos offers these reminders:

- Provide regular communication—not after the fact. You don't even have to call, just fax information. Let people know if you are two weeks behind in shipping, etc.
- Be well educated about your own industry.
- Be responsible for your own customer credit checks. Sales reps will pass credit information about the buyer on to the craftsperson, but it isn't their responsibility to check credit references. Since no client is going to list a company that they haven't paid as a reference, you should call banks directly for complete data.

The following are lists of wholesalers and sales representatives from The Crafts Center database. For information about locating exporters, contact the Global Export Information Office at the U.S. Department of Commerce (Room 7424 HCHB, 14th Street & Constitution Ave., N.W., Washington, D.C., 20230; ph: 800-US4TRADE).

WHOLESALERS

The Alchemists
P. O. Box 1660
Green Valley, AZ 85622
ph: (602) 648-0500

Appalachian Crafts
P. O. Box 104
Irvine, KY 40336
ph: (606) 723-4678

Apple Whimseys
3774 Grove Street, Suite A
Lemon Grove, CA 91945
ph: (619) 469-6903

Artlico
522 Knickerbocker Road
Tenafly, NJ 07670
ph: (201) 567-5094
fax: (201) 567-6906

Basketville
Main Street
P. O. Box 710
Putney, VT 05346
ph: (802) 387-5509

Blackbriar Pottery Limited
1 Meeting House Lane
P. O. Box 430
Old Lyme, CT 06371
ph: (203) 434-8400

Brass Oak Company
6701 Seybold Road, Suite 102
Madison, WI 53719
ph: (608) 274-9700
fax: same

Catamount Glassware
309 County Street
Bennington, VT 05201
ph: (802) 442-5438
fax: (802) 442-5216

Country Folk
18 Rocky Point Road
Rowayton, CT 06853
ph: (203) 655-6887

Country Nouveau
P. O. Box 46
Island, KY 42350
ph: (502) 486-3272

Country Originals
3844 West Northside Drive
Jackson, MS 39209
ph: (601) 366-4229
fax: (601) 366-4294

Country Weavers Unlimited
P. O. Box 1683
London, KY 40743
ph: (606) 864-9532

Country Wholesale
P. O. Box 5405
Glencoe, AL 35905
ph: (800) 345-7923

Custom Designs Jewelry
3070 Alabama Road
Camden, NJ 08104
ph: (609) 962-0127

English Thatch
2912 Suffolk Drive
Houston, TX 77027
ph: (713) 524-7415

Farber Glass
2427 St. Paul Street
Baltimore, MD 21218
ph: (410) 338-0324

Fine Rag Basketry
17 Tacoma Avenue North
Tacoma, WA 98403
ph: (206) 383-6384

Flat Earth Clay Works
5670 North Broadway
Wichita, KS 67219
ph: (316) 838-2774

Flying Colors Ceramic Jewelry
1416 Cole Street
San Francisco, CA 94117
ph: (415) 282-6162

Fortley Potteries
2623 Seville Boulevard, Apt. 203
Clearwater, FL 34624
ph: (813) 461-7669

The Friends
318 East Church Street
Frederick, MD 21701
ph: (301) 695-6126

Frog Park Herbs and Handcrafts
Frog Park Road
Waterville, NY 13480
ph: (315) 841-8636

Genesis Art Glass
P. O. Box 24817
Rochester, NY 14624
ph: (716) 328-6130

Gills Rock Stoneware
12020 Lakeview Road
Ellison Bay, WI 54210
ph: (414) 854-2774

Glass Eye Studio
600 Northwest 40th Street
Seattle, WA 98107
ph: (206) 782-6548
fax: (206) 789-5505

Glass Reunions
1311 East Cary Street
Richmond, VA 23219
ph: (804) 643-3233

Grand Teton Natural History
Association
P. O. Box 170
Moose, WY 83012
ph: (307) 739-3404
fax: (307) 739-3438

Great Falls Metalworks
301 East 22nd Street
Paterson, NJ 07514
ph: (201) 523-6811

The Hands Work-Tinsnips
1585 Tennyson Street
Denver, CO 80204
ph: (303) 534-4251

Hardwood Creations
P. O. Box 542
Davis, CA 95616
ph: (916) 758-6624

The Herb Lady
P. O. Box 2129
Shepherdstown, WV 25443
ph: (304) 535-6570

K and M Crafts of Kentucky
10309 Deering Road
Louisville, KY 40272
ph: (502) 933-8432
fax: (502) 935-6267

Kountry Kreations
1 Washington Street
Towanda, PA 18848
ph: (800) 598-7447

La Botanique
P. O. Box 614
Alpharetta, GA 30201
ph: (404) 475-5435

Liberty Wares
1 Main Street
P. O. Box 5
Liberty, ME 04949
ph: (207) 589-4122

Marble Designs
11625 Columbia Center Drive,
Suite 200
Dallas, TX 75229
ph: (214) 243-1300

The Metal Man
1552 South Euclid Avenue
Tucson, AZ 85713
ph: (602) 792-2220

Metamorphosis
8411 Monroe Street
Stanton, CA 90680
ph: (714) 952-1504
fax: (714) 952-9518

Mountain Light Woodworks
1919 Old Town Road N.W., Suite 3
Albuquerque, NM 87104
ph: (505) 682-2223

North Country Wind Bells
Route 32
Round Pond, ME 04564
ph: (207) 677-2224

Northern Lights Candles
3474 Andover Road
Wellsville, NY 14895
ph: (716) 593-1200
fax: (716) 593-6481

Once Again
10817 Larkmeade Lane
Potomac, MD 20854
ph: (301) 983-1282

Otter Creek Quilt Works
Quarry Road
P. O. Box 23
New Haven, VT 05472
ph: (802) 453-3482

Paper Sharks
3463 State Street, Suite 192
Santa Barbara, CA 93105
ph: (805) 684-1685
fax: (805) 684-4346

Party Animal Celebrations
506 South Silver Lake Street
Oconomowoc, WI 53066
ph: (414) 569-0997

Pillows and Things
17 Lucerne Court
Cherry Hill, NJ 08003
ph: (609) 751-8433

The Pine Works
P. O. Box 22365
Lexington, KY 40522
ph: (606) 268-2453

Pleet Collection
18 Suncrest Drive
Dix Hills, NY 11746
ph: (516) 271-1134
fax: (516) 385-0798

Pod of Edgecomb
P. O. Box 108
Boothbay, ME 04537
ph: (207) 633-5447
fax: (207) 633-5497

The Porcelain Garden
28 Hammond, Suite A
Irvine, CA 92718
ph: (714) 380-0337
fax: (714) 380-8119

Reflections in Glass
P. O. Box 381
Cutten, CA 95534
ph: (707) 443-0135

Rustic Willow Furniture
2970 Negro Creek Road
Brodhead, KY 40409
ph: (606) 758-8587

Santa Fe Stoneworks
3790 Cerrillos Road
Santa Fe, NM 87501
ph: (505) 471-3953

Sculptural Ceramics
12490 Madison Avenue N.E.
Bainbridge Island, WA 98110
ph: (206) 842-9608

Salt Marsh Pottery
1167 Russells Mills Road
South Dartmouth, MA 02748
ph: (617) 636-4813

Sew So Special
Six Ryan Lane
Lincoln Park, NJ 07035
ph: (201) 694-9267

Skyflight Mobiles
P. O. Box 974
Woodinville, WA 98072
ph: (206) 485-0730

Snickerdoodles
P. O. Box 504
Ellensburg, WA 98926
ph: (509) 925-5505

Studio 7 Concepts
526 Raindance Street
Thousand Oaks, CA 91360
ph: (805) 493-1816
fax: (805) 492-6610

The Sunny Window
P. O. Box 199
Southboro, MA 01772
ph: (508) 485-8132

Thimbelina
66 Newtown Lane
East Hampton, NY 11937
ph: (516) 324-0729
fax: (516) 324-0891

Tokens and Coins
295 Lafayette Street
New York, NY 10012
ph: (212) 343-0046
fax: (212) 674-6575

The Tree Factory
5639 Brookshire Boulevard
Charlotte, NC 28216
ph: (704) 399-4446

Trial by Fire Pottery
442 College Highway
Southwick, MA 01077
ph: (413) 569-6975

U.S. Design Groups
21 Madison Plaza, Suite 137
Madison, NJ 07940
ph: (201) 822-8115

Waxen Candles
P. O. Box 422
Mifflinville, PA 18631
ph: (717) 759-2278

The Weaver's Corner
11664 Boston Road
Boston, KY 40107
ph: (502) 833-3240
fax: same

SALES REPRESENTATIVES

American-Craft Brokers
Stillwaters, Box 814
Wendell, MA 01379

Another Catalog Company
P. O. Box 22054
Cleveland, OH 44122

Art Gosz Association
1307 21st Street
Two Rivers, WI 54241
ph: (414) 793-5027

Artists' Marketing Service
160 Dresser Avenue
Prince Frederick, MD 20678
ph: (301) 855-1007

Avita
136 Cedar Street
Corning, NY 14830
ph: (607) 936-6216

Bernard Lowe and Associates
P. O. Box 8704
Spokane, WA 99203

B. K. Enterprises
3833 Schaefer, Suite E
Chino, CA 91710
ph: (909) 628-1291

Bob Baberfeld and Associates
451 East 58th Avenue,
Suite 1250, 1164
Denver, CO 80216
ph: (303) 296-1877

Bonz on the River
11930 Mississippi Drive
Champlin, MN 55316
ph: (612) 427-7929

Britton Sales
P. O. Box 180083
Austin, TX 78718
ph: (512) 836-6998

The Butler Group
1212 Atlanta Merchandise Mart
250 Spring Street
Atlanta, GA 30303
ph: (404) 577-6941

Cambridge Sales
451 East 58th Avenue, Suite 2145
Denver, CO 80216
ph: (303) 296-2664

Charles Zadeh's Creative Toys
International
P. O. Box 41
Glen Head, NY 11545
ph: (516) 759-8479

Chris Starratt and Associates
1591 Vinton
Memphis, TN 38104
ph: (901) 278-6299
fax: (901) 272-0540

CMA
1933 South Broadway, Suite 408
Los Angeles, CA 90007
ph: (213) 746-2163

Coco Company
300 North Elizabeth Street
Chicago, IL 60607
ph: (312) 829-0069

CORROBOREE Australian
Aboriginal Art
509 East 77 Street
New York, NY 10021
ph: (212) 249-7689

Country Couriers
P. O. Box 8143
Prairie Village, KS 66208
ph: (913) 642-2552

Country Workshop Marketing
827 Glenside Avenue
Department CD
Wyncote, PA 19095
ph: (215) 884-7721

Cowboy Sales
305 West Sunset Drive
Riverton, WY 82501
ph: (307) 856-9687

John A. Crum
P. O. Box 61478
Honolulu, HI 96839
ph: (808) 637-6960
fax: same

Cupps of Chicago
831 Oakton Street
Elk Grove, IL 60007
ph: (708) 593-5655

Custom Crafts
54 Pembroke Road
Danbury, CT 06810
ph: (203) 792-0466

Dance of the Ancestors – Traditions
through Art
2645 Maxwell Avenue
Oakland, CA 94619
ph: (510) 261-4321
fax: same

Davol Marketing Company
4 Clinton Avenue
Jamestown, RI 02835
ph: (800) 533-2865

Desert Jewel Company
P. O. Box 336
Cottonwood, AZ 86326
ph: (602) 634-2940

Ed Ibarra Enterprises
2507 North Main Street
Las Cruces, NM 88001
ph: (505) 525-3504

Endless Autumn
P. O. Box 534
Cambridge, MA 02140
ph: (617) 661-1192

ETCO
6100 Fourth Avenue South,
Rooms 218-219-221
Seattle, WA 98108
ph: (206) 762-1707

Famous Peddlers Marketing
Denver Merchandise Mart
451 East 58th Avenue, Suite 26
Denver, CO 80216
ph: (303) 295-0591

Fireburst
Rural Free Delivery 2
Orange, MA 01364
ph: (508) 575-0493
fax: (508) 575-0495

Frank Lennox Associates
3813 Lindy Lane
Weidman, MI 48893
ph: (517) 644-5053
fax: (517) 644-5162

Franzen Enterprises
1308 Wolff Avenue
Elgin, IL 60123
ph: (708) 888-4880

Goldstein and Company
12017 Golden Twig Court
Gaithersburg, MD 20878
ph: (301) 840-3814

Goodfellow Enterprises
10016 Tiffany Drive
New Orleans, LA 70123
ph: (504) 737-1855

A Good Representative
234 Fifth Avenue, 4th floor
New York, NY 10001
ph: (212) 472-2034

Helen Losson Association
1017 Woodmount Drive
New Albany, IN 47150
ph: (812) 948-0532

Hoffman and Hunt
4338 Carter Trail
Boulder, CO 80301
ph: (303) 449-8781

Howard Gibb Associates
11212 Green Dragon Court
Columbia, MD 21044
ph: (301) 997-9225

I. Sales Company – DBA His
Sales Company
230 Fifth Avenue, Suite 1111
New York, NY 10001
ph: (212) 683-4414

Jansco Marketing
P. O. Box 1265
Minnetonka, MN 55345
ph: (612) 473-3382

Joe Tamorello Sales Company
P. O. Box 872
Metairie, LA 70004
ph: (504) 838-9809

Joyce and Associates
P. O. Box 58057
280 World Trade Center
Dallas, TX 75258
ph: (214) 748-7201

Kemp Krafts
288 Flynn Avenue, Suite 2-C
Burlington, VT 05401
ph: (802) 862-4418

Kusek Associates
3104 West Lake Street
Minneapolis, MN 55416
ph: (612) 927-0030
fax: (612) 927-4624

La Rochelle
55 Upper Ritie Street
Piermont, NY 10968

Laughlin Enterprises
2024 Northwest 92nd Court
Des Moines, IA 50325
ph: (515) 225-1980

Laughlin's Country Pride
7326 Winsford Lane
Sylvania, OH 43560
ph: (419) 885-5266

Lineworks
3268 Railroad Avenue
Wantagh, NY 11793
ph: (516) 783-9741

Linking Landscape Culture Art
620 San Francisco Street
Santa Fe, NM 87501
ph: (505) 989-9639

Malmborg and You
2910 Kern Drive
Eau Claire, WI 54701
ph: (715) 839-8700
fax: (715) 839-7600

Marketing Companies
17910 Third Avenue West
Minneapolis, MN 55447
ph: (612) 559-8482

Market Masters
6800 West 115th, Suite 258
Overland Park, KS 66211
ph: (913) 491-0414

Miller's and Company
1067 Osborn Road
Zanesville, OH 43701
ph: (614) 454-8239

The Missing Link
3213 West Wheeler Street,
Suite 179
Seattle, WA 98199
ph: (206) 281-7676

Nelson and Associates
2623 West 27th Avenue
Spokane, WA 99223

New England Gifts Shop
191 Parkerville Road
Southboro, MA 01772
ph: (508) 753-8233

Louis W. Nicosia
Federal Station
Seaman's Unit
Seattle, WA
ph: (206) 441-0905

Northwest Images
6100 Fourth Avenue South,
Room 350
Seattle, WA 98108
ph: (206) 762-1063

Northwoods Trading Company
13451 Essex Court
Eden Prairie, MN 55347
ph: (612) 937-5275

Ozark Gift Mart
Route 1
Box 168
Noel, MO 64854
ph: (417) 762-3812

Pam Lutey and Associates
8128 West Frost Place
Littleton, CO 80123

Paragon Products
451 East 58th Avenue, Suite 1569
Denver, CO 80216
ph: (303) 293-2424

Peddler Sales
134 West Main Street
Tuckerton, NJ 08087

The Penisha Group
49680 West 8 Mile
Northville, MI 48167
ph: (313) 349-1499
fax: (313) 347-6962

PRINTFOLIO
110 West 40th Street
New York, NY 10018
ph: (212) 391-7466

Quality Products
HCR 88
P. O. Box 379
Baker City, OR 97814
ph: (503) 853-2344

Regal Sales
438 East Beech Street
Long Beach, NY 11561
ph: (516) 889-6121
fax: (516) 889-3286

Rideout International
12712 West 119th Terrace
Overland Park, KS 66213
ph: (913) 681-5127

Road Runners
222 Monte Vista Drive
Napa, CA 94559
ph: (707) 255-2683

The Road Show
4152 North Harding
Chicago, IL 60618
ph: (312) 539-0048

Rubell Collection
11666 Goshen Avenue, Suite 325
Los Angeles, CA 90049
ph: (310) 473-2283
fax: (310) 473-9853

Sandra Sciria and Associates
114 B East Lake Road
Auburn, NY 13021
ph: (315) 253-6552

SARMCO
1492 Merchandise Mart,
Number 15-105
Chicago, IL 60654
ph: (312) 527-1688

Siegel Sales
15631 North 50th Street
Scottsdale, AZ 85254
ph: (602) 493-7494

C. Tom Smith
P. O. Box 11503
Lexington, KY 40576
ph: (606) 255-1911

Spencer Enterprises
4355 Oakvista
Drayton Plains, MI 48020

Splash Sales
P. O. Box 511
Freeport, NY 11520
ph: (516) 546-1422

Stang Marketing
P. O. Box 33370
Cleveland, OH 44133
ph: (216) 237-5880

Statements Unlimited
6100 Fourth Avenue South,
Room 263
Seattle, WA 98108
ph: (206) 763-3770

Sterling Representation
Lloyd Sterling Graydon
891 Paseo Ferrelo
Santa Barbara, CA 93103
ph: (805) 564-8401

Tin Originals
P. O. Box 64037
Fayetteville, NC 28306
ph: (910) 424-1400

Traditions
P. O. Box 416
Claverack, NY 12513
ph: (518) 672-4917

Wendell Zellers Association
800 Wolf Drive
Logansport, IN 46947
ph: (219) 722-3507

William Becker Association
14904 Jeff Davis Highway, Suite 208
Woodbridge, VA 22191
ph: (703) 490-0368

WHOLESALE TRADE SHOWS AND TRADE PUBLICATIONS

The American Craft Council (ACC) and the Rosen Group sponsor wholesale trade shows specifically for craft artists and craft buyers. Both organizations jury these shows. The popularity of crafts, however, has inspired a number of general trade shows that have created special areas to highlight crafts. Fees for these show vary greatly depending on the host city, booth location and size, and other factors. These general shows cover various niche markets such as accessories, stationery, fashion, home furniture, and general gifts. Shows can draw a regional or international audience, giving you broad exposure to different kinds of buyers.

International shows, such as the New York International Gift Fair, provide a venue for wholesalers, importers, sales reps, manufacturers, and other producers and craft artists to show their wares once or twice a year to retail buyers in major cities and regions across the United States. This is an opportunity for broad product exposure. Each show has its own procedures and requirements, so it is best to contact the fair organizers directly.

"Supply and demand for crafts is different today than it was at the early shows at Rhinebeck," says Carol Sedestrom Ross, director of craft marketing for the George Little Management, organizers of the New York International Gift Fair. "Back then there were fewer people doing crafts, and buyers used to race up to crafts booths to get what was there. The old concept was to sit back and just let buyers come to you. Too many people are still doing that today, but it won't work anymore." The biggest hurdle for many craftspeople is the concept of actual selling; it is difficult, suggests Ross, because you're selling your ego. "Craftspeople are notorious for not selling their own work. But buyers need to be sold. Today the craft supply is greater. Buyers won't seek you out if you are sitting back with your head down reading a book." Ross advises craftspeople "to stand up and make eye contact. Then follow up. If you take a business card, call the next week. And, if they place an order, don't just send the work—call in three weeks. Ask if everything was received, what's selling, what isn't."

Too many craftspeople leave selling to chance. Buyers are busy and have limited time at trade shows. They want to accomplish as much as possible in the limited time they have. The easiest way to engage a buyer is to talk about your work—the process, the material, the uniqueness. Anything that you can say that romances your craft and educates the buyer will help your work stand out amid all the possibilities at the show. In addition, buyers need information and visuals to take with them; they cannot possibly remember everything they see. Invest money in a professionally designed color catalog, or print color product sheets to hand out with your price list. If you can't afford this, you should, at the very least, have a business card or postcard showing one of your products.

The ability of a craftsperson to be flexible is an appealing quality for buyers today. The climate for crafts has changed and buyers want "more, new, and unique resources," according to Ross. Twenty years ago if a buyer approached a craftsperson and asked about color or design changes, an artist would not respond favorably. "Today, an artist who is willing to work on special commission is very well positioned," says Ross.

Ross also advises craftspeople to know about the markets. If you cater to the retail market, because your work is too labor intensive, then retail fairs are obviously the best choice for you. If you produce for wholesale only, you'll want to try to reach as many buyers as possible. If you cover both the retail and wholesale arenas, a combination trade show may be right for you. Alternatively, you could try both at different times to see which is more profitable. You should also have an understanding of which buyers attend which shows, and what levels of attendance the different shows get.

Many retail buyers subscribe to monthly, bimonthly, or quarterly industry magazines. These trade publications review products and trade shows, suggest trends, and offer advice for craftspeople and retailers (see Catalogs and Special Magazines section). Advertising in these publications allows both companies and artisans to promote their crafts. Product cards inside offer buyers easy access to information for products that may interest them.

The shows listed here are the biggest and best attended, but you might also consider investigating other shows.

WHOLESALE TRADE SHOW ORGANIZERS

AMC Trade Shows
2140 Peachtree N.W., Suite 2200
Atlanta, GA 30303
ph: (800) 285-6278

Americana Sampler
P. O. Box 160020
Nashville, TN 37216
ph: (615) 227-2080

American Craft Enterprises
21 South Elting Corner Road
Highland, NY 12528
ph: (914) 883-6100
fax: (914) 883-6130

American Craft Marketing
P. O. Box 480
Slate Hill, NY 10973
ph: (914) 355-2400

American Gift and Art Show
100 Bickford Street
Rochester, NY 14606
ph: (716) 458-2580
fax: (716) 458-5087

Association and Tradeshow
Management Headquarters
1100-H Brandywine Boulevard
P. O. Box 2188
Zanesville, OH 43702
ph: (614) 452-4541
fax: (614) 452-2552

Atlanta National Gift and
Accessories Market
Atlanta Merchandise Mart, Suite 2200
240 Peachtree Street
Atlanta, GA 30303
ph: (404) 220-3000

Bass Shows
New England Gift Show Association
P. O. Box 369
Brockton, MA 02403
ph: (508) 583-8351
fax: (508) 586-1657

Beckman's Gift Show
Industry Productions of America
P. O. Box 27337
Los Angeles, CA 90027
ph: (213) 962-5424

Chicago Gift, Accessories Mart
222 Merchandise Mart, Suite 470
Chicago, IL 60654
ph: (312) 527-7838
fax: (312) 527-7783

China, Glass and Giftware Association
1033 Clifton Avenue
Clifton, NJ 07013
ph: (201) 779-1600

Cologne International Furniture Fair
40 West 57th Street, 31st floor
New York, NY 10019
ph: (212) 974-8836

Contemporary Crafts Market –
Roy Helms and Associates
1142 Auahi Street, Suite 2820
Honolulu, HI 96814
ph: (808) 422-7362

Creative Fairs Limited
New York Renaissance Fest
134 Fifth Avenue
New York, NY 10011

Dallas Market Center
2100 Stemmons Freeway
Dallas, TX 75207
ph: (214) 744-3131
fax: (214) 655-6238

Denver Merchandise Mart
451 East 58th Avenue
Denver, CO 80216
ph: (800) 289-6278

Douglas Trade Shows
P. O. Box 1087
Kaneohe, HI 96744
ph: (808) 254-3773

Expocon Management and
Association
P. O. Box 915
Fairfield, CT 06430
ph: (203) 374-1411
fax: (203) 374-9667

Fashion Accessory Expo
200 Connecticut Avenue
Norwalk, CT 06856
ph: (203) 852-0500

Festival Productions
2323 Poplar Street
Oakland, CA 94607
ph: (415) 268-8463

George Little Management
10 Bank Street, Suite 1200
White Plains, NY 10606
ph: (914) 421-3200
fax: (914) 948-6180

Gift Association of America
612 West Broad Street
Bethlehem, PA 18018
ph: (215) 861-9445

Helen Brett Enterprises
1988 University Lane
Lisle, IL 60532
ph: (708) 241-9865
fax: (708) 241-9870

The Heritage Market of
American Crafts
P. O. Box 389
Carlisle, PA 17013
ph: (717) 249-9404
fax: (717) 258-0265

Indianapolis Giftware Association
Indianapolis Gift Mart
4475 Allison Road
Indianapolis, IN 46205
ph: (317) 252-5766

Kansas City Merchandise Mart
6800 West 115th Street
Overland Park, KS 66211
ph: (913) 491-6688

Karel Expositions Management
P. O. Box 19-1217
Miami Beach, FL 33119
ph: (305) 534-7469

Kentucky Craft Market
39 Fountain Place
Frankfort, KY 40601
ph: (502) 564-8076
fax: (502) 564-5696

Market Square Shows
Valley Forge Furniture Market
P. O. Box 250
Carlisle, PA 17013
ph: (717) 796-2377

Miami International
Merchandise Mart
777 Northwest 72nd Avenue
Miami, FL 33126
ph: (305) 261-2900

Michigan Association of
Gift Salesman
Northville Square
133 West Main Street
Northville, MI 48167
ph: (313) 348-7890

Minneapolis Gift Mart
10301 Bren Road West
Minnesota, MN 55343
ph: (612) 932-7200

Museum Stores Association
401 South Cherry Street, Suite 460
Denver, CO 80222

The National Needlework Association
650 Danbury Road
Ridgefield, CT 06877

Neocon
222 Merchandise Mart, Suite 470
Chicago, IL 60654
ph: (800) 677-6278

New York Merchandise Mart
41 Madison Avenue
New York, NY 10010
ph: (212) 686-1203

Northern New England Products
Trade Show/Small Business
Development Center
96 Falmouth Street
Portland, ME 04103
ph: (800) 638-6787

North Lakes Gift Shows
208 Mill Road
Manitowoc, WI 54220
ph: (414) 682-6225

OASIS Gift Trade Show
1130 East Missouri Street,
Suite 750
Phoenix, AZ 85014
ph: (602) 230-2717

Offinger Management
P. O. Box 2188
Zanesville, OH 43702
ph: (614) 452-4541

Reber Eriel Company
221 King Manor Drive
King of Prussia, PA 19406
ph: (610) 272-4020

Rome Enterprises
4208 Rivanna Drive
Louisville, KY 40299
ph: (502) 267-7663

The Rosen Group
3000 Chestnut Avenue,
Suite 300
Mill Center
Baltimore, MD 21211
ph: (410) 889-2933
fax: (410) 889-1320

Salt Lake Gift Show
Progressive Exhibitors
P. O. Box 271368
Salt Lake City, UT 84127
ph: (801) 973-7800
fax: (801) 972-1478

South Eastern Exhibitions
805 Parkway
Gatlinburg, TN 37738

Southern Shows
P. O. Box 36859
Charlotte, NC 28236
ph: (704) 376-6594
fax: (704) 376-6345

Toy Manufacturers of America
200 Fifth Avenue, Suite 740
New York, NY 10010
ph: (212) 675-1141

Tradeshow and Exhibit Manager
1150 Yale Street, Suite 12
Santa Monica, CA 90403
ph: (310) 828-1309

Transworld Exhibits
1850 Oak Street
Northfield, IL 60093
ph: (708) 446-8434
fax: (708) 446-3523

Tropical Shows
P. O. Box R Uleta
Miami, FL 33164
ph: (305) 261-1213

Western Exhibitors
2181 Greenwich Street
San Francisco, CA 94121
ph: (415) 346-6666

ADDITIONAL MARKETS

There are a number of other venues that craftspeople can explore for marketing their crafts. They may present great opportunities to generate business, develop contacts, and expand your customer base.

COMBINATION MARKETS AND CORPORATE GIFTS

Craft markets exist in industries that combine their resources. Often two separate businesses such as food and crafts, florists and crafts, or cosmetics and crafts join forces to produce a unique item. For example, you might sell your handmade baskets to a company that would fill them with flowers or food, thus creating a gift composed of the two original products. Joint efforts can create profitable new business possibilities.

Often, company or store owners won't think of combination ideas on their own or don't know where to locate the proper resources, but they would welcome the ideas when presented to them. This is the perfect opportunity for you to approach them with your proposals, especially if you join forces with another craftsperson also looking for new creative options.

Corporate gifts can also be another possible craft venue. Major businesses, corporations, and nonprofit organizations—both local and international—often give their clients, donors, members, or employees gifts. Whether they are end-of-the-year thank-yous or sales incentives, these tokens of appreciation create good will and generate business within companies, and so corporate-gift buyers look for products year round.

If you want to break into this market, you must be able to supply quantity. An order for 500 or even 2,000 pieces is not uncommon. If you can handle these amounts, you might consider producing a separate catalog or sales sheet geared to attract the attention of corporate-gift buyers. Generally, however, it is useful to have a sales representative who sells to this specialized market and already has buyer contacts. You should also consider these other suggestions:

- Advertise in industry journals.
- Contact local businesses.
- Create a database of corporate names and addresses from library reference materials and industry guides.
- Advise your galleries and sales reps of your corporate-gift program.
- Design your business cards with an additional line that reads "Corporate and Executive Gifts."
- Print a separate catalog or information sheet describing your corporate program.

EMBASSIES AND CONGRESSIONAL OFFICES

Embassies throughout the world, and congressional offices in the United States, can offer a showcase for crafts. They provide visibility and prestige for the craftsperson. Sometimes these offices even organize exhibits or publicity campaigns for crafts in conjunction with stores and cultural institutions, and they can assist craft groups in promoting their creative work to local communities and buyers.

Administered by the U.S. Department of State, the Art In Embassies Program (AIEP) is a valuable resource for American craft artists who want to place their work abroad. Curators in this program look for recognizable quality that reflects well on America and doesn't conflict with the culture of the host country. Their address is AIEP, U.S. Department of State, 22 & C Streets, NW, Washington, D.C., 20006 (ph: 202-647-5723).

AIEP searches for work that will complement the environments of the participating embassies. An ambassador's personal vision, combined with a desire to reflect particular ethnic or regional themes or different periods of American art and cultural history, shapes the focus of the collections abroad. With art displayed in 170 American ambassadors' residences and overseas economic agencies worldwide, the program features many quilts, tapestries, sculptures, and ceramics. Working in consultation with the ambassadors and their representatives, curators from AIEP select pieces from various sources, such as slide submissions, art galleries, museums, collectors, craft fairs, and trade publications. On average, AIEP's office receives about 20 unsolicited submissions per week.

When looking for specific artwork or craft designs, curators occasionally place announcements in industry newsletters or trade journals. In addition to the actual work itself, curators consider packaging, fragility, shipping, weight, and other possible constraints. When chosen, artwork is lent for the duration of an ambassador's assignment, which is usually three years. "It is important to remember that this is a loan program," says Dawn Zimmerman, the manager of lender and donor relations. Although no art is for sale, the prestige and exposure could lead to further interest in your crafts. Collectors contact the program about participating artists, and AIEP helps make the connection.

The opportunity for cultural outreach is a source of pride for American ambassadors, and the program takes great care in its organization, maintenance, and installation of the artwork. Available funds and the number of public rooms in each embassy determine the size of each collection. After art is selected, AIEP completes formal loan agreements and arranges crating, insurance, and shipping. It also issues instructions for unpacking, installing, handling, and returning the collection to ensure proper care of the exhibited work.

GLOSSARY

accounting The recording of monetary business activity by summarizing, classifying, and analyzing the results of all transactions.

accounts payable Money that the buyer owes for goods or services received but not yet paid for.

accounts receivable Money due the vendor for goods or services delivered but not yet paid for.

adjustment The correction of an error or misunderstanding to the satisfaction of both the customer and the merchant. This could refer to a price, refund, overcharging, or improper shipping, handling, or recording of a transaction.

advance dating A future date set by the seller when the terms of the sale become applicable. For example, an order placed in January for delivery on March 1 could have payment terms of 2/10 net 30, indicating that the goods may be paid by April 10 at a two-percent discount. *See also* term

airway bill A transportation document and a contract between the shipper and air carrier that identifies the goods being shipped by air to the buyer.

allowance There are a few different types of allowances. *Advertising allowance:* money or credit allotted by a vendor to defray the cost of advertising. *Customer allowance:* a reduction in price offered to a customer to compensate for the sale of unsatisfactory goods, often in lieu of the customer returning the merchandise. *Vendor allowance:* a reduction in price or cancellation of charges by the vendor or producer for defective or unsatisfactory goods, or in lieu of the return of merchandise.

anticipation   An additional discount given by the vendor to the buyer for early payment of an invoice. For example, if payment terms are net 90 days, the vendor may offer buyers a one-percent discount per month early that they pay their bill.

approval sale   A sale of goods subject to future approval that gives the customer unlimited return privileges. *See also* memo billing

assets   Resources owned by a business or individual. These can include property, rights, inventory, and accounts receivable.

assistant buyer   A member of a company's buying staff whose responsibilities include merchandise operations such as reordering products, analyzing sales, price checking, receiving, and following through on purchasing, returns, and marketing details.

assortment   A complete range of product choices within a merchandise line, including variations in price, size, style, color, pattern, and material.

audit   A review or verification of accounting records by internal or external auditors.

back order   The unfilled balance of a customer's order. Both the producer and the buyer can cancel items on back order, depending on the terms of the purchase order and the cancellation date.

back-up order   Frequently placed by large importers and catalog buyers, this is an additional merchandise purchase (ordered at the time of the initial buy) reserved by the buyer, usually for a future date, to guarantee supply and fast delivery on any subsequent demands for the same product.

bad debt   Money, owed for goods or services, which is uncollectable.

balance sheet   A financial statement that indicates the net worth of a business at any given time. It lists assets, liabilities, and owner's equity.

basic stock   Staple products that are in constant customer demand. Often referred to as "bread and butter" items, these are the backbone of a business and should always be in stock and ready for delivery. Stock outs (temporary shortages) on these consistent sellers would result in a loss of business.

bill of lading	A transportation document, signed by the carrier, listing goods shipped; a contract between the shipper and carrier for a shipment.
blanket order	An order, placed before production starts, to meet anticipated needs for a specified time period. A buyer draws smaller orders from the open order (the blanket order) or "calls out" merchandise from the blanket order as needed for the season indicated. This can be for a prearranged quantity or dollar amount.
bonded warehouse	A warehouse that is insured against the loss of stored goods.
book inventory	The value of a store's on-hand retail inventory shown in the accounting records without taking a physical inventory.
bookkeeping	The actual accounting for and record-keeping of all business transactions.
break-even point	The point at which the expenses equal the costs and there is no-profit and no-loss.
budget	A financial operating plan.
buyer	An executive whose responsibilities include, but aren't limited to, product selection, purchasing, pricing, vendor negotiating, training, and merchandising.
buying agent	An individual (or company) who facilitates purchasing and shipping arrangements for buyers and importers. Duties often include planning buyer itineraries; locating suppliers and manufacturers, and handling financial transactions for the buyer; tracking purchase orders and acting as intermediaries on problems, such as quality control and delayed deliveries. Agents receive a commission fee based on the total purchases at cost plus related expenses.
buying plan	A store's monetary budget for each department or merchandise classification to control the purchasing and inventory levels of goods. *See also* open-to-buy
carrier	Any freight handler.
cash discount	A deduction, expressed as a percentage, off the invoice total for early payment of a bill. This is an optional benefit.
cash flow	The amount of actual cash available for use in operating a business.

cash-in-advance	A method of payment for goods prior to receipt. This method is sometimes used as an advance to the producer for material for customized merchandise.
central buying	Group buying activity for area or associated stores, and often for price advantage or other economies of effort.
certificate of origin	A document indicating the country in which a product is made. Required for entry of any product into the U.S.
charge-back	A vendor debit or statement issued by a buyer to a vendor for returned merchandise or other billing adjustments.
CIF	Meaning "cost, insurance, freight," this term is expressed as part of a cost-price quotation. It indicates that the *seller* pays the cost of all expenses related to insuring, shipping, and delivering the goods to an agreed destination, where the *buyer* then assumes responsibility for the merchandise.
claim	A charge to a transportation company for goods damaged in shipment while in the carrier's possession.
classification	A grouping of similar products within a product line.
closeout	A discontinued product or line of merchandise offered at a reduced price for quick sale. Manufacturers often use this to clear slow-moving stock from their inventory.
COD	Meaning "collect on delivery" or "cash on delivery," this indicates that payment is due to the vendor from the buyer upon delivery of the goods.
collateral	Something offered as security to ensure the delivery of goods or payment of a debt.
common carrier	A transportation company that accepts shipments and maintains regular delivery routes and services, at established rates, to move merchandise from one location to another.
confirmation	The official written agreement for a merchandise order. *See also* contract; purchase order
consignee	An individual, agent, or company to whom the goods are assigned or delivered.
consignment sale	A product order owned by the seller but physically transferred to the buyer. Title remains with the seller until the merchandise is sold, and any unsold goods can be returned to the seller without payment within the time period specified on the purchase order. Payment by the buyer is made only on goods sold.

consignor	The originator of the shipment.
contract	A legal agreement that expresses mutual responsibilities between individuals or companies. A contract for goods and services issued by a buyer is called a *purchase order*.
cooperative	A business that is owned, operated, and managed by its employees or an association of customers.
cooperative buying	Affiliated or consolidated buying by a number of stores to save money or economize in other ways.
corporation	An organization bound together legally to establish a business.
cosigner	A joint signer of a loan agreement who is equally obligated to repay that loan.
cost	The wholesale price of an item. *See also* wholesale
cost of goods sold	The price of goods, less discounts and plus transportation and other related costs.
credit	The ability to purchase goods in exchange for a promise to pay at a later date.
customer service	Attention to customer needs, with regard to products bought or services rendered. Customer service should be prompt and courteous, with every effort made to keep promises and provide consistent quality, supply, and delivery.
debit	A record of a debt or charge on the left-hand side of a balance sheet or account; an addition to expenses or a deduction from revenues or net worth.
debit memorandum	A form prepared by the buyer or accounts payable department and sent to the seller seeking a deduction in the amount owed for a specific reason, perhaps a short shipment or damaged goods. It is often deducted from a current or future invoice.
default	A failure to fulfill a legal requirement, financial obligation, contract, or other agreement.
depreciation	A decrease in price or estimated value of a tangible asset over time; also, a normal business expense deducted on taxes as a cost of doing business.
direct mail	Printed mailing pieces that advertise goods, services, or events and are designed to generate business.

discount store	Usually a large retail store using a mass-market merchandising strategy of providing goods with a lower-than-normal markup. These stores have unadorned interiors and limited customer service.
distribution	The allocation of goods to various selling locations.
distributor	A wholesaler; also, a company or individual who acts as a middleman to distribute products (to retailers) for wholesale manufacturers.
documents	Any paperwork (such as invoices, packing slips, bills of lading) that accompanies merchandise shipments.
draft	An order for payment drawn by one individual or bank on another.
drawee	A party (an individual or bank) on which an order for payment is drawn.
drawer	The one who makes a promissory note or writes an order for payment.
drayage	The work or charges for carting goods away from one place to another.
drop shipment	A direct shipment from the manufacturer or vendor to the customer or to some other specified location.
dumping	The act of selling products below prevailing local market prices, creating an unfair competitive advantage.
dun	To make constant demands for payment; also, an urgent request for payment.
EDP	*See* electronic data processing
electronic data processing	Work done by computerized systems. Also referred to as EDP.
ending inventory	Retail stock on hand at the end of an accounting period.
end-of-month dating	A billing term that applies to the discount, off the invoice price, counted from the end of the month instead of the date of the bill.
end user	The final customer.
EOM	*See* end-of-month dating
equity	The money value of or owner's investment in a business.
ex-dock	A price quoted to a buyer that includes the cost of shipping the goods to the import dock.

ex-factory A price quoted to a buyer for goods direct from the point of origin, indicating that the buyer must assume responsibility for all shipping costs.

exporter A person or company responsible for shipping a commodity out of one country and into another.

export license A government document that authorizes the export of a specific quantity of goods to a certain country. If a country has restrictions or a quota system for goods, a license may be necessary.

extra dating An invoice term that refers to deferred dating, giving the buyer extra time to pay the bill.

factor A specialized financial institution that buys accounts receivable.

factoring An accounts-receivable arrangement in which banks or other financial institutions purchase and assume all bill collection responsibility and risk without recourse.

financial statement A monetary record of a company's business status.

fiscal year For accounting purposes, any successive 12-month period.

FOB *See* free-on-board

free-on-board A term applied to the agreed shipping destination where the buyer assumes title of the goods and then pays for continued transportation costs. Also referred to as FOB. For example, *FOB producer* (or *manufacturer)* means the buyer pays for all transportation charges. *FOB destination* (or *store)* means that the seller assumes all freight charges. *FOB shipping point* (or *dock)* indicates that the buyer takes responsibility for transportation costs at the origin of the shipment.

freight bill An invoice for the transportation costs of a shipment of merchandise.

freight collect A term indicating that the buyer pays for the merchandise when it arrives. If the terms of the purchase are FOB destination, the buyer can deduct the freight charges from the vendor's bill.

freight prepaid A term meaning that the seller has already paid the freight charges at the time of shipment. Depending on the terms of the purchase, the vendor can prepay these charges and then add them to the merchandise invoice.

gross margin	The selling price minus the cost of an item; also, net sales less the total cost of goods sold.
guarantee	A promise to repay a loan; also, an assurance or pledge, either written or implied that affirms the quality of goods—as in a "money-back guarantee."
guaranteed sale	An agreement under which the buyer can return goods to the seller for full credit or merchandise exchange. The buyer assumes no risk.
hard copy	A printed copy of a purchase order, report, or other document.
hard goods, hard lines	Merchandise sold in houseware or home furnishing departments of stores.
house brand	A store or company's own merchandise label, which may be a name or logo.
initial markup, initial mark-on	Expressed as a percentage of the retail value, this is the difference between the wholesale price of the goods and the initial retail price. For example, if the wholesale price of a product is $4 and the original retail price (before any markdowns or discounts) is $10, the initial markup is 60 percent.
in-transit	A term describing merchandise that is en route to its destination.
inventory	Physical stock on hand; also, the monetary value of goods on hand expressed at cost or retail.
inventory overage	The amount of stock on hand in excess of the book inventory.
inventory shortage	The difference between the book inventory and the physical inventory on hand for retail sale; also, a loss due to internal or external theft or inaccurate paperwork.
invoice	An itemized bill for goods or services that matches the purchase order.
irregular	An imperfect article of merchandise (sometimes called a *second*).
jobber	A wholesaler or middleman who purchases goods from manufacturers or importers and sells them to retailers. This term is derived from a dealer in job lots.

job lot   An end-of-season surplus or incomplete merchandise assortment offered by a manufacturer to a retailer at reduced prices as a promotional effort. Vendors offer job lots as a method of disposing of the past season's goods to lower their inventories, increase cash flow, and make room for new goods.

journal   A report or log of original transaction entries recorded in sequence prior to entry into respective ledgers.

keystone markup   This markup method establishes the retail price by doubling the wholesale price. For example, an item purchased at a price of $1 wholesale would be $2 retail.

lead time   Time required to produce an item and ship it to a destination.

letter of credit   A letter of financial arrangement issued by a bank on behalf of a buyer that allocates a certain amount of funds for a specified time period for a seller to draw upon for payment of purchased goods. It functions as a guarantee to the vendor of eventual payment for drafts drawn.

liability insurance   Insurance protection against risks for which businesses would be liable.

license   Formal, written permission granted to a business to manufacture goods using logos or trademarks of another company. The manufacturer usually acquires this license to enable them to expand their own merchandise offering and thus increase their sales. For this permission, the manufacturer must pay a royalty to the company that grants the license.

line   A merchandise assortment of various styles, colors, and price ranges.

liquidity   The ability of a business to quickly convert its assets to cash without suffering a loss.

list price   Suggested retail price; also, a printed wholesale-catalog price subject to trade discounts.

loss leader   An item in a store or catalog that is priced below the competition, often advertised and used to generate sales.

mail-order house   A business that sells products through the mail, based on orders received from ads or catalogs.

maintained markup, maintained mark-on	The difference between the cost of goods sold and the net sales figures, expressed as a dollar amount or a percentage.
manifest	A record or form listing all shipping information, such as the description, cost, number, and weight of the packages, and the consignor and consignee.
manufacturer	The producer of finished goods from raw materials.
manufacturer's representative	A professional salesperson who represents and sells a manufacturer's goods to different markets. A representative (also called a rep) often works on a commission basis and shows merchandise from several manufacturers.
markdown	A retail price reduction, expressed in a dollar amount or as a percentage off of the selling price.
markdown cancellation	A price change that raises a discounted price of an item to a higher selling price, usually restoring the original retail price. Retailers often implement markdown cancellations after special sales events.
markdown money	Money that a vendor offers to a retailer to reduce the selling price of slow-moving merchandise.
market	Any place where goods and services are traded or bought and sold; also, a gathering of people for the purposes of trade; a retail establishment of a particular kind; or a trade show, permanent showroom, or merchandise mart (a building) where wholesale goods are exhibited.
market niche	A target audience for a particular type of product.
market potential	The maximum sales opportunities in a particular area or market niche.
market share	The percentage that a company has of the total industry business in a given area or market.
marketing strategy	An extended business plan, for selling a product or service, which anticipates changes and different market conditions.
mark-on	The difference between actual cost and the retail selling price. This is often more popularly, though incorrectly, referred to as markup.
markup	An upward retail-price revision of the initial mark-on. This creates a higher selling price than the original retail one. The term is often used incorrectly to describe mark-on.

memo billing | An agreement in which a buyer orders samples to be billed only on approval, with no obligation to buy. Terms are usually net 30 days, at which point the buyer either returns the samples or keeps them and pays the invoice. *See also* on approval

merchandise | Products and product lines.

merchandise mix | A range of items offered for sale within a particular store or store department.

minimum order | The smallest quantity that a manufacturer will accept for an order. This is usually expressed in dollars, item units, or weight.

net profit | Net or total income remaining after production costs and other expenses are deducted (before taxes). Also referred to as *net operating income.*

net sales | The gross sales less merchandise returns and other deductions, such as discounts and allowances.

net terms | The actual billed amount on the invoice. Payment is expected without cash discounts taken. The term "net 30" on an invoice means that the full payment should be made within 30 days of the billing date. *See also* ordinary dating

net worth | The financial value of a firm, or individual, calculated by deducting any debt from total assets.

nonoperating expenses | Indirect business expenses such as interest payments.

on approval | Buyers select samples to review in their office for usually up to 30 days with no obligation to buy or pay for them until the specified time on the memo-billed invoice. Catalog buyers often need samples to review by committee and often will ask for crafts "on approval." *See also* memo billing

on hand | A term referring to the quantity in stock at a particular location at a particular time.

on order | When something is an open order, or a merchandise order against which there has been no receiving. *See also* open order

open order | An order that hasn't yet been filled by the manufacturer or craftsperson.

open-to-buy	The amount of retail dollars available to purchase merchandise, based on anticipated sales and desired inventory levels. Buyers use this concept as a planning tool to budget their monthly purchases.
operating expenses	All costs incurred in the functioning of a business.
ordinary dating	Also called payment terms, this is an invoice term that refers to the cash discount and the credit period allotted for payment. For example, with the term 2/10 net 60, customers get a two-percent discount on the bill if they pay within 10 days of the invoice date; otherwise, they must send payment within the specified credit period, which is 60 days in this case.
overage	An excess of actual, physical inventory above book inventory; also, an excess of cash. *See also* shortage
overbuying	A situation in which a buyer commits more open-to-buy dollars for purchases than allotted in the buying plan for a specific period. This excess is deducted from a future month's purchasing funds.
overhead	The costs involved in operating a business that are not directly related to the actual production of merchandise. These are fixed expenses, such as rent and utilities.
packing slip	A listing of the items packed in a shipment; often this is a copy of the invoice.
P & L	*See* profit and loss statement
physical inventory	Compiled in dollars and units, this term refers to an actual count of merchandise. Often, businesses take a complete physical inventory once or twice a year on a specific date and match this with book inventory values for accounting and record-keeping purposes.
planned sales	Anticipated sales based on last year's performance, current trends, and any planned increases or decreases estimated on how the business is presently doing.
prepayment	Advance payment of shipping charges by the seller even though the buyer is liable. The charges are usually added to the invoice and then repaid by the buyer.
price point	The dollar amount of an item. Retail store buyers often look for product lines that have a range of price points.
principal	The owner of a business; also, the original amount of a loan (excluding interest).

production	The steps involved in creating and finishing any item, whether it is a one-of-a-kind piece or one of many. The term *production crafts* often refers to handmade objects created as multiples.
product line, product mix	Assortments of items within the same basic group of products. For example, these can be of the same design but with variations in size, style, and pricing.
profit	The income remaining after the deduction of all expenses and taxes.
profit and loss statement	Also known as a P & L or income statement, this is a financial account of income and expenses for a specified time period, usually one year.
pro forma	A term used to describe documents that accompany an order—such as a pro forma invoice.
purchase order	A legal agreement made between the buyer and the vendor that specifies quantities, costs, payment methods, and shipping terms, as well as any other arrangements regarding an order.
quality control	Steps taken to ensure that merchandise meets the production standards and that buyers get the consistent quality that they expect.
quantity discount	A reduction on the cost of a large merchandise order.
resource	The source or merchant from which products are bought. *See also* vendor
retail	The sale of products directly to the end user. The retail price is marked up from the wholesale price. *See also* wholesale
revenue	All income produced by sales.
sales rep	A sales representative or agent who works independently to sell your products on commission. Standard industry commission is 15 percent of the wholesale price of the total sale.
shortage, shrinkage	A difference between the physical inventory and the book inventory. This loss could be the result of actual merchandise theft or of record-keeping errors.
SKU	*See* stock-keeping unit

staple merchandise   Basic stock that sells consistently year after year and that customers expect to be available on a regular basis. Being out of stock on staples can result in loss of sales.

stock-keeping unit   Also called an SKU, this is the lowest level of a unit of merchandise identified for inventory management purposes. Stock-keeping units are the number of items in stock in a given category of wares.

target market   Potential customers for a given product; vendors target markets for sales based on various demographics, such as age, sex, and income.

term   The discount given for different payment methods. *See also* net term; ordinary dating

turnover, turn   The number of weeks or months it takes to sell the inventory on hand. Generally, the faster you sell or turn over your goods, the faster you turn your inventory into cash, and the more profitable your business will be.

uniform commercial code   A document containing common-law principles and uniform laws governing commercial transactions.

vendor   A company or individual who sells merchandise to a buyer. Also called a supplier, source, resource, manufacturer, or producer.

vendor analysis   An analysis of vendors and their products' performance in terms of sales, markups, margins, and so on. Buyers use this to measure product profitability.

venture capital   Money invested in new business enterprises. Investors assume a risk, but expect high payback if their investment is successful. Also referred to as *risk capital.*

visual merchandising   How a store displays and merchandises its stock, using visual props (signage, lighting, fixtures) to tell a story or create a themed look or ambiance within a department or for the store as a whole.

volume   Annual gross sales.

wholesale   The wholesale vendor's selling price to the retailer.

BIBLIOGRAPHY

Benjamin, Medea. "Alternative Trade Organizations." *Co-Op America Magazine,* winter 1988, 11–13.

Borrus, Kathy. "Museum Stores: Your Next Market." *The Crafts Report,* October 1995, 13–14.

Di Angelo, Mary Jo. "Interior Design and Crafts." *The Crafts Report,* January 1995, 14–16.

Dillehay, James. *The Basic Guide to Selling Arts and Crafts.* Torreon, N.Mex.: Warm Snow Publishers, 1994.

Dillehay, James. *Weaving Profits: How to Make Money Selling Your Handwovens.* Torreon, N.Mex.: Warm Snow Publishers, 1992.

Dreezen, Craig. *The Artist in Business: Basic Business Practices.* Amherst: University of Massachusetts Arts, 1988.

Drew-Wilkerson, Kate. "The Ideal Rep." *Lapidary Journal,* January 1996, 103–106.

Fleihman, Rick. "Don't Get Caught in the Web: Can Craft Professionals Really Make Money on the Information Superhighway?" *The Crafts Report,* April 1996, 13, 17, 21.

Ford, Jill Poulson. *Working with Wholesale Giftware Reps.* Capistrano Beach, Calif.: Ford Company, 1991.

Gumpert, David E. *How to Really Create a Successful Business Plan.* Boston: Inc. Publishing, 1990.

Gumpert, David E. *How to Really Create a Successful Marketing Plan.* Boston: Inc. Publishing, 1994.

Gumpert, David E. *How to Really Start Your Own Business.* Boston: Inc. Publishing, 1991.

Heathershaw-Hart, Tamra. "Enter the World Wide Web." *The Crafts Report.* October 1995, 16–17.

Honebrink, Andrea. "Can Shopping Save the World?" *Utne Reader,* January/February 1993, 28.

Kamaroff, Bernard. *Small-Time Operator: How to Start Your Own Business, Keep Your Books, Pay Your Taxes and Stay Out of Trouble.* Laytonville, Calif.: Bell Springs Publishing, 1995.

Kaufman, Laura. "How to Get the Attention of Corporate Art Buyers." Paper presented at The Craft Business Institute, Baltimore, Md., September 1995.

Long, Steve, and Cindy Long. *You Can Make Money from Your Arts and Crafts.* Scotts Valley, Calif.: Mark Publishing, 1988.

National Retail Merchants Association. *The Buyer's Manual.* New York, 1979.

Olson, Sharon. *Directory of Wholesale Reps for Crafts Professionals.* Eden Prairie, Minn.: Northwoods Trading Company, 1994.

Onodovcsik, Maryann. "Buyers: What They Want." *The Crafts Report,* August 1995, 12–14.

Prienitz, Wendy. "Alternative Traders Put People First." *Natural Life,* July 1994, 1–2.

Ramsay, Caroline. *Crafts Development and Marketing Manual.* Washington, D.C.: U.S. Peace Corps, 1986.

Rosen, Wendy. *Crafting as a Business.* Baltimore: The Rosen Group Inc., 1994.

Scott, Michael. *The Crafts Business Encyclopedia: The Modern Craftsperson's Guide to Marketing, Management and Money.* Revised edition by Leonard D. DuBoff. San Diego: Harcourt Brace, 1993.

Seymour, William R. *The Cooperative Approach to Crafts.* Revised by Mary A. Lambert and Gerald E. Ely. Washington, D.C.: U.S. Department of Agriculture, 1991.

Thuermer, Karen E. "Point-Counterpoint." *The Crafts Report,* August 1995, 12–14.

West, Janice. *Marketing Your Arts and Crafts: Creative Ways to Profit from Your Work.* Fort Worth, Tex.: The Summit Group, 1994.

SUGGESTED READING

BUSINESS SKILLS

Caplin, Lee. *The Business of Art.* Englewood Cliffs, N.J.: Prentice-Hall, 1991.
Written for artists; includes two excellent craft-related chapters: one on art materials and health concerns, and a second on craft-show participation

Cochrane, Diane. *This Business of Art.* New York: Watson-Guptill, 1988.
Also written for artists; contains a strong chapter on co-op galleries

DuBoff, Leonard D. *The Law (in Plain English) for Craftspeople.* Rev. ed. Loveland, Colo.: Interweave Press, 1993.
A discussion of the legal issues that affect craftspeople; includes model documents

Gerhards, Paul. *How to Sell What You Make: The Business of Marketing Crafts.* Mechanicsburg, Pa.: Stackpole Books, 1990.
A basic guide to marketing and to maintaining a crafts business

RELATED TOPICS

Korza , Pam, and Dian Magie. *The Arts Festival Work Kit.* Edited by Barbara Schaffer Bacon and John Fiscella. Amherst: University of Massachusetts Arts, 1989.
A detailed pragmatic guide to producing an arts festival

Leland, Caryn. *Licensing Art and Design: A Professional's Guide to Licensing and Royalty Agreements.* New York: Allworth Press, 1990.
Sample licensing agreements annotated with explanations of how each legal clause protects the creative property rights of artists and designers

Meltzer, Steve. *Photographing Your Craftwork: A Hands-on Guide for Craftspeople.* Loveland, Colo.: Interweave Press, 1993.
A technical guide to taking promotional photographs and slides

Snyder, Jill. *Caring for Your Art: A Guide for Artists, Collectors, Galleries and Art Institutions.* New York: Allworth Press, 1991.
Written for artists; contains valuable information on handling, storing, documenting, photographing, and shipping art (and craft) works

INDEX